SACRED FLORENCE
Art & Architecture

SACRED FLORENCE
Art & Architecture

Introduced and edited by
Antonio Paolucci

Texts by
Monica Bietti
Francesca Fiorelli Malesci

BARNES & NOBLE

NEW YORK

Copyright © 2004 for the English edition
SCALA Group, Florence
Hazan Éditions, Paris

This 2006 edition published by Barnes & Noble
Publishing, Inc.
by arrangement with SCALA Group S.p.A.
and Hazan Éditions

2006 Barnes & Noble Publishing

ISBN-13: 978-0-7607-8290-3
ISBN-10: 0-7607-8290-3

Texts:
Antonio Paolucci ("Sacred Florence)
Monica Bietti ("Baptistery of San Giovanni,"
"Santa Maria del Fiore," "San Lorenzo,"
"Santa Croce," "Santa Maria Novella,"
"San Marco," "Santissima Annunziata")
Francesca Fiorelli Malesi ("Badia Fiorentina,"
"Santi Apostoli," "Orsanmichele,"
"Santa Trinita," "Ognissanti," "Santa Maria del
Carmine," "Santo Spirito," "Santa Felicita,"
"San Miniato")

Translation:
Huw Evans

Editorial coordination and graphic design:
Colophon srl, Venice

Photographs:
Archivio Fotografico SCALA Group
The images in the SCALA Archives that
reproduce cultural assets owned by the Italian
State are published by kind permission of the
Ministry for the Cultural Heritage and
Activities

Printed and bound in China

1 3 5 7 9 10 8 6 4 2

pages 2-3:
Florentine painter and mosaicist of the 13th-14th
century (Master of the Magdalen?),
Last Supper, 1275-1300, detail of the fifth row of
the dome. Baptistery, Florence

pages 4-5:
Giotto and Taddeo Gaddi, *Angels Playing
Musical Instruments*, 1328, detail of the
Baroncelli Polyptych. Santa Croce, Florence

pages 6-7:
Lorenzo Ghiberti, *Scenes from the Legend of Adam
and Eve*, 1425-52, detail of the Door of
Paradise. Formerly in the baptistery, Museo
dell'Opera del Duomo, Florence

pages 8-9:
Dome of the Old Sacristy. San Lorenzo,
Florence

pages 10-11:
Masaccio, *Distribution of the Goods of the
Community and the Death of Ananias*, 1427, detail.
Brancacci Chapel, Santa Maria del Carmine,
Florence

pages 12-13:
Michelangelo, detail of a grotesque mask at the
feet of *The Night*. New Sacristy, San Lorenzo,
Florence

contents

Sacred Florence

The churches of Florence are a vast universe that many generations of scholars have scrutinized in depth and on the surface, but which still has surprises in store, still offers unexplored lines of research. Only yesterday came the revelation, after its restoration, of the wonderful *Madonna and Child* in Santa Maria Maggiore, a masterpiece of primitive painting that immediately sparked a lively debate among specialists. Does that gleaming and sumptuous icon stand between the 1260s and 1270s, at a time when Byzantine bas-reliefs encountered the *maiestates* of the West and it almost seems possible to sense, between Coppo and Cimabue, the clash of powerful cultures struggling for supremacy? Is it the "Latin" of Romance Europe beginning to undermine the pictorial hegemony of the Greek, the figurative language of the Italians germinating under the sacred script of the East...? Or should the *Madonna* of Santa Maria Maggiore be dated to a century earlier, to the golden autumn of the Eastern Empire, to the time of Comnenian Byzantium...? If the second hypothesis is correct – and I believe it is – the early history of Florentine art will have to be reconsidered in the light of the presence of authoritative painters from Constantinople; a presence that was already "ancient" in the days of Cimabue and of Dante.

But these are questions for the experts. My only reason for citing the case of the "Greek" icon in Santa Maria Maggiore is to show that Florence's churches are an unexhausted reserve of research and discovery. Studies are piled on studies in a continual process of investigations and amendments. It is barely a year since the publication of the many volumes that the international academic community has dedicated to Santa Maria del Fiore, the cathedral of the Florentines, on the seventh centenary of its foundation (1297). If we were to assemble all the works that have been written over the centuries on the city's religious buildings (from the monumental undertakings of Richa and W. and E. Paatz to individual monographs, guidebooks and abstracts from specialized journals), even a middle-sized library would not be enough to hold them all.

There is nothing surprising about this if we consider that Florence has long been regarded (to pick a date, at least since Giorgio Vasari's *Lives*, 1568) as the cradle of Western civilization between the Middle Ages and the Renaissance, and that the churches, rather than the museums, of that artistic period are its natural historical containers. However, all this constitutes a substantial obstacle – theoretical even more than practical – for anyone trying to squeeze a religious, civil and artistic history stretching for sixteen centuries into a single book. Anyone who wished to cover the churches of Florence in an exhaustive and systematic manner, utilizing a topographic criterion (quarter by quarter, street by street), a historico-chronological one (from the year AD 393, when Ambrose, the bishop of Milan, consecrated the *martyrion* of the deacon Lawrence on the outskirts of Roman "Florentia" to the restorations of recent years) or, finally, an alphabetical one by works and artists (from the Albertinelli, Mariotto of the *Crucifixion* in the Charterhouse to the Zuccari, Federico of the frescoes

of the Apocalypse in the dome of the cathedral), or even juggling all three criteria, would end up with nothing more than a reproduction of the Touring Club's *Red Guide*. A very useful, indeed invaluable book for the cultured traveler, but radically different from what this volume sets out to be. It is my intention to approach the world of Florentine churches from selective points of view, dipping into it here and there and seeking to use a general key of interpretation that will function as a passe-partout for the various sectors (art history, religious history, history plain and simple) to which the churches of Florence provide access.

If is true that stones (and with stones, marbles, bronzes, paintings) speak, let us put them in a position where they can do so. The key I have chosen is that of *instructiveness*. It is a line of interpretation – at one and the same time of analysis, disaggregation and assembly – which I consider particularly effective since a distinctive feature of the Florentine artistic heritage is that it appears to be divisible into groups of perfect

exemplarity. Let me give an example. Go to Florence Baptistery, *umbelicus urbis*, heart of the city's civil and religious history, and limit yourself, for the moment, to walking around it, admiring its three bronze doors one after the other: first Andrea Pisano's, facing Via Calzaioli, then the first of Ghiberti's, opposite Via Martelli, and finally the last, the "golden door" opening onto the cathedral, now replaced by a copy.

No textbook of art history could give you a better explanation of what happened in Florence in those crucial years between the revolution of Giotto and the "perspective" Renaissance of Masaccio and Alberti than those three doors, seen in chronological order. First the plastic measure of Giotto enclosed in the elastic frame of the Gothic multifoil (Andrea Pisano's door with *Scenes from the Life of the Baptist*, 1330-36); then the melodious elegance of the first Ghiberti door, which adapts late-Gothic rhythms to produce effects I would call Neo-Hellenistic (the North Door with the *Life of Christ*, 1401-24); lastly (on the third door, the one Michelangelo called *La Porta del Paradiso*, 1425-52), we find the "Albertian window" opening onto the colorful perspective of the new world revealed by the Renaissance.

Vincenzo Danti, *Beheading of the Baptist*, 1569-79. Baptistery, Florence

Perhaps only the three *Maestà* of Duccio, Cimabue and Giotto now in the Sala dei Primitivi at the Uffizi constitute, in their visible demonstration of the gradual emergence of the figurative language of the Italians, an equally exalted and instructive series.

And what to say of the statues that crown the three doors? Over a span of seventy years, from Andrea Sansovino (1505) to Rustici (1511) and Danti (1569-79), the fundamental tendencies in 16th-century Florentine sculpture are exemplified. First the severe classicism of the early 16th century in Andrea Sansovino's *Baptist*, flanked by Vincenzo Danti's *Christ* and Innocenzo Spinazzi's *Angel* (above the Door of Paradise, where the group has now been replaced by a copy), where the figure of the Precursor appears to be a three-dimensional translation of Andrea del Sarto's image in the Scalzo Cloister. Then the naturalism and psychologism derived from Leonardo in Giovanni Francesco Rustici's bronze group of the *Preaching of the Baptist* above Ghiberti's North Door. Finally, in Vincenzo Danti's *Beheading of the Baptist*, crowning Andrea Pisano's door, you will see the lesson of Michelangelo translated into the captious, supremely formalistic style of the *ultima Maniera*. Simply by walking around the baptistery, looking at the three doors and the sculptures above them, you will have grasped the fundamental "tendencies" of Florentine (and therefore Italian and European) art between the 14th and 16th century, from Giotto to Michelangelo.

Of course understanding the history of art is not quite so simple. Examples, however sublime, are not enough. But for anyone who wishes to make a study of our discipline, those examples, arranged in perfect chronological sequence around Florence Baptistery, are paradigmatic and indispensable. It is easy – if you learn to find your way around the marvelous labyrinth of "sacred Florence" – to join up the threads of religious history and the Christian message with those of political history and civil mythmaking. Consider the colossal silver altar dedicated to John the Baptist that once stood in the baptistery and is now housed just a few meters away, in the Museo dell'Opera del Duomo. Imagine it performing its original function. When, on the saint's feast day, it sparkled with reliquaries, ornaments and precious vestments at the center of the *bel San Giovanni* and the whole city paid homage to it as the most glorious symbol of its history.

Certainly, time has passed for the baptistery and its city, obscuring symbols and values. Michelozzo's *Baptist*, in the middle of the niche of the altar, is indicating something and someone with his hand, held out and lifted slightly. *Ecce Agnus Dei ecce qui tollit peccata mundi* ("Behold the Lamb of God who takes away the sins of the world"). These are the words of the liturgy that accompany the gesture and give it meaning. Today, in the aseptic setting of the museum, it is difficult to relate the gesture to the words and either of them to Christ the Savior of whom the baptistery is a symbol and the Baptist the precursor and witness.

It was not like that when the altar stood at the center of San Giovanni, on the patron's feast day, with the nobles of the Signoria, the officials of the guilds, the feudal vassals of subject castles, the rulers of tributary cities, the priests and the rest of the population, for then that gesture was revealed in all its eloquence. The *Saint John* cast and chiseled in silver by Michelozzo (1452) pointed at Pollaiuolo's cross (1457-59), set above the altar to signify that the Resurrection passed through the sacrifice of Christ and – beyond the cross – to the gleaming mosaics on the vault representing the mystery of the Apocalypse: Christ coming again to judge the living and the dead. He will come for everybody on the last day, he will come for each person at the end of his or her earthly existence. Once even the most illiterate citizen of Florence was able to understand the Baptist's gesture at the center of the silver altar and the system of symbols that lent meaning to that gesture. And knew that the doors, read in iconographic and not chronological sequence, provided a summary of sacred history. First the eve of Salvation depicted on Ghiberti's *Golden Door* with the scenes from the Old Testament and prefigurations of the Messiah; then Andrea Pisano's door with *Scenes from the Life of Saint John*, link between the Old and the New Law and almost a "lamp" – as the ancient theologians called him – placed by God to illuminate both the Time of Waiting and that of the Revelation; finally Ghiberti's first door, symbolically the most important (and in fact originally located in front of the cathedral) as it tells of Christ's entry into history to bring humanity into the universe *sub gratia* introduced by the sacrament of Baptism.

At times it is extraordinarily useful to compare similar iconographies, not just to see the shifts in style and understand the course of artistic history but also to grasp the changes that have taken place in theology and religious imagery over time. Not everyone knows that Florence houses two great cycles devoted to the Apoc-

Giovanni Francesco Rustici, *Preaching of the Baptist*, 1506-11. Baptistery, Florence

following pages
Andrea Sansovino, Vincenzo Danti, Innocenzo Spinazzi, 1502, 1569, 1792, 16th-18th century, *Baptism of Christ*. Formerly in the baptistery, Museo dell'Opera del Duomo, Florence

alypse, separated by about three centuries and located a few tens of meters from each other. They are the *Last Judgment* in mosaic on the ceiling of the baptistery (datable to between the 13th and 14th century) and the vast *Judgment* (just under a two and half acres of wall painting) that Giorgio Vasari and above all Federico Zuccari painted between 1572 and 1579 inside Brunelleschi's dome in Santa Maria del Fiore.

The first cycle, the work of craftsmen of various origins and poised between the predominant Byzantine tradition and stylistic features that are already Romanesque, offers a hieratic and merciless interpretation of the *Last Judgment*. Christ is a frosty autocrat borne on clouds in the sky to judge the living and the dead. He is the bearer of terrible justice, surrounded by angels armed like praetorians. Paradise is as dazzling and cruel as the court of Byzantium and Hell looks like a "slicing machine" (Longhi). It is clear that the age that produced those mosaics was a time of strict hierarchies, metaphysical fears and brooding anxieties.

How much more optimistic, in comparison, Vasari and Zuccari's *Last Judgment*! Here too Hell is described with vivid realism, but there are also hosts of benevolent saints and a Madonna, merciful mother, who will certainly do her utmost to help her poor sinning children. Above all there is a Christ whose severe expression does not exclude the possibility of clemency. In short it is evident that behind the apocalyptic cycle in the dome, expression of a by now "international" Mannerism, there is the Church of the Counter Reformation; a popular, educational, persuasive church that wished to make the route to Salvation comprehensible and therefore accessible to all.

But here the bloody history of the republic enters the cathedral on horseback and in parade step. Among the famous horsemen of art history, alongside the *Marcus Aurelius* on the Campidoglio, Donatello's *Gattamelata* and Verrocchio's *Colleoni*, we must place the two *condottieri* who file, one after the other, in fresco and at full length, on the left-hand wall of Florence Cathedral. They have been part of our basic mental imagery since our schooldays. There is no manual of art history that does not reproduce them. They represent the mercenary leaders John Hawkwood and Niccolò da Tolentino: the first is by Paolo Uccello, the second by Andrea del Castagno. Twenty years separate them, as the image of John Hawkwood dates from 1436, that of his companion from 1456. Both represent well (and this is where the political and economic history of the city enters the church) the attitude of the Florentine financial oligarchy toward military affairs. Unlike their Venetian colleagues, who – having a colonial empire to defend and the Turk in their home waters – were obliged every now and then to die like heroes on the decks of their galleys or the bastions of their fortresses in the Levant, the merchants and bankers of Florence did not practice the art of war. Not out of cowardice or lack of patriotism but simply because they did not think it logical to waste time and business opportunities when they could pay professionals to wage their wars. And so they hired – on short-term or open-end contracts – the leaders of *condotte*, i.e. of mercenary armies. Those *condottieri* who served the republic well received, in addition to their professional "fee," special rewards (today we would call them bonuses) and prestigious honors, of which the highest was a memorial in the cathedral. The captains of fortune portrayed in Santa Maria del Fiore obtained the sought-after homage for having played an objectively important historical role. For example, the English mercenary John Hawkwood, known as Giovanni Acuto in Italy, saved Florence simply by passing (during the War of the Eight Saints and in exchange for a higher fee) from the pope's service to that of the republic.

The two *condottieri* ride toward the high altar to bring the tribute of their victories to the Madonna of the Florentines. Just like everywhere in the Catholic world, but more obviously in Florence than elsewhere, secular history is inextricably interwoven with religious history. Here too, what counts for the art historian is the instructiveness of "exemplary masterpieces." For Paolo Uccello's "metaphysical" horse, frozen in its stereometric

Antonio del Pollaiuolo, *Silver Reliquary Cross*, 1457. Museo dell'Opera del Duomo, Florence

facing page
Florentine painter and mosaicist of the 13th century (circle of Meliore), *Christ the Judge*, 1260-75, detail of the dome. Baptistery, Florence

majesty, is a direct precedent for the chargers of Constantine in Piero's frescoes in San Francesco at Arezzo. While Andrea del Castagno's *Niccolò da Tolentino*, with its lively characterization of the man's features and his muscular and psychological force, opens the door to the innovations of Verrocchio, Pollaiuolo and Leonardo. In its civil and political administration Florence has always been a lay city. The Gospel principle of "render unto Caesar the things that are Caesar's, and to God the things that are God's" has been applied even in the urban structure. In fact the center of religious power (baptistery, cathedral, archbishop's palace) is sharply distinguished from the center of political power (Piazza della Signoria with Palazzo Vecchio). The Florentines chose to locate their religious and civil governments at the opposite poles of the ancient "quadrangular" city of Florence, which had grown up on the orthogonal grid of the Roman colony. And yet, exactly halfway between Piazza della Signoria and Piazza del Duomo, there is that singular cube of stone Orsanmichele, the ancient church of the guilds. In this church, which looks more like a fortress, Art, History and Faith are once again fused into an inseparable whole. Between the House of Power (Palazzo Vecchio) and the House of God (the cathedral) stands the House of Work, which wealthy Florence felt should have no less dignity.

The art historian will explain to you that around Orsanmichele is ranged the most important anthology of 15th- and 16th-century sculpture (though much of it has been replaced by copies today). Almost all the great masters of the Florentine Renaissance (Ghiberti, Donatello, Nanni di Banco, Verrocchio, etc.) are present – in marble or bronze – in the tabernacles of the Major and Minor Guilds.

A historian of economics will tell you that this church encapsulates Florence's golden age. When the gold florin (Dante's "alloy stamped with the Baptist") was the principal currency used in the markets of Europe and the Mediterranean, when Florentine merchants, at the summit of an already "globalized" economy, dealt in Ukrainian grain and Welsh wool, silk and spices, shipping charter fees and bank rates, the insurance of goods and foreign loans raised abroad; with a range of operation that extended from Via Calzaioli and Piazza del Mercato to the fairs of Champagne, the markets of Flanders and the bazaars of Damascus. And then, wandering around the niches of Orsanmichele, you will realize that the money which permitted the great flowering of Florence's art and monuments (even Giotto's campanile, even the "magnificent and swelling" dome rising against the heavens to "cover all the peoples of Tuscany with its shade," to use Alberti's unforgettable words), came from the labor of the men and women that the saints of the guilds, and of this church, have protected over the centuries.

A few more examples of the didactic exemplarity of Florentine churches. Entering Santa Croce you will realize immediately that there are two main keys to its interpretation. One, the most popular and comprehensible to all, partly because of memories of our schooldays, is the "Romantic" one put forward by Ugo Foscolo in *Dei sepolcri*. It is an imaginary route leading from the tablets set in the floor that the feet of millions of tourists are inexorably wearing away (attempts are made to protect them with coverings and hurdles, even though we know this runs counter to the desires of the medieval dead, who wanted precisely this, their memory trampled on, consumed, reduced to dust: *memento quia pulvis es et in pulverem revertis...*), a route that leads – as I was saying – from the penitential burial register of the floor to the sepulchral monuments of the Renaissance (Bernardo Rossellino's *Leonardo Bruni*, Desiderio da Settignano's *Carlo Marsuppini*), where the glory of the deceased is set under a Roman arch of triumph as if they were Livy's heroes, and to the memorials of celebrated Italians of the past. These last are the "great spirits" whose mortal remains lie in Santa Croce (Michelangelo, Vittorio Alfieri, Niccolò Machiavelli, Galileo Galilei, etc.) or who are present only in effigy (Dante Alighieri).

Passing from the memorial tablets in the floor to the marble tomb of Vittorio Alfieri (a masterpiece by Antonio Canova) and to that of Ugo Foscolo, the poet who sung of the *Pantheon* of Santa Croce, what better occa-

Exterior of the church
of Orsanmichele

sion to reflect on the immortal themes of the History that consumes everything, of the Fame that outlasts History and Art and through which the otherwise ephemeral memory of men endures in time?

The other guiding thread that allows us to "read" Santa Croce like a textbook is the historical and artistic one. It is sufficient to enter this church to relive the "heroic" age of Italian painting through its greatest masterpieces. Commencing with Cimabue's painted *Cross*, we arrive at the Giotto of the Bardi and Peruzzi Chapels, continue with the most significant tendencies of Giotto's legacy (the "Master of Figline," Maso di Banco and the great Taddeo Gaddi, who in the frescoes of the Baroncelli Chapel lights up the night of the shepherds woken by the Angel) and finish with Agnolo Gaddi's *Legend of the Cross*, last glimmer of that school.

In Santa Croce more than in any other place in Florence or Italy, you will be able to "see" and thus "understand" the significance of the revolution in painting wrought by Giotto and described by Cennino Cennini and Giorgio Vasari: the "Greek" of the Byzantine tradition being consumed and transfigured into the "Latin" of the West, accompanied by the birth, with the discovery of Life and the certainty of measurable Space, of the new figurative language of the Italians; the one that was to lead from Giotto to Masaccio, Piero della Francesca, Raphael and Caravaggio.

Master of the Bardi St. Francis, *Saint Francis and Scenes from His Life*, 1245-50. Santa Croce, Florence

There is one place in Santa Croce that demonstrates, in an absolutely instructive way, the radical nature of Giotto's revolution. This place is the Bardi Chapel. On the walls there are Giotto's fragmentary frescoes representing *Scenes from the Life of Saint Francis*. On the altar stands the image of the saint himself, in the form of a hieratic icon, painted by an unknown artist from the mid-13th century whom scholars call the "Master of the Bardi Saint Francis."

About seventy years separate the panel from the wall paintings, but it is as if they belonged to two remote ages, two civilizations, two ways of understanding and therefore representing humanity and the universe. It is not so much a question of quality (sublime in Giotto, less than mediocre in the icon painter of late Byzantine culture), but of radically different conceptions of the World of Divinity and History.

For the 13th-century painter St. Francis is a hierogram, a sacred symbol. For Giotto St. Francis is a man like us, living in a world just like ours, amidst the marvelous variety and verity of the visible universe, surrounded by the emotions of other human beings. It is clear that the road that would lead to Raphael, Titian, Caravaggio and thus to modern art could only start from here.

If you go to the Uffizi you can admire some of the most beautiful altarpieces of the 15th and 16th century. But to see the Renaissance altarpiece in its original location, in the same architectural space and light that the artist who painted it saw, measured and evaluated when he planned it and then placed it on the altar, to see it in its authentic frame, with its frontal, patron's device and explanatory inscription, you must go to one of two places in Italy. One is Pienza Cathedral, where the pictures of Sano di Pietro, Giovanni di Paolo, Vecchietta and Matteo di Giovanni (the finest collection of late 15th-century Sienese painting) are still there, complete with frames and coats of arms, on the very altars for which they were commissioned by Pope Pius II Piccolomini, the man who gave the city its name.

Old Sacristy, San Lorenzo, Florence

facing page
interior of the church
of Santo Spirito

The other place capable of conveying the same sensation of a perfect harmony between architecture and painting, of absolute coherence between the image represented, the space that houses it and the history that has brought it there, is the ambulatory of Santo Spirito. Walk from right to left past the patronal chapels, designed by Brunelleschi, that encircle the transept and apse of Santo Spirito with an unbroken series of niches, and you will be presented with the most perfect "museological" display of sacred painting and sculpture from the Renaissance (Filippino Lippi and Andrea Sansovino, Raffaellino del Garbo and Donnino and Agnolo Del Mazziere, Cosimo Rosselli and Francesco Botticini) that you could imagine.

The instructive exemplarity of these ensembles, come down to us intact after centuries, will be found in the Capponi Chapel in Santa Felicita, a masterpiece by Jacopo Pontormo with the collaboration of Agnolo Bronzino (two of the *Evangelists*). You will find it in the Pazzi Chapel in Santa Croce, designed and commenced by Filippo Brunelleschi in 1443. This is of one of the most harmonious interiors in Renaissance architecture, justly admired and celebrated by the critics as an example in stone of the aesthetic ideals of Humanism. Very simple in its structure and of an almost mathematical rigor, the decoration is based on the relationship between the plaster and *pietra serena* and the splendor of Luca della Robbia's glazed terracottas. Exemplary, in the church of the Carmine, is the Brancacci Chapel with the frescoes of Masolino and Masaccio. Here, in the 1420s, the two great figurative cultures that ushered in the modern era (the naturalistic and luminous one of Masolino but also, in the same period, of Gentile da Fabriano, the Limbourg brothers and van Eyck, and the other, volumetric and perspective one of Masaccio, but also of Brunelleschi, Nanni di Banco and Donatello) confronted one another, distinguished themselves and were reflected in each other.

The periods in the history of art that the textbooks call "Late Gothic" and "Early Renaissance" have, in the Brancacci, their most effective illustration.

The absolute peak of instructive exemplarity is to be found in the Old Sacristy of San Lorenzo, the first nucleus of Brunelleschi's intervention in that majestic basilica, patronized by the Medici family. The small room is a masterpiece in itself as well as a concentration of supreme masterpieces. Brunelleschi had already designed and partly built it between 1428 and 1429. It is the manifesto of the Renaissance in architecture. It is geometry turned into measurable order and musical proportion. It is perspective in architecture given habitable form, a harmonious and extremely precise organization of space. The Old Sacristy has the same importance that the Brancacci Chapel has for the history of painting. And yet it was here, in the same years, that a challenge to the "order" of the Renaissance also took shape. For inside the sacristy we find Donatello, who was Brunelleschi's partner and friend but also, in a sense, his antagonist. The stuccoes with *Scenes from the Life of Saint John* in the tondi of the dome, like the images of Medici patron saints (Lawrence and John, Cosmas and Damian), are Donatello's work. And he also made the bronze doors, characterized by such an aggressive and transgressive plasticity that they were criticized by Antonio Manetti, who was in all likelihood echoing the opinion of his teacher Brunelleschi. Renaissance and "anti-Renaissance," proportion and excess, classical order and its "Manneristic" subversion are already present *in nuce* in the Old Sacristy of San Lorenzo.

If it were necessary, because of some nuclear catastrophe, to save just one bit of Florence in its entirety, I would suggest putting the Old Sacristy in some indestructible container and sending it to another planet. For there is no more beautiful and significant record of Florentine civilization.

The churches of Florence are not just "Renaissance." All the styles that have been laid down one on top of the other in that sumptuous superfluity which is typical of Catholic places of worship are represented. Except that we do not find the sad and puristic restorations of the modern era (whose effects, luckily, have been felt less in Florence than elsewhere).

Masolino de' Panicale, Masaccio, Filippino Lippi, frescoes of the Brancacci Chapel. Santa Maria del Carmine, Florence

The culture of the baroque has left exquisite churches in our city, worthy of Rome, such as San Firenze and San Gaetano. It has entered venerable Gothic monuments like Santa Maria del Carmine (I am thinking of the Corsini Chapel, frescoed by Luca Giordano in 1682 and decorated by Giovan Battista Foggini and Balthasar Permoser). It has clad Michelozzo's original structure of the Santissima Annunziata, Florence's ancient and much venerated Marian shrine, with polychrome marbles, stuccoes and gilded wood, as well as wall paintings and sculptures.

At the Annunziata you will find the lesson in art history of which I have spoken so often. You will find it in the cloister called the "Chiostro dei Voti" with the frescoes of Andrea del Sarto, Franciabigio, Pontormo and Rosso Fiorentino: the finest "permanent" exhibition of Florentine Mannerism that has ever been. While inside the church, in the chapels, the paintings, the sepulchral monuments, the memorial tablets and the aedicule of the Virgin filled with silver votive offerings, you will find the history of the city, the history of the dynasties and families that have lived in it and ruled it, the history of the Florentine people who have always loved and venerated its miraculous Madonna.

To understand just what an extraordinary interlacing of history (individual history, political history, social history and economic history) can be found in an old Florentine church, visit the Feroni Chapel, the first on the left as you enter. Go in, look around carefully, and you will realize that this small space tells an extraordinary story of personal success, of political and financial ventures and international enterprise. The funerary chapel of Marchese Francesco Feroni is an exquisite little theater of the baroque. Under Foggini's direction the saints of the Catholic "pantheon" face one another and hold a dialogue (Camillo Caetani's *Saint*

Francis, Marcellini's *Saint Dominic*), alongside allegorical representations of unusual Virtues: *Fidelity* and *Diligence* by Antonio Francesco Andreazzi and Isidoro Franchi, *Thought* and *Fortune at Sea* by Giuseppe Piamontini. Into this exquisite "exhibition" of the best Florentine sculpture of the late 17th century a wholly unexpected Modernity bursts with a plaque and an emblem. The plaque, in Latin, tells how Francesco Feroni won honor and fortune sending his ships to Africa and India. The emblem is the ocean-going ship modeled in bronze by Massimiliano Soldani Benzi. It is the "tramp" that permitted Francesco Feroni, a man of very humble origin, to make more money than the Corsini princes and all the other aristocrats of Florence had ever dreamed of.

You can love a ship like a woman. I like to think that Francesco Feroni, at the end of his days, decided to entrust Massimiliano Soldani Benzi with the memory of one particular ship, the queen of his fleet, captured by French pirates in August 1677. That "beautiful, sturdy and large vessel" had cost 58,600 florins and was called *San Giovanni e San Cosimo*: sailing under the flag of St. Stephen and with the passport of the grand duke of Tuscany, she carried black slaves to the Spanish colonies in America with the *asiento* of the Catholic king. Francesco Feroni, the son of a dyer from Empoli who had become a wealthy shipowner and banker in Amsterdam, and whom Grand Duke Cosimo III had then persuaded to return to Tuscany by offering him the title of marchese, the stole of senator and the office of general depositary (the equivalent of a finance minister today), presents two objectively revolutionary concepts in his mortuary chapel. He declares that success and therefore money are acquired with the favor of Fortune but, above all, with *absiduo labore mentis*. He places the instrument of his profession in the foreground and exalts it as worthy of honor: for him, the slave

following pages
Donatello, *Resurrection of Christ*, 1465, detail of the pulpit on the right. San Lorenzo, Florence

ship. It took courage to assert such things in the bigoted Florence of the last Medici. Francesco Feroni had that courage and the Santissima Annunziata provides a splendid testimony of it.

For me one of the most fascinating aspects of the ancient churches of Florence is their capacity to hold a dialogue with the city. A dialogue that is visibly urbanistic (the portico of the Santissima Annunziata replicated by the Innocenti and the front of the Serviti, the façades, campaniles and domes of Santo Spirito, Santa Maria del Carmine and San Frediano al Cestello which "are" the iconographic but also the psychological and spiritual identity of the Oltrarno district, San Miniato al Monte transformed by 19th-century restorations and by Poggi's avenues into the most perfect emblem of "Room with a View" Florence, an exquisite pre-Raphaelite jewel); but that is also, very often, a subtle dialogue made up of allusions and reflections.

Inside the cathedral, in Domenico di Michelino's painting, Florence with its walls, dome, campaniles and

Filippino Lippi, *View of the Borgo and Porta San Frediano*, 1488, detail of the *Nerli Altarpiece*. Santo Spirito, Florence

towers faces the gate of Hell; between them stands Dante, the exiled prophet. In this case Florence enters the church in allegorical form, as an eschatological warning. At other times it enters in its everyday reality. In the background of Filippino Lippi's *Nerli Altarpiece* in Santo Spirito, we see the Borgo di San Frediano and its gate, practically unchanged since then. Looking at the people the artist has depicted in the street, it is easy to identify with the man – Nerli himself, owner of the chapel – who, before mounting his horse to ride to Pisa (where, as diplomatic envoy of the Signoria, he will meet King Charles VIII of France in an unsuccessful attempt to forestall the invasion of Florence), affectionately kisses the little girl who has come out to say goodbye to him at the door of the house.

Florence is like a play of mirrors. You see things in paintings in the churches, and then find them again as soon as you go outside. In San Lorenzo, next to the Old Sacristy, there is a painting by Filippo Lippi. It represents the *Annunciation of the Virgin*. There are two details in the panel which cannot fail to catch our attention. In the foreground there is a still life, a glass vase with a flower in it: one of the purest and most intense pieces of realistic painting in the history of art. And then, in the background, there is a garden with brightly colored buildings in the Brunelleschian manner. Look at them carefully and then go out into the cloisters of San Lorenzo. You will feel as if you are still inside Filippo Lippi's *Annunciation*, so precisely is the painted perspective mirrored in the measure, light and rhythm of the real architecture.

You can look at the churches of Florence through the eyes of the art historian or of the historian plain and simple. You can enjoy their beauty with the curiosity and enthusiasm of the aesthete. But there is another way (and one that is more effective as it comprises and enhances all the others) to approach the churches of Florence, with the culture and sensibility of a Christian. If it is true, and it is, that Florence has been for centuries one of the great centers of Western civilization, it has also been one of the great centers of theological thought and thus of its religious affirmation in figurative form.

At the beginning of the 13th century the great mendicant orders, the Dominicans and the Franciscans, arrived in Florence and settled there. With them were born the majestic churches of Santa Croce and Santa Maria Novella, masterpieces of Italian Gothic. On the frescoed walls and in the painted panels of Santa Croce and Santa Maria Novella the art of the 13th- and 14th-century masters was placed at the service of a new spirituality and a new theology.

The age of the communes and the political rise of the city burghers has, in religion, the voice of St. Francis and St. Dominic. Thanks to them the dualism of a Manichean character that tended to separate the Kingdom of Heaven from the things of this world – transient, illusory and therefore contemptible – went into decline. Increasingly emphasis was placed, in doctrine and preaching, on the Gospel message that proclaimed the goodness of creation and the preeminence of Christ's humanity in the story of Salvation. The highest result of this crucial theological evolution, destined to open the door to modern religiosity, can be seen in the *Cross* that Giotto painted in Santa Maria Novella around 1290. With the capacity for acceleration and synthesis typical of genius, "in the cross of Santa Maria Novella Giotto leaps beyond the iconographic tradition of Giunta and Cimabue, which made the Crucifix a sort of heraldic symbol of the Passion, and, for the first time in history, paints a man, a real man, crucified" (Previtali). Again in Santa Maria Novella (church of the Dominicans, the most learned order in Church history), the incipient Humanism of the Renaissance attempted to give visual expression to the mystery of the Trinity. The result was Masaccio's celebrated fresco (*circa* 1425), a true theological meditation on human destiny and the Eternal. Inside a mock work of architecture – the first *trompe-l'oeil* in the history of art constructed according to the rigorous scientific rules of Brunelleschian perspective – is set the image of the Trinity. At the sides of the tabernacle, rapt in contemplation of the mystery, kneel the two donors. At the feet of this sublime architecture of figures lies the skeleton, recalling, by its presence and by the inscription ("What you are, I once was..."), the inescapable fate of every mortal.

Florence has always been a city of intense but troubled spirituality, sometimes in the vanguard, at others transgressive. All this is amply reflected in the religious art of the churches. I will give just one example. The bronze pulpits of San Lorenzo that Donatello modeled in the last years of his life are so unusual in their conceptual profundity and iconographic originality that we ought perhaps to call them the "Passion and Death of Our Lord according to Donatello," as if they were a new gospel to be added to the canonical ones. I have always been struck, looking at the bronzes in San Lorenzo, by the great freedom that the Church allowed its artists in this period. When people talk to you of iconographic prescriptions, of the dogmatic control of figurative expression, suggest they take a look at the reliefs of the pulpits and tell you if it is possible to be freer (and more transgressive) than this.

On the north pulpit he has represented the *Resurrection of Christ*, climax of the whole narration. Traditional iconography has always assigned an aura of triumph and glory to the episode. Not Donatello. Christ emerges with difficulty from the sepulcher, leaning on his standard, as if climbing a ladder of pain. He is still wrapped in the bands of the shroud. He is burdened with death, visible in his stiff body, in his dull and unfocused expression. It is as if he were mired

Filippo Lippi, *Architectural View*, 1437-41, detail of the *Martelli Altarpiece*. San Lorenzo, Florence

in death, but struggling out of it to carry out an unpleasant duty. There is no trace of glory in Donatello's *Resurrection.* His Christ (as Pope-Hennessy once wrote in an apt metaphor that was particularly eloquent in the postwar years) is like some poor man released from a concentration camp. The Christ who leaves his tomb in an almost furtive manner, weighed down by the misery of the human condition, so sorrowful and devastated that you feel he doubts the utility of his rising again, and at the same time obliged to do so by the fatality of a love that no one among the living deserves, is an image highly revealing of the sculptor's pessimistic faith, of his dramatic vision of the story of Salvation.

In Florence the Dominicans were not just at Santa Maria Novella but also at San Marco. For centuries San Marco was a center of high spirituality as well as the first experimental laboratory, in Italy and Europe, of a consciously, programmatically "sacred" art, conceived and realized for edificatory and catechetic purposes. Painters like Fra Bartolomeo, Albertinelli and Sogliani were molded in the spirit of San Marco. The first and most intelligent standard bearer of this ambitious project was the friar and painter Giovanni da Fiesole, better known as Fra Angelico. He tried to adapt the perspective revolution and Humanistic values of the figurative Renaissance to suit the purposes of a "theological" painting that would be a fusion of dogma and reason, as well as doctrine in figures and "visible prayer." To grasp just how extraordinary were the poetic results achieved by Fra Angelico, you need to visit the Museo di San Marco, which is nothing but the former Dominican monastery, taken over by the State in the 19th century.

San Marco was also the residence of Girolamo Savonarola, the Dominican friar whose activities on behalf of democracy and against the Medici and unbending and reformist zeal led to his being burned in Piazza della Signoria on May 28, 1498. Savonarola's execution burned for a long time in the Christian conscience of Florence and its indirect reverberations lent a very special character to religious art in the age of the Counter Reformation. For a glimpse of the way the spirituality of the 16th and early 17th century was expressed in Florentine churches, I would suggest, among the many possibilities, three emblematic places: the Charterhouse, Santo Spirito and San Salvatore in Ognissanti.

Now in the museum but originally in the cloister of the Charterhouse – a true monastic citadel high above the city – we can see Pontormo's "Lutheran" version of the Passion of Christ. These are the frescoes that the artist painted between 1523 and 1525 under the threat of the plague raging in Florence and the stimulus of an obsession with Dürer's prints. The strenuous formalism and lucid intellectualism of those paintings clearly express the spirit of the dramatic years that saw the definitive breakdown of the religious unity of the West. Toward the middle of the century, the painter who best represented the sorrowful spirituality of his city and succeeded in articulating the "devout" and somewhat fanatical severity of Florentine Catholicism was Pier Francesco di Jacopo Foschi. In the three altarpieces in Santo Spirito (the *Disputation over the Conception, Resurrection* and *Transfiguration*), all dating from before 1550, Foschi, moving in the exclusive milieu of the local tradition of Andrea del Sarto and Pontormo, scaled some of the most breathtaking heights in religious art of the century. The drab, bleak tones, those of sand and ashes, the hyperbolically elongated figures, the spurning of perspective and the crowded compositions are elements of style that seem to be deliberately intended to prompt reflections of desolate contrition, to induce a mood of gloomy mysticism.

If Foschi's paintings reflect the rigorist grip of the Counter Reformation, the cloister of Ognissanti with its cycle of frescoes datable to the beginning of the 17th century is an expression of a rediscovered optimism, of an eager desire to explain and persuade with warmth and naturalness. The painters who frescoed the cloister of Ognissanti (Jacopo Ligozzi, Giovanni da San Giovanni and others) were given the task of recounting the life and miracles of St. Francis. They did so with such a variety of accents and such skilful dramatization and naturalism that a visit to the cloister of Ognissanti is like entering a color film or the pages of a historical novel. The 16th and 17th centuries were a period of narration by images on a vast scale. From Santa Maria degli Angeli to Santo Spirito, from Santa Maria Novella to San Marco, from Santa Croce to the Compagnia di San Pierino at the Annunziata, everywhere in the ancient monastic complexes of Florence, in the cloisters and the cenacles, there is a continuous itinerary of religious stories. Even though many of those buildings have now been turned into museums, barracks or universities, the cycles of frescoes survive to bear witness to the great effort made by the Church of the Counter Reformation, in Florence, to promulgate Faith, to teach History, to instill an appreciation of Beauty.

At the end of this long journey, of necessity anthological and disjointed, through the churches of Florence, a concluding reflection is called for. People come to this city to visit its museums, but there are few other places in Italy where what is the distinctive characteristic of our country, the only one that makes us really unique and the envy of the world, is so evident as here: the fact that the museum (in Florence, as in Siena, Venice, Rome, as in all the ancient cities of Italy) emerges from its confines, occupies the squares and streets and spills over into the places of worship. The most beautiful Pontormo in the world is not in the Uffizi, as one might expect, but in the Capponi Chapel of Santa Felicita. Donatello is in the Bargello, but also (as we have seen) in San Lorenzo. You cannot understand Masaccio without going to the Brancacci Chapel at Santa Maria del Carmine or to Santa Maria Novella, nor Ghiberti without a lengthy study of the doors of the baptistery. The Florentine painting of the 14th century is well documented in the Museo dell'Accademia, but it is even better represented in the frescoes of Santa Croce.

Notwithstanding the expropriations, abolitions and confiscations that have taken place in the modern era, the artistic heritage preserved in the churches remains, for its variety, for its instructiveness, for its excellence, the basic manual of great Florentine and therefore Italian art. This signifies that in Florence the museums and churches form an inseparable whole. Sometimes the museum is physically located in all or part of a religious building following institutional annexations or amputations, as in the case of San Marco, the Medici Chapels in San Lorenzo and the expropriated refectories of former monasteries (Sant'Apollonia with Andrea del Castagno's frescoes, San Salvi where the absolute masterpiece of Andrea del Sarto is located, Ognissanti with Ghirlandaio's *Last Supper*).

All this means that "sacred Florence" is outside the museums and inside the museums. In confirmation of the decisive role that religious inspiration has played in the artistic history of a city that has been a flower and model for the whole of the Christian West.

ANTONIO PAOLUCCI

Pier Francesco di Jacopo Foschi, *Disputation over the Conception*, 1540-45. Santo Spirito, Florence

Baptistery of San Giovanni

"Umbelicus urbis" from temple of Mars to heart of the city's civil and religious history.
Filled with mosaic decorations, it is characterized on the outside by marble in two colors
and three bronze doors which, along with the groups of sculptures set above them, bear witness
to the fundamental tendencies in Florentine art between the 14th and 16th century.

Michelozzo, *Saint John the Baptist*, 1445-47, detail of the altar of San Giovanni. Museo dell'Opera del Duomo, Florence

facing page
Florentine painters and mosaicists of the 13th century, *Dominations and Angels of the Last Judgment*, 1250-60 and 1260-75, detail of the second and third row of the dome

Piazza del Duomo

Built in the late classical period, modified in the Romanesque period

Canons of Florence

Viewed from above, the most striking thing about Florence Baptistery is its white marble roof. From the octagon run eight segments culminating in a polygonal lantern at the center, and the brilliance of the whole contrasts strongly with the terracotta tiles used to clad the roofs of the other monuments and houses of Florence. Anyone walking around it cannot help but be impressed by the elegance and proportion of the decoration of white and green slabs of marble, arranged in a geometric and regular pattern. And then the interior is a blaze of light, since the gilded and colored tesserae of the mosaics in the dome reflect the natural light that enters through the lantern. Entering you get a sensation of transcendent centrality, almost of mental confusion, so brilliant is the glow of the *Christ Pantocrator* and the *Scenes from the Gospels* that are represented. It is the largest and most magnificent baptistery constructed or reconstructed in the Romanesque period, probably on late classical foundations. The central role, proportions and morphological characteristics of the interior are in line with those of buildings erected between the 4th and 5th century AD, but also with the Pantheon (2nd century), which has always been indicated as the model for its proportions. It is likely that Florence Baptistery was decorated on the inside during the brief period of Byzantine rule (553-70): this is suggested by the women's galleries, where the adornment of the capitals is very similar to those of the Neonian Baptistery at Ravenna. During the 11th, 12th and 13th centuries the *bel San Giovanni* was completely clad with polychrome marble on the outside and lined with golden mosaics on the inside, becoming the symbol of the city itself, in keeping with its central and prominent position in religious life. Located at the nodal point of the city, it remained the baptistery of the Florentines up until the 1980s, the place where they received their first *viaticum* on the road to eternal life, and everything in its history and decoration reflects this central function of its existence.

The sacred city. Recent studies have shown that the central axis of the baptistery corresponds with that of the cathedral and that there used to be a colonnade linking the two constructions, called the "paradise," while the bishop's palace was built in line with the rectangular apse. All these buildings, which constituted the religious center of the city, were arranged in parallel to the Roman walls, whose north gate stood where Via Borgo San Lorenzo now passes, while the "cardo" ran along Via Roma. There were also precise relations between baptistery and basilica, with apses of identical proportions and a match between the measurements of the "paradise" and the bishop's palace, in accord with a plan that some have traced back to Constantine (compare the Holy Sepulcher and Anastasis in Jerusalem,).

The origins. It is highly likely that the construction of the baptistery, but not its decoration, took place before the visit of St. Ambrose to Florence (394 AD). In fact the iconography of the whole, which included

the ritual of washing the feet, seems to be linked to Ambrose's catechesis. Inside lamps were lit close to the baptismal tub, the central point of light of the whole building, according to the precise theology of baptism. Then the chosen catechumens arrived, entering from the north door (coming from the night and going, through the bath, into the realm of light). From the opposite, south side, the place of light, entered the clergy and bishop, each going to his allotted place. The catechumens stayed in the dark part, beyond the columns; they took off their old clothes to enter the pool naked and then received white robes and had their heads anointed. The clergy and bishop stood by the basin, located outside the colonnade. The presbyters washed the neophytes and the bishop went to his throne toward the apse to administer the sacrament of the Confirmation. At the end a procession was formed to the cathedral, leaving from the east door and passing through the "paradise" into the basilica, where the baptismal Eucharist commenced. Although the baptistery's origin remains uncertain (it is first mentioned in the documents in 897 and there is a record of a new consecration by Nicholas II in 1059 or 1061), we can be sure that its moment of greatest splendor was the one when it became the new symbol of the rich and greatly expanded city. The external decoration of polychrome marble that is so characteristic of Florentine Romanesque was executed in the 11th and 12th centuries, along with the internal mosaics and flooring, the apse and the new baptismal font. Finally the oculus at the center of the dome was closed with a lantern in 1150. Thus the baptistery became a municipal symbol as well as a religious one: the commune was to choose it as the place to keep its *carroccio* or "war chariot" and to deposit the most significant trophies of its military success. St. John would become the patron of the city and a symbol of its wealth (his image appeared on the florin, the ancient gold coin of Florence).

The exterior. The building, which can be described as an octagonal although not regular prism (the rectangular apse sticks out from the perimeter), is decorated with a geometric pattern of white (from Luni)

and green marble (from Prato). For the most part the facing is original (although many restorations are documented, the most substantial directed by Luigi del Moro in 1896) and datable to the Romanesque period, like that of San Miniato al Monte, which it closely resembles in its decorative motifs and proportions. In elevation, the baptistery is divided by projecting moldings into three tiers, of which the lower two correspond to the height of the internal subdivisions. Each side of the octagon is underlined by ribs at the corners, decorated in parallel bands. Each face is split into three and presents geometric motifs on two rhythmic and repetitive tiers. The second tier is architecturally complex and filled with citations of antiquity, making it a source of inspiration for Renaissance artists, from Ghiberti to Brunelleschi to Michelangelo. Divided into three, in continuity with the one below, by two-color polygonal pillars standing on plinths and supporting three round arches, it has three windows of different shapes and sizes: a central single-light window framed by half-columns topped by an arch, flanked by two rectangular ones enclosed by moldings in alternating colors and framed by triangular tympana resting on pilaster strips. The third tier under the dome is adorned with an unbroken pattern of rectangles. The decoration was executed around the turn of the 12th century and, we are told by Villani, finished in 1293 at the behest of the guild known as the Arte di Calimala. The roof of marble segments terminating in a lantern was commenced in 1150 and completed in 1174 (the date is inscribed on the base, but may have been added in a 19th-century restoration). The magnificent doors, executed at different times, blend into this architecture without disturbing its harmony in the slightest.

The doors. Until the 14th century the three doors of the baptistery appear to have been made of wood. When the Arte di Calimala had finished decorating the interior in mosaic the decision was taken to move on to a suitable ornamentation of the exterior. In 1329 the door on the east side (the one in front of the cathedral) was executed by Andrea Pisano on the model of the door of San Ranieri in Pisa Cathedral. From 1330

to *circa* 1336, the sculptor worked on the bas-reliefs representing the *Life of Saint John Baptist* (twenty panels) and *Virtues* (three theological, four cardinal and *Humility*). Twenty-eight scenes set inside a quatrefoil and mixtilinear frame, called *a compasso* and copied in the 15th century. Over both leaves runs the inscription: "ANDREAS UGOLINI NINI DE PISIS ME FECIT A.D. M CCC: XXX." Stylistically the door is influenced not only by the sculpture of Nicola and Giovanni Pisano, but also by the lesson of Giotto. At the beginning of the

and cast of a quatrefoil panel representing the *Sacrifice of Isaac*. Brunelleschi and Ghiberti's panels have survived (Museo Nazionale del Bargello, Florence). As is well known, the competition was won by Ghiberti. From 1403 to 1428 Ghiberti worked, with numerous assistants (including Donatello, Michelozzo and Paolo Uccello), on the two leaves of the door, which was dedicated to the *Life of Christ*. The general scheme, based on the one used by Andrea Pisano, comprised twenty-eight panels whose subjects were divided into

From left to right
Andrea Pisano, South Door, 1330-36

Lorenzo Ghiberti, North Door, 1403-28

Lorenzo Ghiberti, *Porta del Paradiso* ("Door of Paradise"), 1425-52

facing page
Lorenzo Ghiberti, Scenes from the Story of Esau and Jacob, 1425-52, detail of the Porta del Paradiso. Formerly in the baptistery, Museo dell'Opera del Duomo, Florence

15th century Andrea's door was moved to the north side of the baptistery and replaced by Ghiberti's; on that occasion the fine leaf in gilded bronze with plant shoots in relief alternating with little animals and figures in an antiquarian style was executed, again by Ghiberti's workshop. In 1424 the door was placed on the south side, where it can still be seen.

The procedure for the assignment of the second door (originally intended for the east façade, but then located on the north one) was very complicated. In 1401 the Arte di Calimala held a competition in which the best sculptors of the day took part (Ghiberti, Brunelleschi, Jacopo della Quercia, Simone da Colle, Niccolò d'Arezzo, Francesco di Valdambrino, Niccolò Lamberti). They were required to produce the model

two distinct parts: the eight in the bottom two rows represent *Evangelists* and *Doctors of the Church* (i.e. the foundation of the entire ecclesiastical structure), while the twenty in the upper five rows depict episodes from the *Life of Christ*. Above the first two scenes runs the inscription: "OPUS LAURENTII FLORENTINI." Around the squares containing the *compassi* is set a magnificent motif of ivy garlands with heads standing out in full relief at the junctions (one can be recognized as a self-portrait of Ghiberti). The door was transferred to the north side, where it is still visible, in 1452.

In 1425 the execution of the third door (east wall) was entrusted to Ghiberti again. The wax models were finished in 1429 and the casting of the ten panels of the so-called *Porta del Paradiso* in bronze was completed in

Master Jacopo (Jacopo Torriti?), *Mystic Lamb, Candeliere and Prophets*, 1225, detail of the ceiling of the rectangular apse

facing page
Ceiling of the baptistery

1437. The finishing took another two years, with the help of pupils like his son Vittorio, Michelozzo and Benozzo Gozzoli. In 1452 the door was ready and was located on the east wall after 1455, where it was replaced by a copy in the 1990s. Set between the two columns of the portal and two more columns in porphyry, a gift from the Pisans in commemoration of the naval victory over the Saracens in the Balearic Islands (1117), the golden door or *Porta del Paradiso* was recognized as the sculptor's absolute masterpiece. The iconographic program was drawn up by the chancellor of the Florentine republic Leonardo Bruni and Ghiberti composed ten large square panels, five for each leaf, with themes taken from the Old Testament. Each scene is set in a perspective space and the refined technique, shading from bas-relief to almost full relief, permitted the application of the most recent spatial theories. In the frame twenty-four full-length figures of personages from the Bible alternate with twenty-four heads in full relief (here too we find portraits of Lorenzo and Vittorio Ghiberti). The jambs and lintel are decorated with a continuous bronze frieze richly worked in plant wreaths and trophies, interspersed with animals, among them the eagle of the Calimala guild. Above each door were set sculptures by Tino di Camaino, removed by the Arte di Calimala and replaced by specially commissioned sculptural groups. On the south façade is the *Beheading of the Baptist*, executed by Vincenzo Danti from 1569 on and installed

in 1571. For the north one Francesco Rustici carved, from 1506 to 1511, the *Baptist* preaching to a Pharisee and a Levite. On the east front was set the *Baptism of Christ*, executed by Andrea Sansovino between 1502 and 1505 but left incomplete and finished by Vincenzo Danti (1569) and Innocenzo Spinazzi with the addition of the *Angel* in 1792.

The interior. The masonry structure of the baptistery is contained within an octagonal ring covered by a dome, with a double cavity wall. On the inside, in the lower part, stand sixteen columns, fourteen of them in granite and two in antique marble. They are followed by eight large corner pillars, two of which are hollow and contain the stairs leading to the women's galleries and dome. The corner pillars are repeated on the sec-

ond tier, where the women's gallery is located. The third tier forms the base of the double-shell dome. Everything inside is decorated: the floor with polychrome marble; the walls with green and white marble between columns and pillars with geometric and decorative motifs from various periods; the women's galleries with three two-light openings or "tribunes" adorned with geometric motifs in marble and rich mosaics on the inside, also dating from various periods; and the dome, clad in its entirety with mosaic tesserae representing the *Last Judgment*. The architectural subdivision described above does not apply to the western side with the rectangular apse, in which the altar is located. Here the structure of the wall opens up to form a large round arch resting on corner pillars, whose curved head rises to occupy the level of

The Floor

At the beginning of the 13th century the original flooring in *opus signinum* was replaced by the sumptuous marble floor we see today, which used to cover the whole area of the octagon before the alterations for the baptism of Filippo di Francesco de' Medici made by Buontalenti in 1577 led to the destruction of the central part, where the ancient font mentioned by Dante stood. The division into variously decorated sections follows no precise scheme, but a criterion of juxtaposition reminiscent of the rugs of Islamic mosques. A series of more or less rectangular panels set side by side and composed of green, white and red tesserae forming serpents, triangles and diamonds interspersed with circles, naturalistic elements, fantastic creatures, dragons, griffons and the disc of the Zodiac. Under the floor lies that of the preexisting temple, whose decoration can be dated to the 3rd century.

Wheels with Birds, Griffons and Lions, 12th century, detail of the floor

the women's galleries. In the rectangular apse the corners are reinforced by four columns salvaged from Roman buildings, in different kinds of marble.

The mosaics. The decoration of the dome of San Giovanni is without doubt one of the oldest and most important figurative cycles in Florence. Many studies have been carried out, even in recent times, into the chronology, attribution and iconography of the mosaics. An inscription in the apse gives the date of the beginning of the work, May 21, 1225, and the author, a Franciscan friar called Jacopo whose origin is unknown and whom some believe to have been Roman and others Venetian. Jacopo was responsible for the main figures, while the rows of a more narrative character, begun in 1271 and finished after the first decade of the 14th century, are attributed to some of the finest Florentine artists active at the time (Meliore, the Masters of the Magdalen and the Bardi St. Francis, Cimabue, Coppo di Marcovaldo).

The mosaics should be read from top to bottom. Below a border of moldings with a frieze of palmettes is set a band resembling a velarium in which heads are represented inside tondi, like medals, separated by symbolic pairs of animals. In the band underneath are *Hierarchies of Angels* (one in each segment, with the seraphim and cherubim gathered around Christ). The three rows under these are dominated by the imposing image of *Christ the Judge* inside a variegated circular nimbus (west segment); the two adjoining segments (northwest and southwest) are dedicated to the *Last Judgment*, with angels holding symbols of the Passion at the top, the chosen with the Madonna and St. John in the middle and the resurrection of the flesh with Heaven and Hell at the bottom. The remaining five segments are split into four rows, of which the one at the top under the *Hierarchies* contains, counterclockwise, *Scenes from Genesis*, the next *Scenes from the Story of Joseph the Patriarch*, the third *Scenes from the Life of Mary and Christ* and the fourth *Scenes from the Life of the Baptist*. At the base of the dome openings to let in light alternate with panels containing busts of bishop and deacon saints. In the archway beneath Christ, leading into the apse,

there is a row of busts at the sides of the central *Baptist* under a decorative border. *Prophets* are represented on the soffit. In the vault of the apse four telamones kneeling on dosserets support a central wheel enclosing figures of *Prophets and Patriarchs of the Old Testament*; the *Madonna* and *Saint John* are seated on two thrones set symmetrically at the sides.

Relatively few of the works commissioned for the baptistery over the centuries remain inside the building. The magnificent silver and enamel altar executed from *circa* 1366 to 1483 is now in the Museo dell'Opera, as are the wooden *Magdalen*, a late work by Donatello, and the hanging designed by Pollaiuolo.

Of those that are left the most important is without doubt the monument erected in honor of the antipope John XXIII, i.e. Baldassarre Coscia or Cossa, who died in 1419. Deposed by the Council of Constance, Coscia was given the title of cardinal by his successor, Martin V. He left the money needed for his tomb, which he wanted in Florence, and in 1428 the Signoria commissioned the monument from Donatello, who executed it in collaboration with Michelozzo, his partner at the time.

Set between two imposing columns, the monument is surmounted by a canopy that appears to hang from a large ring in the center of the space. Underneath is a valve enclosing an image of the Virgin, whose presence protects the slightly foreshortened bier with the deceased.

The figure is wearing bishop's robes and lying on a "faldstool" bed with lion's paws and heads. The space behind is decorated with three panels. The bier stands on a sarcophagus with two funerary cherubs in relief holding the dedicatory inscription. Underneath this is set a socle adorned with festoons and angel's heads and a bas-relief with three niches containing the three Theological Virtues (carved by Michelozzo).

Donatello was responsible for the general idea and the execution of the antipope's sepulchral monument, a gilded bronze sculpture which is a true portrait rich in naturalistic details. These are also to be found in all the decorative elements (such as the fabric of the canopy and cushion), executed with the great sculptor's customary freedom.

IOANES QVODAMPAPA
XXIII·OBIITFLORENTIEA
ÑODÑIMCCCCXVIIIIXI
KALENDASIANVARII

The Altar of San Giovanni Battista

Work continued on the magnificent altar, in embossed and chased silver with cast elements and enamels, for over a century (*circa* 1366-1483). Parallelepipedal in shape, it is divided by eight pillars into twelve panels, eight on the front and two on each side. Along the upper part runs an unbroken series of niches with statuettes of *Saints, Prophets and Sibyls*. In the middle of the front is set the figure of the Baptist in full relief, flanked by scenes from his life. The date of the beginning of the work, 1366, is recorded in the inscription along the altar's base. The altar can be considered a votive offering made by Florence to its patron saint for the victory over the Pisans (1364), which had ensured the city's access to the sea and a revival of

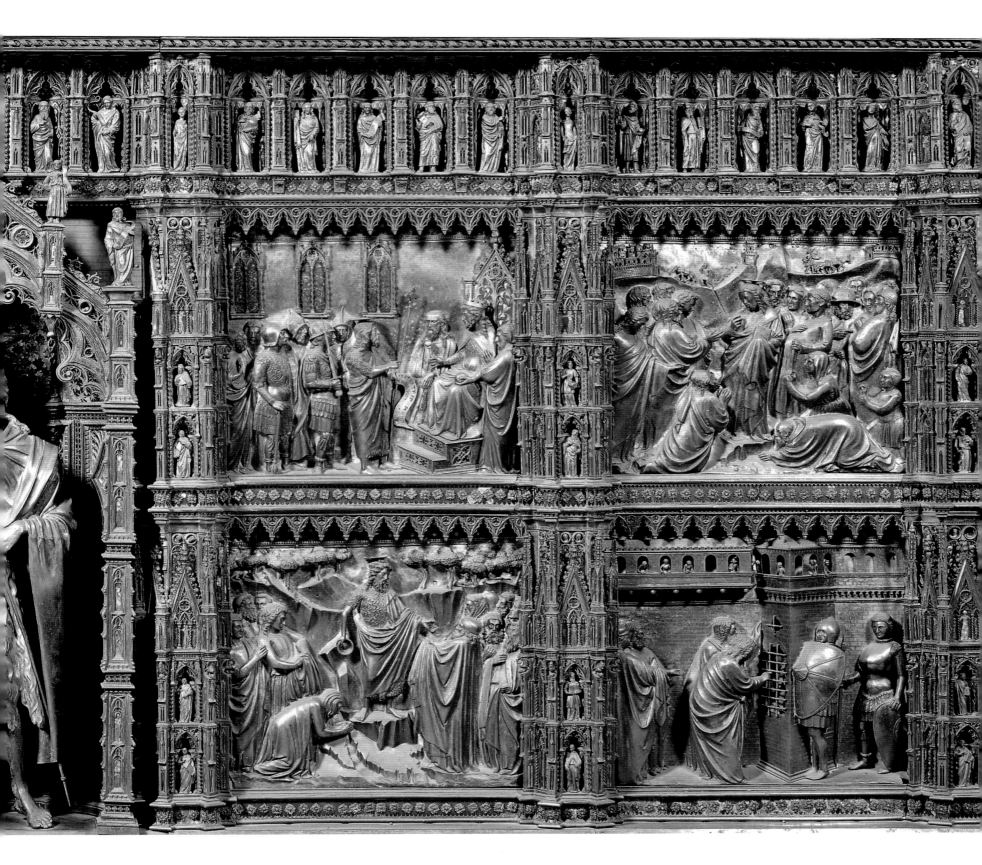

trade. In the early years the work was done by the Florentine goldsmiths Betto di Geri and Leonardo di ser Giovanni. The most significant interventions were carried out in the 15th century: in 1445-47, when Michelozzo executed the statue of the Baptist and Lorenzo Ghiberti's son Tommaso worked on the bas-reliefs with the life of the saint, and in 1477-83 when other bas-reliefs were executed by Antonio del Pollaiuolo, Bernardo Cennini and Andrea del Verrocchio (left-hand side) and by Antonio di Salvi and Francesco di Giovanni (right-hand side). At the times it was put on display, up until its transfer to the Museo dell'Opera in the 19th century, the altar was adorned with all the liturgical treasure of San Giovanni.

Florentine sculptors of the 14th and 15th century, *Altar of San Giovanni Battista*, c. 1366-1483. Museo dell'Opera del Duomo, Florence

Santa Maria del Fiore

The cathedral, proud and instantly recognizable mark of Florence's wealth and power.
Brunelleschi's dome constitutes the towering Renaissance standard
raised to make it visible far beyond the confines of the city

Crest of the city of Florence.
Chapel of the Princes,
San Lorenzo, Florence

facing page
Florentine painter and mosaicist
of the 13th century (Master of
the Magdalen?), *Coronation of
the Virgin*, c. 1280-90, inside
wall of the façade, detail

Piazza del Duomo

*Cathedral church of Florence.
First dedicated to St. Reparata,
it was rebuilt from 1284 onward*

Canons of Florence

*Patrons: Consoli di Calima and
Arte della Lana*

Florence Cathedral is located at the nerve center of the city, in line with the baptistery. The building is characterized by Brunelleschi's dome, which makes it visible and recognizable from every part of Florence. It must have looked even more imposing when the city was surrounded by nothing but open countryside and hills, from which the red brick of its roof and the white ribs that delimit and define its space can still often be seen. A towering standard raised to make it visible far beyond the confines of the city, "covering all the peoples of Tuscany with its shade" as Leon Battista Alberti put it.

Ancient history. The discovery, following the excavations of 1965-73, of the existence of the early Christian basilica (perhaps originally dedicated to the Savior, but soon afterward to St. Reparata) underneath Santa Maria del Fiore, together with the conviction that it had the same late classical origin as the *bel San Giovanni* (a belief that has never faded in the city's historical memory and is supported by many scholars), inevitably led to the suspicion that the two buildings, baptistery and basilica, formed part of a single project, dating from the final period of late classical antiquity. At the time the two buildings were located close to and parallel with the walls that marked the northern boundary of *Florentia*, the colonial Roman city founded in the 1st century BC. Inside the first ring of walls stood the original church dedicated to St. Reparata, which may have been constructed, according to the evidence brought to light by the excava-

tions, immediately after the baptistery (already in existence before 535) and been closely connected with it and with the layout of the religious center. The period that stretched from the beginning of the Gothic War of Justinian to the Longobard conquest of Florence (535-70) must have seen a suspension of the work, which was resumed in the brief period of Byzantine rule (553-70), judging by several floor mosaics found in the basilica. For historical reasons, the project was then abandoned for almost two centuries, but in 724 there is reference to activity around the basilica. It is not clear whether it immediately assumed the role of cathedral or if, as some historians claim, this function was performed, at the time of St. Ambrose, by the basilica of San Lorenzo, consecrated by the bishop of Milan. According to tradition the body of St. Zenobius, the first bishop of Florence, was buried in San Lorenzo when he died in 397 and only later moved to Santa Reparata. Legend has it that a dead tree blossomed on that occasion, and the site of the miracle is now marked by the column of San Zanobi.

The demolition of the Carolingian walls and the rapid demographic and economic growth of Florence in the 13th century, which had led the commune to decide to build a third circle of walls (1285) only a hundred years after the last one (1173-75), quadrupling the size of the city, also made necessary the erection of a series of churches belonging to the new monastic orders (Santa Croce, Santa Maria Novella, Ognissanti, etc.) and, obviously, the creation of a suitable cathedral. So in 1294 work started on the building, to a design by

Arnolfo di Cambio and at the expense of the Commune of Florence. The construction of the church commenced from the apsidal part, permitting the use of the old one until the new and much larger building was ready. Thus the old church was gradually incorporated into the new one, culminating in the demolition (1375) of the section closest to the new façade. In 1331, the year the body of St. Zenobius was identified, responsibility for the work on Santa Reparata was entrusted to the Consoli di Calimala (the guild of bankers and cloth merchants) and the Arte della Lana (wool guild), who became the patrons of Florence Cathedral, contributing to the funds allocated by the Commune of Florence for the building of the Duomo, as the cathedral is called in Florence. Thus it became a showcase of municipal glory at the center of a square that was redesigned to set off the imposing building, on the axis of the new Palazzo Pubblico, constructed in those same years. The mosaic lunette on the inside wall of the facade, which is the oldest decoration in the cathedral, dates from this time. It depicts the *Coronation of Mary* and can be attributed to an artist in Cimabue's circle. The *Polyptych of Saint Reparata*, painted on both sides and distinctly Giottesque in style, dates from not long after, executed at the turn of the 13th century by a close follower of Giotto, called "Giotto's relative" by the critics.

The marvelous quality of the architecture of Santa Maria del Fiore is fully revealed if you take a walk around the outside, from where the manner in which the various sections of the building interlock is immediately apparent, setting one another off and enhancing the overall effect through the contrast between the broken forms of the geometric solids and the convex volumes of the cupolas and between the marble facing of white and green slabs of marble and the fired-brick tiles of the cupolas. Each of the three apses, arranged in a tricorn pattern, is in the shape of an octagon, from which three sides have been removed where it connects with the main body of the cathedral. The cupolas above abut onto the wall of the drum, but stand out from it, accentuating the drum's isolation and height. The third and last cupola of the apse was completed amidst great rejoicings in

1421. The cathedral's facing of polychrome marble (white, green, black and red) echoes that of the baptistery, but at the same time diverges from it, reflecting the change of style that occurred over the long period it took to execute the external ornamentation of the sides and apse of the cathedral. The oldest part is the one close to the join with the façade and was built before 1310 by Arnolfo himself. The marble inlay covers the entire surface, creating a dazzling effect, and comprises the ribs, the windows and the magnificent doors, the oldest of which are the ones on the south and north sides, located close to the façade. Known as the Porta del Campanile and the Porta dei Cornacchini or di Balla, they recall Arnolfo's scheme of composition and are enriched with sculptural elements, some of which are now in the Museo dell'Opera. On the north door, the Porta dei Cornacchini, is set the group of the *Annunciation* attributed to Niccolò di Pietro Lamberti (1402). The other two side doors are called the Porta dei Canonici (south) and the Porta della Mandorla (north).

The Porta della Mandorla. This is perhaps the most artistically significant. Work started on it in 1368, but the architectural structure was not completed until 1397. On the lintel is set the celebrated mandorla with a sculpture representing the *Virgin Handing the Girdle to Saint Thomas*, surrounded by angels, attributed to Nanni di Banco, author of the *Four Crowned Ones* in a niche on Orsanmichele. On the pinnacles at the sides are figures of prophets, one of them attributed to a very young Luca della Robbia. Giovanni di Ambrogio, Piero di Giovanni Tedesco, Niccolò Lamberti, Jacopo di Piero Guidi, and Antonio and Nanni di Banco worked on the reliefs. The *Man of Sorrows* in the pentagonal panel set in the key of the arch is attributed to either Donatello or Nanni di Banco. The *Our Lady of the Annunciation* and *Announcing Angel* formerly in the tympanum and replaced by the *Annunciation* in mosaic by Domenico and David Ghirlandaio in 1487 (now in the Museo dell'Opera), have been attributed to the young Jacopo della Quercia. The shift in the style of sculpture from the Gothic to the Renaissance is clearly

The Façade

Work on the façade had been commenced around 1310 to a design by Arnolfo di Cambio. However, it never got beyond the third tier of decoration, as is clear from a drawing by Bernadino Poccetti, now in the Museo dell'Opera del Duomo. We know that it comprised the splendid sculptures by Arnolfo that can still be seen in the same museum. Above the main portal, for example, was set the *Madonna and Child Enthroned*, which Arnolfo carved in a style completely in harmony with Giotto's painting of the same years and thus strongly influenced by ancient and in particular Etruscan statuary. In 1587 Bernardo Buontalenti was commissioned by Francesco I de' Medici to make a wooden model of a new façade in keeping with changing tastes to replace Arnolfo's. The magnificent model, along with the designs that preceded it and the many that followed, up until the last and definitive one produced by De Fabris in 1871-86, is also in the Museo dell'Opera del Duomo. After Buontalenti had come up with his design a competition was held for the construction of the façade. The most famous architects of the day took part, from Dosio to Cigoli and Giambologna, submitting projects that reflected the simplification of style called for by the Council of Trent. The last design was drawn up in 1633 by a group of members of the Florentine Academy. This was used as the basis for the construction of the façade in 1636, as it appears in a painting now in the Misericordia in Florence. Harsh criticism induced the grand duke to call a halt to the work, and in 1688 Ercole Graziani executed a painted façade to make up for the lack of decoration of Florence's principal church. The present façade was built between 1870 and 1887 to a design by Emilio De Fabris, whose project was chosen from among the many presented at the time, of which the drawings and models are preserved in the Museo dell'Opera. Other competitions were held for the three bronze doors, finished in 1903. In the dense ornamentation of the new façade, the decorative elements are linked iconographically with the history of the cathedral and its dedication to the Virgin. The Marian and Christological themes are flanked by figures drawn from holy scripture (*Apostles* etc.) or important personages of the Church (*Popes, Bishops,* etc.). The statues were carved by some of the most famous sculptors of the day (Sarrocchi, Fantacchiotti, Ximenes, Carnielo, Romanelli, Amalia Dupré) from 1879 onward. The completion of the façade was celebrated with great festivities attended by all the Italian and foreign nobility present in the city.

reflected in this decoration and the planned restoration will certainly make it easier to understand the role played by the various sculptors in the work of decoration, which was not finished until 1423.

The campanile. It was designed by Giotto (the drawing is now in the Museo dell'Opera del Duomo in Siena) and work began on its construction in 1334, lasting up until 1387 and absorbing much of the Vestry Board's financial resources. Giotto was in charge from 1334 until 1337, when his place was taken by Andrea Pisano, who had collaborated on the decorative panels of the campanile. He retained the role of master builder until 1343, reaching as far as the second tier of decorations. He was succeeded, for a short time, by Taddeo Gaddi and finally by Francesco Talenti, who finished the work, adding the pairs of two-light windows, the third level with a three-light window on each side and the crown in the form of a balcony.

The building is a tall bell tower, located to the right of the cathedral, whose form and decoration are fully in keeping with that of the baptistery and the original façade. Quadrangular in section and taller than any other construction in Florence at the time, it is freestanding and completely detached from the structure of the cathedral. The form of the tower is underlined by four vertical edges that have been reinforced for its entire height by four pillars with an octagonal section. The base is clearly marked by continuous moldings while the top consists of a projecting and deeply shaded, accessible balcony, formed out of corbels and parapets of finely worked marble.

In the lowest and oldest part of the campanile are set hexagonal (at the bottom) and rhomboidal (the ones higher up) panels with figurations linked to the theme of humanity's redemption from original sin through work and knowledge, over the course of a Christian life illuminated by Grace. On the basis of a subdivision that was later adopted by Scholasticism, the *Mechanical Arts* are represented at the bottom, together with the *Creative and Inventive Arts.* Above them are set the *Liberal Arts* of the Trivium and the Quadrivium, along with the *Cardinal* and *Theological Virtues* and the *Sacraments.* The whole of this part of the decoration,

replaced by copies in 1965, is now in the Museo dell'Opera and can be attributed to Andrea Pisano and his collaborators, such as his son Nino and Maso di Banco. Five panels were carved by Luca della Robbia around 1437-39, after the demolition of the bridge between the cathedral and the campanile.

The niches of the third tier used to hold imposing statues in full relief, which have also been removed for reasons of conservation and can be seen in the Museo dell'Opera. They represent *Kings, Patriarchs, Prophets* and *Sibyls* of the Old Testament, symbolizing the preparation for the Redemption to be attained through the Christian Sacraments. On the side facing the baptistery were located the *Saint John the Baptist* attributed to Donatello (1420-23), *Habakkuk,* also by the great sculptor (1434-36), and *Jeremiah* (1423-27) and *Abdias,* carved by Nanni di Bartolo (1422). On the portal of access on the east side were inserted figures of *Prophets,* executed around 1410 by Nanni di Bartolo, Niccolò Lamberti or perhaps the young Donatello.

The Renaissance. It is obvious that the updating of style which was changing Florentine and Italian art could not fail to leave its mark on the principal church of Florence. From the first decade of the 15th century and right up to its end many works were commissioned. The earliest, already referred to, was the Porta della Mandorla, clearly reflecting the shift in style. This was followed by a large number of stained-glass windows, sculptures, paintings, wooden inlays, hangings and pieces of gold work commissioned by the members of the Vestry Board and executed by the most important artists in Florence. A program of general renovation that did not clash with the contributions of the past but blended in with them, renewing the church and bringing it up to date with the extraordinary balance that characterizes the development of art in Florence. The grandest of these works was without doubt the dome, but the sculptures of Luca della Robbia and Donatello, the paintings of Paolo Uccello and Andrea del Castagno and the inlays of Giuliano da Maiano confirm this harmony of artistic feeling. Given that they are all gen-

Donatello (?), *Prophet*, 1406-09. Porta della Mandorla

facing page
The tympanum of the Porta della Mandorla

uine masterpieces we have decided to devote a separate section to each of them, which can be read by itself or in the chronological context of the church.

The dome. The dome was designed by Brunelleschi in the same spirit as shaped the architecture of his predecessors: the ribs of white marble, set on the eight joints, are an ideal continuation of the corner pillars of the drum and come together at the top to form the base of the "lantern." On this last, built entirely of marble, the accentuation of the eight joints continues right up to the base of the terminal cone, culminating in a gilded ball. Even though founded on the well-established design of domes that had already been built, the structural system employed by Brunelleschi was so innovative that it astonished his contemporaries, and even today those who have investigated its construction and who are responsible for its maintenance and restoration cannot agree over the methods used. The documentation, still preserved in the archives of the Vestry Board and published in large part by Cesare Guasti in 1857, records the various stages of the undertaking, from the competition to the execution of the external finishings (the decoration of the drum, the lantern). The dome rests on the drum (constructed between 1413 and 1417 in solid masonry) and is made up of two shells – an outer and an inner – of different thickness, rendered solid by spurs (twenty-four in all), of which the ones at the corners form the ribs clad with marble. Horizontal arches create a link between the spurs and the two shells have sections of walling binding them together, with walkways constructed to permit inspection. The sides, or segments, trapezoid in shape, are constructed on a plane that curves as it rises toward the top, where they are united by the keystone, on which is set the lantern in the form of a tempietto.

Brunelleschi, consulted in 1417, began to study the problem of the dome's construction together and in competition with other master carpenters and mathematicians. The Vestry Board accepted Brunelleschi's design, presented in collaboration with Donatello and Nanni di Banco and in competition with Ghiberti. Brunelleschi started to erect the dome without formwork in 1426. By 1432 the work had reached an advanced stage and in 1436 the two shells were completed and blessed by Bishop Federighi.

The four *tempietti* or blind galleries set at the height of the drum and serving as buttresses were designed in 1439, but constructed from 1445 onward. Each consists of five niches with conch-shaped vaults, framed by Corinthian columns. From 1460 to 1512 the facing of the drum was executed, in white and green marble (never completed), in which are set the "eyes" with deep splays decorated with polychrome inlays. The lantern, designed from the outset, was not built until 1445. It has eight faces, in each of which is set a tall and narrow window; at the corners stand pairs of pilaster strips, from which run the buttresses. Above is set the pyramidal finial with curved faces. Brunelleschi was unable to finish the lantern: he died in 1446 and the responsibility for its construction passed to Michelozzo and then Ciaccheri and Rossellino. The crown, in the shape of a golden sphere, was made by Andrea del Verrocchio in 1467. It was brought down by lightning in 1601 and put back in place in 1604. The clock set on the inside of the façade was painted by Paolo Uccello between 1440 and 1443. It consists of a central face with twenty-four divisions corresponding to the hours of the day and is read like a sundial, starting from the time of sunset (i.e. if the hand indicates two, it means two hours have gone by since sunset, obviously at different times in different seasons). The faces of the four Evangelists are set at the corners, inserted in circles painted in perspective, like medallions.

Giovanni Acuto. The monument was frescoed in green earth by Paolo Uccello in 1436, to commemorate the English mercenary John Hawkwood, hired by the republic in 1364 and famous for leading the Florentine forces to victory over the Pisans at the battle of Cascina. The imposing image, restored a short time ago, presents the captain of fortune on horseback and in parade armor. The figures of the rider and horse, in green monochrome, simulate bronze and the harness, in ocher, imitates gilding. The "statue," painted to look like a solid volume, stands on a base recalling a sarcophagus and bears an inscription in Roman letters: "IOANNES ACUTUS

View of the campanile

facing page
Detail of the campanile showing the panels representing
The Virtues, Arts and Crafts

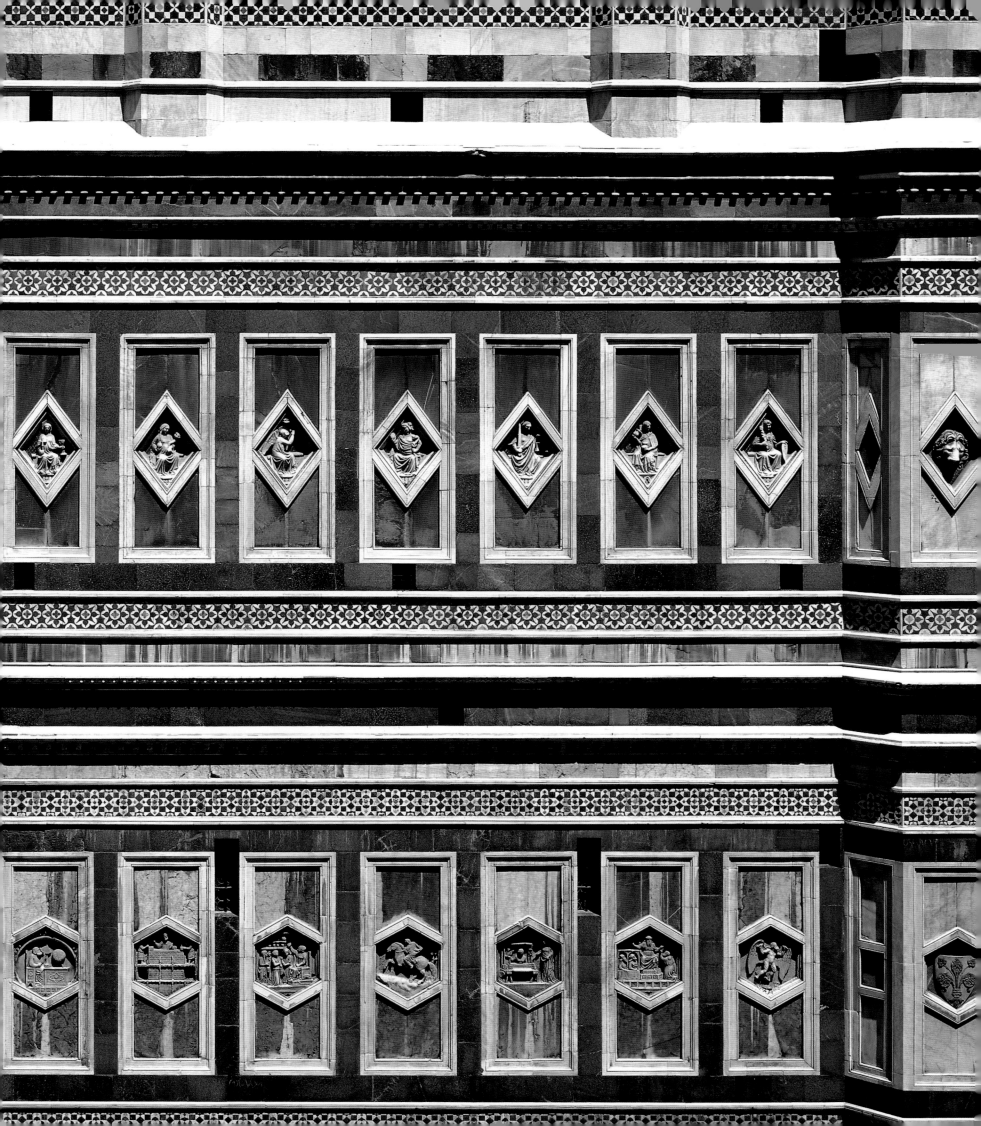

Dome of Santa Maria del Fiore

EQUES BRITANNICUS DUX AETATIS S/UAE CAUTIS-
SIMUS ET REI MILITARI PERITISSIMUS HABITUS EST."
The whole thing is set on a deep console painted in
sotto in su perspective and decorated with coffers,
supported by three large volutes interspersed with
the *condottiere*'s coat of arms. Paolo Uccello preserved his name for perpetuity by writing it in capital letters in the middle of this console (PAULUS
UGIELLI OPUS). The background is an imitation of
red porphyry and is bounded by a frame decorated
with *candeliere* and geometric elements at the corners
and in the middle of each side, painted in the early
16th century. For reasons of conservation, the fresco
was transferred onto canvas in 1842.

Niccolò da Tolentino. Located next to *Acuto, Niccolò da Tolentino* was painted by Andrea del Castagno
between 1455 and 1456. The *condottiere*, winner of
the battle of San Romano in 1432, was buried in the
cathedral in 1435. Castagno's memorial is painted in
gray monochrome on a blue-green ground, imitating serpentine. The mercenary's pose is similar to
that of Sir John Hawkwood, making it look as if they
are on parade, but horse and rider are vividly
depicted in all the detail of their muscles and of the
harness, armor, cloak and hat, in flowing and curling
lines that reach their climax in the knotting of the
horse's tail. The plinth on which the monument
stands is flanked by two warrior geniuses bearing the
family arms and imitating sculpture in white marble.
The sarcophagus has a scale roof and decorations in
porphyry and gold. The central slab is also in imitation porphyry and bears an inscription set on a
white tablet, flanked by two small columns of the
type used in balustrades. A sort of large shell,
between two consoles with plant motifs, supports the
base for the sarcophagus and monument. The
frame, underlined with geometric elements just like
the previous one, is adorned with palmettes like the
fascia of the sarcophagus. The fresco was detached
in 1842 and transferred onto canvas. Another
restoration in 1954, followed by a very recent one
(2000), have given the painting back its planarity
and legibility.

Paolo Uccello, *Giovanni Acuto*
(*John Hawkwood*), 1436

Andrea del Castagno
Niccolò da Tolentino, 1455-56

following pages
Domenico di Michelino, *Dante with the Divine Comedy*, 1465

NEL MEZO DE
L CHAMINO
DI NOSTRA
VITA MI RI
TROVA PE
R UNA SEL
VA SCURA
CHE LA DIRI
TTA VIA ER
A SMARITA
E QUANTA
DIR QUAL E
RE COSA D
URA QUE
STA SILVA
SILVAGGI
ASPRA ET
FORTE CH
E NEL PEN
SIERI NO

The Divine Comedy Illuminates Florence. This canvas, painted in honor of the great Florentine poet Dante Alighieri, was designed by Alesso Baldovinetti, but executed by Domenico di Michelino, who finished it in 1465. Dante appears at the center at full length, holding the open poem. On his left is the city of Florence, surrounded by walls, inside which we can recognize the cathedral with Brunelleschi's dome, Palazzo Vecchio and the campaniles of the Bargello and Badia. On his right is a view of the Inferno based on Dante's description, while in-the background we see Purgatory with the entrance to the golden door of Paradise. Above this sort of pyramid Adam and Eve are represented in the Garden of Eden with the apple of original sin, and higher still the heavens, an allusion to Paradise, in accordance with the Ptolemaic conception.

The sacristies. Two spaces of not very large size open to the north and south of the choir respectively: the sacristies of the Masses and the Canons. The first, from *circa* 1436 to 1457, was completely lined with stalls of inlaid walnut made by various master craftsmen headed by Agnolo di Lazzaro, who collaborated with Scheggia (Masaccio's brother) and Antonio Manetti, Brunelleschi's assistant and biographer. The inlays were completed, between 1463 and 1468, by Giuliano da Maiano and collaborators. The sacristy of the Canons, above whose entrance was set Donatello's *Cantoria*, now in the Museo dell'Opera, houses Renaissance paintings and sculptures from the altars of the church. They include Lorenzo di Credi's splendid *Michael the Archangel* and Giuliano and Benedetto da Maiano's wooden *Crucifix*, revealed in all in its magnificence by the recent restoration.

Luca della Robbia and Donatello. In 1688, on the occasion of the baroque preparations for the wedding of Ferdinando and Violante of Bavaria, the celebrated *Cantorie*, or *Singing Galleries*, now in the Museo dell'Opera del Duomo, were removed from their position above the entrances to the sacristies. Luca's *Cantoria* (1431-38), in white marble, originally above the sacristy of the Masses, is supported by five consoles decorated with acanthus leaves that frame four reliefs with putti, maidens and angels playing musical instruments. On the parapet are set six similar reliefs alternating with pairs of fluted responds. Above runs a frieze with an inscription in Roman capitals that recalls the verses of Psalm 150, an allusion to the power of Christ and the Resurrection. Still *in situ* are the lunette in glazed terracotta depicting the *Resurrection* executed by Luca della Robbia in 1442-44 and the later lunette with the *Ascension* (commissioned in 1446 but installed in 1451), set above the sacristy of the Canons where the *Singing Gallery* carved by Donatello between 1433 and 1439 used to be located as a companion to Luca's. The two marble pulpits were supposed to adhere to a unitary conception, as complements to the new organs commissioned in 1432. But Donatello departed from the proposed scheme, sculpting a deep and continuous frieze on the faces, resting on five large consoles adorned with acanthus leaves and plant motifs. The background and the pairs of columns that punctuate the frieze are covered with gold and colored tesserae and create an effect of vibrant preciosity.

Two candle-holding angels in glazed terracotta were commissioned from Luca in 1448. The life-size figures, each carved in one piece, covered with white enamel and finished in gold, are now in the chapel of San Zanobi. The bronze door of the sacristy of the Masses was the fruit of a long and complex gestation and was executed by Luca together with Michelozzo and Maso di Bartolomeo from 1435 to 1474. The ten reliefs of which it is made up represent the *Doctors of the Church, Evangelists, Virgin* and *Saint John the Baptist*, following Donatello's prototype for the Old Sacristy of San Lorenzo.

The chapel of San Zanobi. The most important of the chapels from the liturgical viewpoint, the one in the middle of the east tribune, was dedicated to St. Zenobius in 1428, with the intention of erecting an

top
Luca della Robbia, *Cantoria*, 1431-38. Museo dell'Opera del Duomo, Florence

bottom
Donatello, *Cantoria*, 1433-39. Museo dell'Opera del Duomo, Florence

facing page
Luca della Robbia, *Singing Angels*, 1431-38, detail of the *Cantoria*. Museo dell'Opera del Duomo, Florence

The Stained-Glass Windows

A total of forty-four stained-glass windows filter the light that enters the great Gothic basilica, tinting it with magical reflections. A cycle dedicated to Marian and Christological themes and to the most important saints in Florence's history, executed from *circa* 1394 to 1444 and designed by the city's greatest artists. The first windows to be installed were the ones in the nave and aisles. The window by the door of the Canons bears the date 1394 and represents *John the Baptist*, *Louis of France*, *Bishop Barnabas*, *Pope Victor*, *Anthony of Vienne* and *Miniatus*. The frieze on the intrados was painted by Mariotto di Nardo. The stained-glass window next to the door of the campanile dates from 1395. It depicts *Zenobius* and *Reparata*, the deacons *Eugenius* and *Crescentius* (linked with St. Zenobius), a probable *Bernard degli Uberti* and *Catherine of Alexandria*. The painted frieze is by Francesco di Tommaso. The other two late

14th-century windows were executed by Mariotto di Nardo and Agnolo Gaddi between 1395 and 1396. Three large oculi with stained glass executed to a design by Ghiberti light up the inside of the façade with scintillating colors. The oldest represents *Our Lady of the Assumption* (1405) and is set in the central oculus, while *Lawrence* and *Stephen* are depicted in the ones at the sides (1412-15). The oculi in the drum of the dome all date from the 15th century and represent scenes from the *Life of Christ*. The cartoons were produced by painters and sculptors like Donatello, Andrea del Castagno, Paolo Uccello and Ghiberti from 1433 on. The first, in chronological order, was the oculus with the *Coronation of the Virgin*, executed in 1434-37 to a cartoon by Donatello. This was followed by the windows commissioned from Ghiberti: the *Ascension*, *Presentation in the Temple* and *Agony in the Garden* (1443-44). Paolo

Uccello worked on the *Nativity*, *Resurrection* and *Ascension* in the same period. The *Annunciation* executed by Paolo in 1445 has been lost, while Andrea del Castagno's window depicting the *Lamentation over the Dead Christ* (1444) has survived. The windows of the chapels in the apse are devoted to Marian themes and the lives of the most important saints for Florence, based on Jacobus de Voragine's *Legenda Aurea*, a text that circulated from the 13th century on. In the chapels, in fact, the *Virgin* is surrounded by *John the Baptist*, *Reparata*, *Miniatus*, *Zenobius* and the principal saints of the Church, including *John the Evangelist*, *Peter and Paul*, *Simon and Jude*, *Philip* and *James the Lesser*, as well as *Kings*, *Ancestors* and *Prophets*.
The authors of the stained-glass windows belonged to the circle of Ghiberti and were close to Alesso Baldovinetti and Maso da Finiguerra.

Paolo Uccello, *Nativity*, 1443-44, window in the drum

Lorenzo Ghiberti, *Presentation in the Temple*, 1443-44, window in the drum

Lorenzo Ghiberti, *Agony in the Garden*, 1443-44, window in the drum

Andrea del Castagno, *Lamentation over the Dead Christ*, 1444, window in the drum

Paolo Uccello, *Resurrection*, 1443-44, window in the drum

Lorenzo Ghiberti, *Ascension*, 1443-44, window in the drum

facing page
Andrea del Castagno, *Lamentation over the Dead Christ*, detail

View of the choir

facing page
Baccio Bandinelli and Giovanni
Bandini, *Prophets*, 1547-65,
detail of the choir

altar in it to hold a casket for the remains of the venerated Florentine saint. Brunelleschi designed a crypt to house the bronze casket executed by Lorenzo Ghiberti and finished in 1442. The urn-shaped casket with a lid is visible today underneath the altar and on the main front represents the *Raising of a Child* by the saint, a splendid carving using the technique of *rilievo stiacciato*, so that the figures in the foreground stand out in full relief but the image is gradually flattened into the very low relief of the architectural background.

The choir and the Counter-Reformation decoration. The central area of the choir is devoted to the high altar. In 1547 Duke Cosimo I de' Medici entrusted the Michelangelesque sculptor Baccio Bandinelli with the reconstruction of the octagonal enclosure of the choir, formerly in wood. This was the first Medicean commission for the cathedral and, as well as Bandinelli, Giuliano di Baccio d'Agnolo, Battista Lorenzi and Giovanni Bandini worked on it, creating a structure composed of a marble base enclosing the altar and seats, surmounted by an architraved Ionic colonnade. The outside of the pedestal was decorated with panels carved with prophets and apostles in relief, and behind the altar stood imposing sculptures of *Adam and Eve* (in

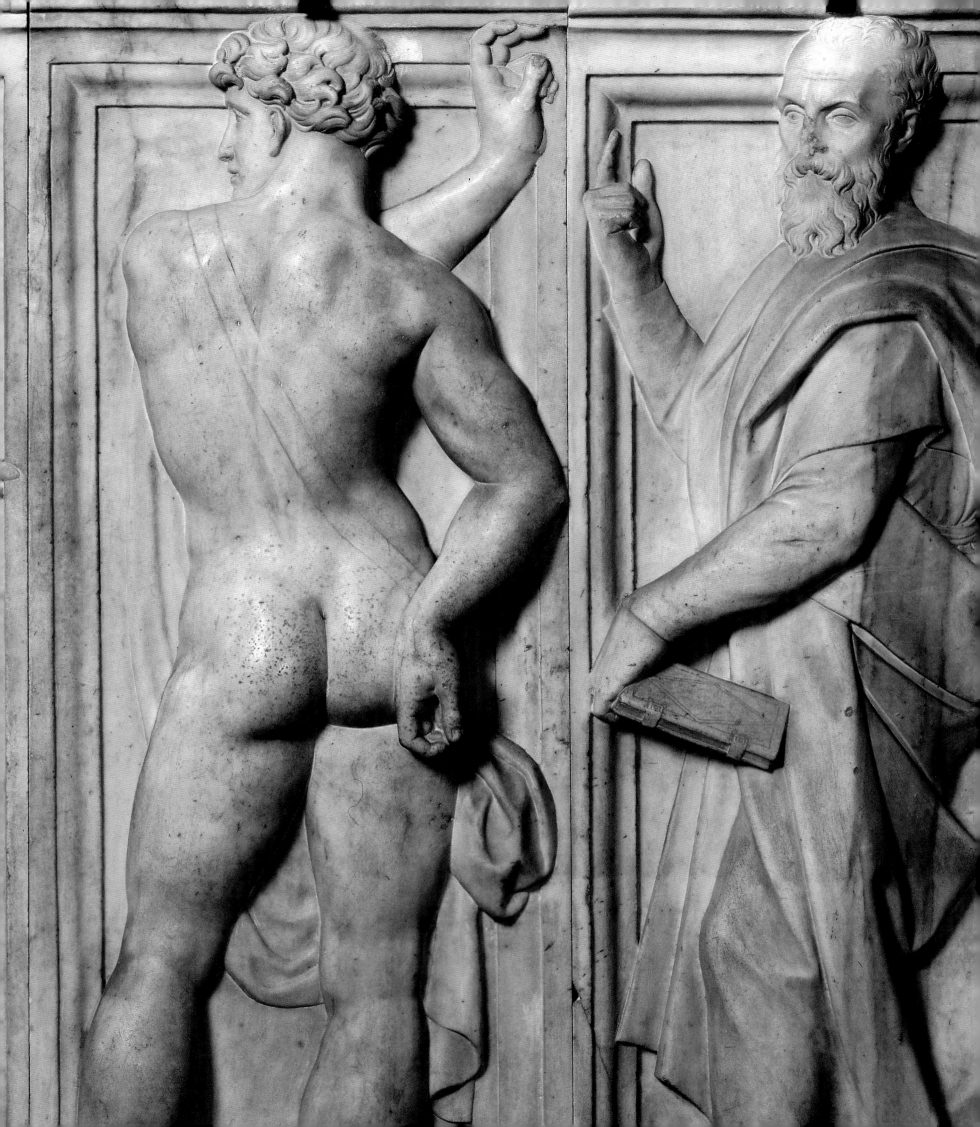

two versions, the first now at Boboli and the second in the Bargello), the *Tree of Good and Evil* (left at the state of a model in wood and stucco) and *God the Father*, also in two versions (one at Boboli, transformed into *Jupiter*, the other, with the dead Christ and an angel, placed on the altar in 1552 but then moved to Santa Croce). Of the three hundred reliefs planned, Bandinelli and his assistants executed only eighty-eight, now divided between the Museo dell'Opera and the choir: they are figures of Michelangelesque inspiration that clearly reflect the influence of the great master on the sculptors. Bandinelli's workshop also produced the large marble candelabras that crown the architrave and the altar with vases adorned with pairs of sacred and profane winged figures. Completed in 1572, the choir was immediately criticized and partly dismantled in 1722, under Cosimo III de' Medici. The figures of *Adam and Eve* were replaced by Michelangelo's *Pietà*, now in the Museo dell'Opera. A late masterpiece (1549-53) that the artist had carved for his own tomb and in which he portrayed himself in the figure of Nicodemus.

The subsequent disposition of the choir is the product of Gaetano Baccani's restoration in 1842, when Benedetto da Maiano's wooden *Crucifix*, completely coated with bronze in those years, was placed on the altar.

The wall paintings of the dome. The cycle of paintings with the *Last Judgment* was begun by Giorgio Vasari in 1572 and left unfinished on his death in 1574. Federico Zuccari resumed the work in 1576, completing it in 1579. The ambitious undertaking was commissioned by Grand Duke Cosimo I de' Medici, who since at least 1568 had hoped to see the decoration of the inner surface of the dome, which it had been the intention to adorn with paintings or mosaics even in Brunelleschi's time. Don Vincenzo Borghini, prior of the Innocenti and a classical and ecclesiastic scholar, was entrusted with the iconographic program. Vasari worked on it from the winter of 1571-72 to the June of 1574, when he died, alternating the production of drawings and cartoons in Rome with periods of painting on the scaffolding of Santa Maria del Fiore, helped by various assistants. At the time of his death the upper band with the twenty-four *Elders* seen by John at the foot of the throne of God inside the *Tabernacle of the Covenant* had been completed. In the central part, intended for the Tribunal of God, he had painted only the eastern sector with *Christ the Judge*. He had also prepared numerous drawings for the zone intended for *Hell*, but had not been able to execute them. Grand Duke Francesco I, succeeding his father Cosimo I (who also died in 1574), gave the job of completing the work to Federico Zuccari from the Marche, who was assisted by several painters from the Accademia Fiorentina, including Passignano, Pieri and Carducci. Zuccari brought the composition very up to date, as is evident from the part with the powers of the earth, which Vasari had designed as a solemn assembly of ancient kings and Zuccari converted into a lively gallery of contemporary figures where, alongside picturesque personages drawn from his travel sketchbooks (beggars, peasant girls, fortunetellers), appeared the portraits of relatives and friends: his parents, his brother Taddeo, Passignano, Vasari, Giambologna, Borghini and many others.

Even in the representation of *Hell* Zuccari replaced the figures in the style of Michelangelo drawn by Vasari by ones set in an Empyrean derived directly from Raphael's Stanze. Hell is divided into blazing

sectors, where sinners are cruelly punished. In the background are set pale scenes of the *Resurrection of the Flesh* in a greenish-blue landscape. In the angles *candeliere* alternate with corpses that symbolize the condemnation of the Islamic schism and were intended as an explicit and ominous warning against the Lutheran heresy. Lucifer (a figure about five meters high) dominates the circles of hell.

The dome was unveiled in 1579: the Florentines greeted it with the critical spirit they have always displayed and in the 19th century there was even talk of whitewashing it. The decision was taken to keep the decoration, although the question was raised again in the mid-1980s. The extraordinary restoration carried out from 1981 to 1994 has put an end to the debate, creating the premises for a positive reappraisal of this gigantic work that marks the transition from the Florentine "Manner" derived from Michelangelo to the simple and grandiose "reformed" style based on Raphael, introduced by a painter of European standing like Federico Zuccari.

The 19th-century interventions. From 1824 to 1860 Gaetano Baccani held the post of architect of the cathedral. The mark of his neoclassical style is clearly visible in the first works he directed, relating to the reorganization of the zone of the Canons. In 1838 he embarked on the restoration of the cathedral's exterior and interior, an undertaking that culminated in the commission to build a new façade for the church from a committee set up specially for the purpose. The work of restoration of the cathedral, much of it completed by 1842, appears to have been inspired by a restrained and respectful neo-medievalism. In particular, it focused on the elimination of those ornaments that, according to the taste of the time, jarred with the medieval vision of the church. Thus the wooden tribunes erected in place of the singing galleries in 1688 were removed and replaced with Neo-Gothic elements; Bandinelli's choir was simplified and at the center of the altar was set a splendid wooden *Crucifix* by Benedetto da Maiano, coated with bronze for the occasion.

Giorgio Vasari and Federico Zuccari, *Last Judgment*, 1572-79, decoration of the dome

San Lorenzo

Called the Ambrosian basilica as it was founded by St. Ambrose in 317 and then "caput Ecclesiae florentinae," it is today, for everyone, the manifesto of the Renaissance in architecture. Rebuilt by Filippo Brunelleschi, it owes its present form to Medici patronage and a number of absolute masterpieces to Michelangelo.

Donatello, *Saint Lawrence*, 1442-43, detail of the Porta dei Martiri. Old Sacristy

facing page
Filippo Lippi, *Martelli Altarpiece*, 1437-41, detail

Piazza San Lorenzo

Built before 393. Reconstructed to a design by Filippo Brunelleschi from 1421 onward

Collegiate church and parish church of the canons of the Laurentian basilica

Patrons: the Medici

Documented as early as 393, San Lorenzo is one of the oldest and most prestigious churches in the city, having been Florence's first bishop's see and College of Canons. The Medicean place of worship *par excellence*, as it was the parish church of the family, whose residence was on Via Larga, it was also the setting, from the Middle Ages up until after the unification of Italy, for grand celebrations linked to its patron saint and to Sts. Cosmas and Damian, to liturgical festivities, to the baptisms, weddings and funerals of members of the Medici family, to great artists (Michelangelo's memorial service was held there), to the potentates of the world and to triumphal entries into the city. Events staged with temporary decorations and theatrical scenery capable of attracting the attention of rulers, placing Florence in the foreground of European politics and San Lorenzo at the center of its celebrations. Forming an inseparable whole, the complex of San Lorenzo is made up of the church proper and its annexes, the Medici Chapels with Michelangelo's New Sacristy and the chapel of the Princes, the Biblioteca Mediceo-Laurenziana and the Biblioteca d'Elci, all now state institutions.

Ancient history. The first reliable record of a Florentine episcopal see dates from 313, the year of Emperor Constantine's edict of tolerance. But the first mention of San Lorenzo in the documents was not until 393, the year in which Bishop Ambrose of Milan consecrated the Florentine basilica, dedicating it to the martyr Lawrence, who had died on August 10, 258. The building had been constructed in the 4th

century, on a slight elevation very close to the northern gate in the city's first circle of walls, at the expense of a Jewish woman called Juliana who had made a vow to erect a church if her prayers for a son were answered. Her son Lawrence was duly born, along with the church that became the city's first cathedral. St. Zenobius was buried in San Lorenzo and it was only after the construction of Santa Reparata that his remains were transferred to the new cathedral. The church was consecrated for a second time in 1060 by Pope Nicholas II (formerly bishop of Florence, under the name Gerard), after a radical refurbishment. It became the parish church and in 1191 was still the largest place of worship in Florence. An idea of the great early-Christian and Romanesque basilica can be gained from the image of it in the Rustici codex, predating the renovations of the 15th century. In the drawing it has a portico in front, a tripartite façade and therefore a nave and two aisles, and no crossing, and is characterized by a tall campanile. The tradition of making a pilgrimage to the church every Wednesday began shortly after the construction of the second circle of walls. This led to the emergence of a market to supply the pilgrims, a tradition that has now been transformed into a daily tourist attraction. On December 22, 1418, the Chapter of the Canons asked the Signoria for permission to enlarge and restore the basilica, which entailed occupying the street in front and demolishing several houses. This marked the beginning of the third and most important transformation of the building, with work commencing on the feast

below
View of the complex of
San Lorenzo

Marco di Bartolomeo Rustici,
San Lorenzo, 1447-48.
Codex in the library of the
Seminario Maggiore, Florence

Cloister of San Lorenzo

day of St. Lawrence in 1421, under the patronage of Giovanni di Bicci de' Medici. From that moment on the church was indissolubly tied to the favor of Florence's most powerful family and became, in a manner of speaking, the "state basilica."

Medici patronage. The strength of the link between the Medici family and the primary church of their quarter became plain when Giovanni di Bicci decided to finance its reconstruction, entrusted to Filippo Brunelleschi. The mark left by the Medici is what still characterizes the large church today, with its nave and two aisles, transept and presbytery with two chapels on each side. There are similar chapels in the short arm of the crossing and the pattern is repeated in the succession of crossings in the aisles, creating a harmonious and well-proportioned form based on the repetition of mathematical modules. The construction took many years and when Brunelleschi died in 1446 his place was taken by Michelozzo. The latter was responsible for the building of the cross-headed transept and part of the nave and aisles, characterized by a series of columns in *pietra serena* with Corinthian capitals, topped by pulvins or dados bearing the Laurentian symbol of the gridiron, which support round arches decorated by arched lintels of *pietra serena* carved with a garland of laurel. The nave is taller and illuminated by round windows. It has a magnificent coffered ceiling with the Medici coats of arms at its center. The dome (later painted by Meucci) was built by Manetti, who took over from Michelozzo.

A door in the left transept leads to the sacristy, also designed by Brunelleschi and called the Old Sacristy to distinguish it from the other one (the New Sacristy) built by Michelangelo, again at the behest of the Medici, to the right of the transept and symmetrically opposite the first. Behind the apse was built the Medicean Pantheon, the so-called chapel of the Princes, comparable in its importance, style and significance to the Escorial constructed by Philip II of Spain a short distance from Madrid.

To the left of the church, with an access from its interior as well as from the outside, is located a first large quadrangular cloister, filled with light, for the use of the canons of the basilica. It was built to Michelozzo's design by Antonio Manetti, in 1457-62. At the center of the cloister still stand, as in the 15th century, the great lemon and orange trees that, in the silence, allow us to imagine what the Florentine *hortus conclusus* of the Renaissance must have been like. The arches are supported by columns of *pietra serena* with capitals with volutes of the Ionic type. Above runs a loggia, also supported by columns, but more slender ones, set on top of the lower ones and with similar capitals. The loggia provides access to the magnificent Biblioteca Laurenziana, the first large secular library to be created. It was constructed by Michelangelo from 1524 onward for Giulio de' Medici, just elected pope, to house the collection of family codices he had brought back to Florence.

A second, rectangular cloister, with 14th-century columns and capitals, dates from the phase prior to Brunelleschi's intervention and connects the canons' apartments to some common facilities.

The façade. The imposing but incomplete façade is built of unplastered stone and has three entrances, one leading into the nave and the others into the aisles. These are covered with pitched roofs, of which the central and taller is characterized by a large niche set above the main portal. A strong and austere image that conceals the secret of the riches inside. Its history coincides, in many ways, with that of the façades of other famous and important Florentine churches (Santa Maria del Fiore, Santa Croce), which saw a succession of projects intended to improve the obviously important external appearance of the church. But unlike the other two buildings, whose façades were constructed in the 19th century, the designs of that time for San Lorenzo were not accepted, and it was left as we see it today. It was a set of unfavorable political circumstances that prevented the realization of the project for which a competition was held in 1515, attracting submissions from Raphael, Michelangelo and Giuliano da Sangallo. But other fine designs were drawn up for the façade of San Lorenzo later on, and yet none was ever implemented. It has to be wondered if this reluctance was in any way connected with the custom of "array-

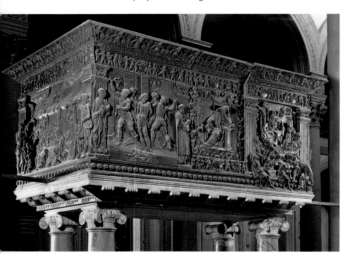

ing" the church for each festival or celebration, periodically compensating for the bareness of its image and with the advantage of being able to use the latest style. This may have been why no need for a definitive façade was felt, at least up until the 19th century. The façades of Santa Croce and the cathedral were built over the course of the 1800s, but it is not clear if the abandonment of Pasquale Poccianti's grandiose plan (1837) was due to a lack of funds or to the fact that it, and the later one by Cesare Bazzani (1905), were not found convincing. The inside of the façade, on the other hand, was executed by Michelangelo (1531-32) and is designed to perform the function of displaying precious relics, by means of a tribune with three small doors that communicate with the area in which they are conserved.

The interior decoration of the church. The decoration of the interior is characterized by the same architectural rigor. The eye is immediately caught by the two pulpits located just before the screen, architectural inserts themselves, supported by columns in verd-antique marble topped by capitals in white marble, with Ionic volutes and ovuli, given their present form between 1558 and 1565. They are faced with finely chased and damascened bronze panels, late works by Donatello. Left partly unfinished on the master's death, the pulpits were continued by his pupils Bellano and Bertoldo, but were not completed until the 17th century, with wooden bas-reliefs. On the pulpit on the left (looking toward the high altar) are depicted scenes from Christ's Passion: *The Agony in the Garden, Christ before Caiaphas and Pilate* and the *Crucifixion, Descent from the Cross* and *Deposition in the Tomb*. On the right-hand pulpit: the *Martyrdom of Saint Lawrence, Three Marys at the Tomb, Descent into Limbo, Resurrection, Ascension* and *Pentecost*. The dense and dramatic composi-

tion of the scenes reflects Donatello's overall design and the hand of the sculptor – whose signature and the date 1465 are carved on the pulpit on the right – is recognizable in many scenes, such as the large bronze panel with three scenes, the *Descent into Limbo*, the *Resurrection* and the *Ascension*, in which the figure of the Risen Christ, still covered with the shroud, moves as if torpid with sleep, displaying an expressive and evocative power on a par with other extraordinary inventions of Donatello. Also by Donatello is the tomb of Niccolò and Fioretta Martelli, "a wickerwork chest, shaped like a cradle, to serve as an urn" as Vasari describes it, located in the family chapel along with Filippo Lippi's panel representing the *Annunciation*, commissioned by Niccolò Martelli between 1437 and 1441. The predella of the altarpiece depicts *Scenes from the Life of Saint Nicholas of Bari* (following the common practice of representing eponymous saints in sacred pictures) executed by Fra Diamante and Francesco Pesellino. The panel with the *Annunciation* is architecturally conceived. In the foreground the space is divided up by two arches of a portico that open onto a deep perspective view of buildings framing a garden with a central vanishing point. On the right is the sacred representation with the Virgin standing and drawing back behind a lectern and the angel kneeling and holding the lily, symbol of purity. Another allusion to purity is the extraordinary image of the glass bottle half filled with water and set in a special recess in the step between the two main figures. On the left, on a higher step, are painted two singing angels, one of them looking toward us. There is a lively play of colors which, in the angels, contrasts the white of the robes with the alternating red and green of their cloaks and wings. The singing gallery in the left-hand aisle is also attributed to Donatello. It is similar to the one he carved for Florence Cathedral, with panels of polychrome marble and slender columns supporting the cornice with marine motifs of dolphins and shells. Behind it is one of the oldest organs in Florence (1502), bearing witness to the long musical tradition of this basilica.

Around 1453-55, Desiderio da Settignano carved the marble ciborium in the right-hand aisle, flanked by

Filippo Brunelleschi, Old Sacristy, 1422-28, detail of the interior

facing page
Pesello, *Signs of the Zodiac and Star Chart*, 1442. Dome of the Old Sacristy

at the beginning of the following decade. Between 1428 and 1432 much of the stucco decoration of the chapel was carried out by Donatello, who must have first executed the bas-reliefs in the tondi on the walls with *Scenes from the Life of Saint John* and then, between 1442 and 1443, the figures of the saints above the bronze doors. The conception of the decoration was undoubtedly linked to Brunelleschi's design, but the liberties taken by Donatello must have immediately created disagreements and misunderstandings that led to his dismissal (and departure for Padua) and the conclusion of the work by his collaborators (some see the hand of Michelozzo, others that of Luca della Robbia). The recent restoration of Donatello's stuccoes has revealed a skillful technique based on a familiarity with Vitruvius. The coloring was obtained by mixing earths of different tints with the mortar. The backgrounds behind the saints are executed with the *buon fresco* technique. In the rectangular apse there is an unusual representation of the celestial hemisphere, datable to the second quarter of the 15th century. It is an accurate depiction of the heavens based on the studies of the astronomer Paolo dal Pozzo Toscanelli – who had close ties to Cosimo I the Elder – painted, in all probability, by Pesello, an artist who is little known now but was very famous in his own time. The signs of the Zodiac and map of the stars are executed in gold and white lead, as in books of hours, on the blue ground, painted with the precious azurite pigment. According to recent studies, the map represents what could be seen from San Lorenzo on July 4, 1442, a date that was undoubtedly connected with a particular circumstance of which we are ignorant.

The only addition to the interior of the hall is the magnificent tomb of Piero il Gottoso and Giovanni de' Medici, executed between 1469 and 1472 by Andrea del Verrocchio. Exploiting and enlarging an existing door that linked the sacristy with the chapel of Santi Cosma e Damiano, Verrocchio placed the sarcophagus under an arch decorated with marble bas-reliefs and separated from the adjoining space by a broad rhomboidal mesh of bronze. The sarcophagus is made of precious porphyry with a serpentine medallion at

candleholder angels. It is conceived as a high relief in which a coffered hallway with a central vanishing point leads to the door of the Sacrament (no longer *in situ*). Inside this structure there are groups of angels; above is set a lunette with the Infant Jesus standing on the chalice, flanked by two adoring angels. On the altar frontal the sculptor carved a bas-relief of the *Pietà*, inserted between two responds decorated with *candeliere*.

The Old Sacristy. In the autumn of 1422 work started on the sacristy and the chapel of Santi Cosma e Damiano, and was completed by the end of the 1420s, so that they were ready to house the mortal remains of the client, Giovanni di Bicci de' Medici,

the center (carved with the names of the deceased) surrounded by a wreath of laurel in bronze, and the ends of the casket and the lid are adorned with acanthus leaves and lion's paws, also in bronze. The sarcophagus is set on a white marble base, on which are carved the clients' names (Pietro's sons Lorenzo and Giuliano, 1472), standing in turn on the back of four bronze turtles. The splendid wooden cabinets with benches, made by a Florentine workshop and comparable in proportions and decorations to those of the sacristy of the Masses in Florence Cathedral, were part of the sacristy's original fixtures. Commissioned by the Medici, they were probably executed between the middle of 1450s and the 1460s, in two different stages, first the benches and then the backs. The rectangular apse houses a marble washstand carved between 1465 and 1469 and attributed to Antonio Rossellino and Andrea del Verrocchio, decorated with the heraldic device of Piero de' Medici (who died in 1469).

The design of the Old Sacristy is based on a central plan, to which are added the composite one of the central chapel, or apse (a square in which a central circle cuts out three niches in the walls), with two small rooms at the sides that echo the early-Christian pattern of the diaconicon and prothesis. The main part roughly corresponds to a square and the proportion between the other parts is comprised in modules all linked to that geometric figure. The larger room is covered by a dome with twelve sides, each containing an oculus. The precision of the relations between height, width and depth bears witness to Brunelleschi's knowledge of Vitruvius's text.

The New Sacristy. Symmetrical to the Old Sacristy, it echoes its proportions, but the organization of the space inside makes it look completely different. Michelangelo intervened in Brunelleschi's scheme, carrying out a patient work of counterpoint. He emphasized its height by superimposing a second order of Corinthian pilaster strips that taper toward the top, in accordance with the rule of the golden section. The architectural order is comparable in the well-proportioned geometry of its elements, but the considerable variation in heights bestows a different rhythm on the spaces. Although the commission was received by Michelangelo prior to the death of Pope Leo X, it was not confirmed until later, by Cardinal Giulio, the future pope Clement VII. At first the sacristy was only intended to house the tombs of Giuliano and Lorenzo the Magnificent (at the center of the chapel, as the many preparatory studies show), but then those of Giuliano, duke of Nemours, who died in 1516, and Lorenzo, prince of Urbino, who died in 1519, were added. The architecture was completed between 1520 and 1524. By 1526 many of the sculptures had been executed, but as a result of the expulsion of the Medici and the siege of Florence, Michelangelo did not resume the work until 1531 and then supervised it until 1534, the year he left for Rome. At that date the decoration was not yet complete, and it was finished around 1555 by Vasari and Ammannati.

The main room, with a square plan, is covered by a large dome with five rows of coffers on the model of the Pantheon in Rome and terminating in a glazed lantern, letting in light from above. Alongside this dome is set that of the rectangular apse, plastered in its entirety and with the structure marked by an architectural molding in *pietra serena*, which also decorates the four blind oculi of the vaulting cells. The overall effect of the very tall space is majestic and striking for the breadth of its architectural lines. The pattern of white and gray, in which the latter marks the nodal points of the structure, forms the basis of the architecture of the walls, in the middle of whose east-west sides were set the tombs of Duke Giuliano of Nemours, and Duke Lorenzo of Urbino: sarcophagi with lids of broken and flowing lines topped by the representations of four times of day and the full-length figure of the warrior hero seated in a trabeated recess flanked by two pairs of pilaster strips and two mock windows covered with depressed arches. This harmonious composition is, in its turn, inserted in a large arch underlined by stone ribbing and flanked by similar fluted pilaster strips surmounted by Corinthian capitals. In the second order windows to let in the light are set at the sides of the arch, inserted in spaces again marked by pilaster strips and bounded by cornices with saddleback tympana. The third order is the base of the dome and houses

more windows (with depressed-arch tympana) to let in light. The illumination was designed to obtain the best result as the light varied during the day and the same outcome, despite the monochromatic materials, was achieved through the use of different kinds of statuary marble and the treatment of the surfaces of the sculptures. Thus on Giuliano's tomb the *Night* is carved from a marble of dazzling whiteness whose shiny surface produces an effect of moonlight, while the *Day* is luminous at the center, with a polished and brilliant body, but remains roughcast in the face, emerging from the material as if awakening. *Duke Giuliano of Nemours* is powerful and vigorous. Under his armor we can discern an athletic body and his face, with its unfocused gaze, is young and heroic: thick hair with neat curls, fine fleshy lips and an extraordinarily long neck set on a muscular trunk. At the center of his breast is set, like a large brooch, a whiskered sea monster in the grotesque style, much in vogue in those years.

The *Dawn* is limpid and rosy, with finished and polished surfaces in every part of the figure, while the material, also pinkish but rough, of the *Dusk* suggests the colors and atmosphere of that time of the day, when edges grow blurred and vague. The two figures flank the sepulcher above which, in an analogous and symmetrical manner to that of Giuliano, is set the statue of *Duke Lorenzo of Urbino*, a pensive hero who, despite his military attire, has the appearance of a sensitive and meditative youth. Symbols and details help in the identification of the subjects, for which various philosophical interpretations have been put forward by scholars. All, however, agree that they are allusions to the passing of time and of life, and to its transience.

Later the bodies of Lorenzo the Magnificent and Giuliano de' Medici were placed in a large sarcophagus on the wall opposite the apse and altar, forming a simple base for three groups of sculptures, with the *Madonna and Child* in the middle and *Saints Cosmas* and *Damian* at the sides. Preparatory studies for the Virgin date from 1521 or 1524, while the two saints were executed to Michelangelo's models by his pupils Montorsoli and Raffaello da Montelupo respectively.

16th-century paintings and the years of the Council of Trent. The second chapel on the right, belonging to the Ginori family, houses one of the masterpieces of early Mannerism: the *Marriage of the Virgin*, painted by Rosso Fiorentino in 1523, shortly before his departure for Rome. The crowded scene displays evident parallels with the contemporary painting of Pontormo and even with the typical characteristics of engravings, especially those of Dürer. In 1546 Pontormo was given the task of frescoing the chancel of San Lorenzo. The themes of the decoration were the *Legend of Adam and Eve*, *Martyrdom of Saint Lawrence*, *Ascension of the Souls* and *Resurrection of the Bodies*. The frescoes, which were destroyed when the apse was rebuilt in 1742, were not well-received and created problems of an iconographic and theological nature from the moment of their execution. In 1565 Cosimo I had commissioned Bronzino to paint a *Martyrdom of Saint Lawrence* on the wall at the beginning of the left-hand aisle, where it can still be seen. The scene, set in a visionary Roman city, is filled with figures huddled around the martyr, bound to the gridiron. The influence of Michelangelo is very evident in this composition, whose overall effect is too rich and discordant.

The late decoration of the church. Much of the work done in the 18th century was due to the electress palatine Maria Luisa de' Medici, the last descendant of the family who bequeathed all its art treasures to the city of Florence (the *Electress* is portrayed in a monument by Raffaello Salimbeni, erected on the back of the church close to the Medici Chapels in 1995). Between 1738 and 1742, Maria Luisa and her brother Giuseppe had Ferdinando Ruggieri consolidate the spaces under the church where many Medici tombs were located; they had a cladding added to the church's dome, which was decorated with the *Glory of the Saints of Florence* by Vincenzo Meucci in 1742, and the campanile built next to the New Sacristy. She was also responsible for the reconstruction of the chancel, resulting in the loss of Pontormo's frescoes, although they had already been plastered over. The fine *Crucifixion* by Francesco Conti (1709) also dates from the years of the last of the Medici

line, while the high altar was installed under Lorraine rule: designed by Gaspare Maria Paoletti, it was made by the Opificio delle Pietre Dure (1787) and panels designed by Poccetti and Cigoli were set in the altar frontal. Florence's brief period as capital of Italy saw, in addition to the never realized projects for the façade, the redecoration of the main chapel to a design by Baccani in 1860. In those same years (1864) the main organ was donated by the House of Savoy, which declared San Lorenzo the "Royal Basilica." In

Pietro Benvenuti, *Scenes from Genesis to the Last Judgment*. Chapel of the Princes, paintings of the dome

facing page
Interior of the chapel of the Princes

addition, several important sepulchral monuments were erected inside the church, such as the one to *Aristodemo Costoli* by Pietro Benvenuti (1852) and the one to *Berta Moltke Withfield*, carved by Giovanni Dupré in 1864. The most recent work that we would like to mention is Pietro Annigoni's picture of *Saint Joseph the Carpenter and the Infant Jesus*, painted in the 1970s and bearing witness to the vitality and modernity of this great collegiate church.

The chapel of the Princes. It was Cosimo I who had the idea of creating a third and more monumental family chapel, after the two sacristies, entrusting the task to Vasari between 1561 and 1568. But the project was not completed until the reign of Ferdinando I who, following a competition held in 1602, chose the design by Don Giovanni de' Medici (son of Cosimo I and Eleonora degli Albizi) over those of Buontalenti and Gherardo Silvani: it was submitted in collaboration with Matteo Nigetti who, in practice, supervised the whole of the work from 1604 to 1650. Its designers wanted the building to have a solid and powerful appearance on the outside, as was suited to a dynasty that set out to challenge eternity, but to resemble a precious casket on the inside, where the architectural form is lost under the baroque and multicolored incrustation of ancient marble and prized stone. The central plan recalls classical constructions, but the octagonal geometry is an explicit reference to the baptistery of San Giovanni as well as an allusion to the eight stars of the constellation of Capricorn, Cosimo I's birth sign. It is entered from the low crypt built by Nigetti in 1608, where two flights of stairs in *pietra serena* lead up to the mausoleum proper. On each side of the octagon are set the tombs of the grand dukes, surmounted by niches which should have held full-length portraits of the Medici. However only the statues of *Ferdinando I* and *Cosimo II* were executed, by Tacca. The installation of the inlays of semiprecious stones produced by the Opificio delle Pietre Dure, founded by Cosimo I, which lend the chapel of the Princes such a magnificent appearance continued for over a century and were not even finished by the time of the electress palatine's death. The drum of the dome with its large bell-shaped windows was built by Ferdinando and Giuseppe Ruggieri in 1740.

The interior of the dome, originally to be decorated with lapis lazuli, was instead painted with eight scenes from *Genesis* to the *Last Judgment* by Pietro Benvenuti between 1828 and 1837. Since 1869 the chapel of the Princes has been an integral part of the Museo delle Cappelle Medicee, set up by the Royal Galleries and Museums as a celebration of Florence's selection as capital of Italy.

The Biblioteca Laurenziana

Prior to the construction of the present library another one stood on the same site, and its 15th-century portal has been preserved. It was Clement VII who commissioned the new Biblioteca Laurenziana from Michelangelo, to house the collection of books assembled by Cosimo I the Elder and added to by his sons Piero and Lorenzo. When the Medici were driven out of Florence (1494), the collection was confiscated by the Signoria and entrusted to the Dominicans of San Marco. Cardinal Giovanni de' Medici, later Pope Leo X, reclaimed the books (1508), taking them to Rome. Clement VII decided to return the library to Florence and work commenced on the building in 1524, but was then interrupted by the political developments that led to the siege of Florence. By the time of Clement's death and

Michelangelo's departure from Florence in 1534 the work was in no way complete. Cosimo I was to finish the project (*circa* 1559-70) with the help of Vasari and Ammannati, to whom Michelangelo continued to send instructions for the execution of the sumptuous setting from Rome. The vestibule is characterized by a broad flight of steps in *pietra serena*, built by Ammannati to Michelangelo's design from 1559 on. The handling of the space in the large hall of the library echoes the rhythm of the vestibule. It can be described as being made up of fifteen bays, clearly defined on the ceiling and floor as well, with a division into three orders marked by the benches at the bottom, openings with rectangular frames in the middle and similar quadrangular panels at the top, in an alternating pattern of

plastering, i.e. of voids and solids, a rhythm that is repeated in the decorations of the extraordinary terracotta floor and the wooden ceiling. A portal with a tympanum in the center of the right-hand wall leads to the Biblioteca d'Elci, with its neoclassical rotunda built by Poccianti (1841). The room has a very harmonious appearance despite having been executed at different times: the ceiling was carved by the famous Florentine craftsmen Giovan Battista del Tasso and Antonio di Marco di Giano, known as Carota, in 1549-50; the floor was laid by Sante Buglioni using clays of different kinds and colors, to a design by Tribolo, in 1549-54, while the stained-glass windows, the only ones to have survived in an ancient library, with grotesques and Medici coats of arms, are by Marcillat and date from 1558-68.

Badia Fiorentina

*Temple of the Counts of Tuscany and the first major Benedictine complex
on the perimeter of the oldest circle of walls.
Built by Arnolfo and filled with Renaissance masterpieces.*

Marco di Bartolomeo Rustici, *Badia Fiorentina*, 1447-48. Codex in the library of the Seminario Maggiore, Florence

facing page
Master of the Chiostro degli Aranci (Giovanni di Consalvo?), *Scenes from the Life of Saint Benedict, c. 1440.* Chiostro degli Aranci, detail of the frescoes

Via del Proconsolo

Built and altered from the 10th to the 17th century

Order: Cluniac Benedictines; since 1998, Monastic Brotherhoods of Jerusalem

The image of the large Benedictine abbey in the first book of Marco di Bartolomeo Rustici's codex – now in the library of the Seminario Maggiore in Florence and datable to 1447-48 – shows us what the Badia looked like in the 15th century. On the left the small church of Santo Stefano del Popolo, where Boccaccio had given the first readings of the *Divine Comedy* in 1373; in the middle the towering hexagonal campanile, interrupting the perspective view of the church with its side entrance. Set slightly back, a large building and behind it the upper part of the façade, with a large rose window. On the right side a line of constructions and large enclosed spaces that suggest the dormitory, refectory, chapterhouse and other facilities of a monastic community. The external spaces open onto the area that extends from what is now Via Alighieri to the cathedral, bounding to the north the 14th-15th-century church that faced onto Piazza San Martino, but turned through ninety degrees with respect to the present.

This is the building that Marco di Bartolomeo Rustici saw around the middle of the 15th century, but not the monastery of Santa Maria, according to tradition founded by Hugo of Tuscany, or more precisely his mother Willa – daughter of Duke Boniface of Spoleto and wife of Hubert of Provence – around 978, and reconstructed, according to Vasari, by Arnolfo di Cambio in 1284.

While all that survives from the ancient church founded by Willa are a few parchments, the church on which her son Hugo of Tuscany lavished riches and imperial favors would be the one that reflected, more than any other, the complex and troubled history of the city center. The original orientation was preserved in the building of 1284 when, at the time of the construction of the last circle of walls and the nearby palace of the podestà, the small church, dating from the year 1000, was enlarged, giving it an appearance similar to the one we see in the Rustici codex and which was to endure, with numerous alterations and enlargements, until the 17th century. Thus we can imagine the apsidal chapels decorated with frescoes and polychrome majolica floors, as well as many paintings on a gold ground, including a polyptych by Giotto that stood on the high altar. Relegated to a room in front of the refectory in 1568, perhaps because it was already in poor condition, it was moved to Santa Croce in the 19th century and then to the Galleria degli Uffizi, where it can now be seen. Owing to the deterioration of the painted surface it is just a shadow of what it must have been on the Badia's high altar, although we know it was already in a poor state of preservation in the middle of the 15th century, as a result of the flood of 1333, when the water reached "up to the foot of the high altar," but above all of frequent cleanings in the past. Puccinelli, in his *Cronica* of 1664, provides the interesting information that the altarpiece had ovals at the bottom in which Giotto had portrayed Hugo of Tuscany and Willa holding a model of the ancient Badia. The polyptych has been tampered with many times: originally cuspidate, it was squared off in 1451 and adapted to support a cross and candlesticks at the end of the century. An attempt to repair the damage

Giotto, *Badia Polyptych*,
c. 1300. Galleria degli Uffizi,
Florence

was made in 1958, when the polyptych was restored, as far as possible, to its original form.

Despite the lack of evidence with which to reconstruct the church's structure between the 10th and 14th century, the fragmentary remains – three underground apses, painted wooden trusses, vestiges of frescoes on the cavity walls, portions of flooring – supported by references in the documents allow us to discern, in the picture in the Rustici codex, the orientation, supporting structures and complexity of the building. The Badia

was the first Benedictine settlement, abutting onto the ancient ring of walls, which from Porta San Piero to Porta Aurea, along what is now Via del Proconsolo, limited the expansion of the abbey, and from which the populace used to hear, partly from the many workshops attached to the monastery, the striking of the hours that regulated their life and work, as Dante records in the *Paradiso*: "Florence, within her ancient ring of walls / that ring from which she still draws tierce and nones / sober and chaste, lived in tranquility."

The 15th century. Decay and rebirth. The beginning of the 15th century found the complex of the Badia expanded, but in profound decay. Following the Black Death of 1348, when the population of the city was reduced, along with its cultural and commercial activities, and large numbers of hospitals and almshouses were founded, only the grand construction of the cathedral went ahead – even though it was not until the second decade of the 15th century and the appointment of Filippo Brunelleschi that it was roofed with a dome – and the Badia went through one of the darkest moments of its history. The period from 1419 to 1439, when the Portuguese Gómez of the congregation of Santa Giustina, an illustrious Humanist, friend and collaborator of Ambrogio Traversari, whom he had succeeded as head of the Camaldolensian congregation, was abbot of the monastery, put an end to the mainly spiritual decadence into which it had fallen. With the revocation of the *commendam* imposed by Pope John XXII in 1327, which had permitted the exploitation of the monastery's property by the abbots, the Badia returned to its original discipline and forgotten observance, with the result that Pope Martin V, then in Santa Maria Novella for the Council, praised its respect for religion and principle. This spiritual revival was followed by a cultural, economic and architectural rebirth: obvious examples are the construction of the cloister of the Oranges in 1435 and Antonio Corbinelli's bequest of his library to the Badia in 1424. This legacy of around three hundred Latin and Greek codices from Corbinelli, a pupil of Emanuele Crisolora, the first professor of Greek at Florence University, marked the beginning of the constitution of the monastic library and the cultural renascence of the Florentine complex, in line with other Florentine and Italian monasteries. A corollary to this moment of revival was the compilation of an inventory, in 1441, listing the abbey's furnishings room by room and offering an insight into the structure of the large monastic complex, including the numerous workshops that were occupied chiefly by flax dressers, stationers and public notaries.

The erection of the Chiostro degli Aranci, or cloister of the Oranges, and the much vaunted but never implemented intervention by Cosimo I the Elder, who before going into exile in 1433 had Brunelleschi draw up a project for a new abbey, give us an idea of the fervor for construction that marked the following decades. The cloister, which we know was built between 1435 and 1438 by Antonio di Domenico with the collaboration of Bernardo Rossellino, is one of the earliest examples to have survived from the Renaissance period. It has a trapezoidal plan with a loggia and two tiers of depressed arches standing on slender columns with capitals with plant motifs. The walls are decorated with *Scenes from the Life of Saint Benedict* attributed to an anonymous painter called the "Master of the Chiostro degli Aranci." The name of the documented artist of Portuguese origin, Giovanni di Consalvo, has also been put forward. Most of the work had been carried out by the end of the 1440s. The style is a skilled balance of Flemish limpidity and the renewal of color brought about in Tuscany by Fra Angelico.

Along with the new cloister several annexes were built, including a dormitory, cells, an infirmary and the guests' quarters, all structures that had become necessary to house the large number of monks that

View of the Chiostro degli Aranci (cloister of the Oranges)

facing page
Master of the Chiostro degli Aranci (Giovanni di Consalvo?), *Scenes from the Life of Saint Benedict*, c. 1440. Chiostro degli Aranci, detail of the frescoes

the Badia now held, following the end of the period of depression that had characterized it up until the second decade of the 15th century.

The tomb of Hugo of Tuscany, whose remains had first been stored in an iron coffin and then in one made of porphyry, was also given its definitive form by the monks in the 15th century. The memorial was completed by Mino da Fiesole in 1481 and located in the main chapel, where it stayed until the reconstruction in the 17th century, when it was moved to the left-hand arm.

The picture of the 15th-century church would not be complete without a mention of the large *Hanging* – discovered and put on display in 1981 – woven for the Badia in the second half of the 15th century and used to cover the walls of the church during festivities or at times of particular importance. The splendor of the fabric – crimson velvet brocaded with gold bouclé on a ground of gold cloth – and the good condition in which it has been preserved (it was found in a cabinet in the sacristy that had been built expressly to store it) have drawn attention to an often forgotten aspect of Florentine Renaissance architecture: the fact that the white and gray pattern of the walls was overlaid by the marvelous colors and brilliant gold of these gorgeous hangings, whose patterns were often copied by contemporary painters in drapes or sumptuous robes. Decorated with the motif of a pomegranate inserted in a multilobate leaf, called *a griccia*, the large sheets of cloth have been subjected to various alterations over the centuries, so as to adapt them to changes made to the church, right up to the last transformations in the 17th century.

The 17th-century reconstruction. In 1587, about a century and a half after the inventory of 1441, a new one was drawn up in which the objects were again listed by room, showing that, in essence, the spaces of the monastery had remained the same: structurally, therefore, the complex of the Badia had not changed. In our summary of the complicated history of the Benedictine abbey, this inventory preceded the definitive and substantial transformation of the building – and the church in particular – that was carried out between 1628 and *circa* 1650 at the behest of Abbot Serafino Casolani by Matteo di Marco Segaloni, assisted by Felice Gamberai, who carved the beautiful wooden ceiling and the two singing galleries of the organs.

The unusual structure of the Badia Fiorentina – now a Greek cross – reflects the innumerable interventions to which the building has been subjected, rendering it, between additions and continuities, particularly difficult to interpret and comprehend. It is not easy to make a summary of the works that it houses today, but which originally came from different locations and thus arrived there by different historical and artistic routes, and which the 17th-century reconstruction has thrown together in a sort of jumble of preexistences. The protagonists of these wanderings were the great tombs and many of the paintings, such as Giotto's polyptych, Nardo di Cione's triptych depicting the *Descent of the Holy Spirit*, Vasari's large panel of the *Assumption* and Filippino Lippi's *Apparition*, painted for the convent of the Campora, near Porta Romana.

Although he described himself as an architect-antiquarian, Matteo Segaloni decided to make major alterations to the structure: the volumes to be rebuilt would be larger than the ones preserved, something that did not please many of the families who patronized the church, who saw centuries of commissions and works "disappear," along with the traces of their forebears.

To create the vestibule which now precedes the entrance to the church from Via del Proconsolo – after passing through the imposing portal designed by Benedetto da Rovezzano – alterations were made to what had been the northern side of the old church, where the Pandolfini had built a vestibule and chapel in the 15th century. Giovan Battista Pandolfini commissioned Benedetto da Rovezzano to erect the vestibule and family chapel in the space occupied by the ancient church of Santo Stefano. Covered by a

Mino da Fiesole, *Sepulchral Monument to Hugo of Tuscany*, 1481

facing page
Filippino Lippi, *Apparition of the Virgin to Saint Bernard*, c. 1480, detail

issus est angelus
gabriel adeo in
ciuitatem galilee: cui
nomen nazareth ad
uirginem desponsa
tam uiro. cui nomen
erat ioseph de domo
dauid. et nomen
uirginis maria:
et ingressus an
gelus ad eam dixit

Aue gratia plena dominus.
tecum Benedicta
tu in mulieribus. Et
cum audisset tur
bata est in sermone ei
et cogitabat qualis
esset ista salutatio. Et
ait angelus ei. Ne timeas
maria inuenisti
enim gratiam apud deum.
Ecce concipies in utero

hemispherical dome and with tombstones set in the floor, the chapel has architectural forms underlined by stone ribs, while slabs of marble decorate the walls.

Entering the church we see, on the left-hand wall, Filippino Lippi's large panel with the *Apparition of the Virgin to Saint Bernard*, one of the highest achievements of the Florentine Renaissance. It is a painting that "accomplishes the arduous task of fusing a highly analytical but impeccable drawing with a varied and lavish coloring" (L. Berti).

In 1568 Giorgio Vasari painted the panel with the *Assumption and Saints* to be set on the high altar in the place of Giotto's polyptych, on the occasion of the repairs made to the chapel following a fire. The 17th century work, on the singing gallery on the left, is a fine example of the artist's formal virtuosity and technical and compositional skill.

In the 17th and 18th century – during the complex work of reconstruction – several new works were executed, some of which are still entirely visible: the baroque chapel dedicated to St. Bernard with its vault frescoed by Vincenzo Meucci and, on the altar, Onorio Marinari's picture of *Saint Maurus*, on the walls of the apse, where some of the stalls of the 16th-century choir made by the del Tasso workshop have been placed, the views of Pietro Anderlini and the airy wall paintings of Gian Domenico Ferretti open up a sweeping perspective, of considerable dimensions, in the rigorous Greek cross that defines the church.

The choir, executed by the del Tasso woodcarvers, formed part of a complex wooden structure that occupied the apse of the 16th-century church, including a cabinet for vestments and ornaments and a monumental tabernacle. All that is left today are some of the stalls, moved to the new choir after the 17th-century rebuilding, which demonstrate the high level achieved by the workshop, active in Florence in the middle of the 16th century.

The works of the 17th century were the last ones of significance to be carried out in the old church of the Badia. The same cannot be said, however, of the other structures of the monastery where, following the final abolition (1810) and right up to the early part of the 20th century, what had once been the silent and industrious cloistral spaces were adapted to meet the demands of the most varied functions of secular life.

Del Tasso workshop, wooden choir, 16th century, detail

facing page
Filippino Lippi, *Apparition of the Virgin to Saint Bernard*, c. 1480

Filippino Lippi's *Apparition of the Virgin to Saint Bernard*

The work, originally in the convent of the Campora outside Porta Romana, was moved to the sacristy of the Badia for safety reasons during the siege of 1529. Commissioned by Piero del Pugliese (1430-98) for his father Francesco, portrayed on the right at prayer, it is a splendid example of Filippino's art, painted sometime after 1480. The picture represents Mary's appearance to Bernard of Clairvaux, a monk and theologian who lived in the 12th century. The saint, seated in a rocky study and surrounded by books, is busy writing, glancing to his right at the Gospel of St. Luke, open at the account of the Annunciation. At the same time the gazes of the Virgin and the saint meet and their hands almost brush in mute conversation. Piero del Pugliese, portrayed by Filippino in the *Raising of Theophilus's Son* in the Brancacci Chapel of Santa Maria del Carmine (third figure on the left) and later in the *Adoration of the Magi* for the monastery of San Donato at Scopeto, now in the Galleria degli Uffizi, was a wealthy merchant, enrolled in the Wool Guild in 1453, and great patron of Filippino, Botticelli and Fra Bartolommeo. He held numerous public posts, including those of Gonfalonier of Justice for the Oltrarno on several occasions and Prior of the Libertà in 1474.

Santi Apostoli

*Ancient church hidden away in the medieval center of the city.
Built on the site of a Roman necropolis, it houses stones brought from the Holy Sepulcher.*

Benedetto da Rovezzano,
Altoviti Crest, detail of the
*Sepulchral Monument to
Oddo Altoviti*

facing page
Benedetto da Rovezzano,
*Sepulchral Monument to
Oddo Altoviti*, 1507, detail

Piazza del Limbo

Built in the 11th-12th centuries

Patrons: Altoviti family from
1532, Capitani di Parte from
1553

Descending the few steps that lead from Borgo Santi Apostoli to the small Piazza del Limbo, onto which faces the church from which the quarter takes its name, is a suggestive experience. This secluded corner of the city's medieval center – preserving its lowest level – bounded by Via Porta Rossa, Via Por Santa Maria and Lungarno Acciaiuoli, where legend has it that the church was founded by Charlemagne in 805, offers an essentially complete view of the complex succession of its historical and urbanistic transformations. The original cemetery for unbaptized children, which gives the square its name; the ancient Roman baths from which two of the capitals in the nave were taken; the neighborhood outside the old circle of walls, the so-called "Borgo di Sant'Apostolo"; the 16th-century Palazzi Altoviti, on the right of the church; and the imposing Palazzo Borgherini, later Rosselli del Turco, still linked with the church by an opening with a grate: these are all fundamental to a modern understanding of the ancient urban space.

The Altoviti, a rich family of bankers and merchants who commissioned a lot of the works inside the church, became its patrons in 1532. Many of its members were buried there, even after 1553 when Cosimo I, after expelling Archbishop Antonio from the city and declaring Bindo Altoviti a rebel, accusing them of belonging to the faction opposed to the Medici during the war with Siena, transferred the patronage of the church to the Capitani di Parte.

This transfer of patronage to the city's magistrates marked a turning point in the life of the church, leading to a substantial renovation of the interior and the execution of new vestments and ornaments.

The stone façade of the church has a saddleback design with a central two-light window. It used to be adorned with a small fresco of the *Madonna and Child* by Paolo Schiavo at its center, but all that now survives is the *sinopia*, transferred into the first chapel on the left, and a marble scroll recording the traditional Carolingian foundation. On the lower level two side doors, surmounted by narrow windows, flank the marble portal by Benedetto da Rovezzano, with pilaster strips and a lintel decorated with the Altoviti coats of arms.

Following its restoration in the early 20th century, the interior, divided into a nave and two aisles by columns in green marble from Prato, presents the characteristics of the basilica constructed in the 11th and 12th centuries. In fact this is the church that has come down to us, although there was undoubtedly a preexisting building, described as very old in 11th-century documents, erected with the same layout of a nave and two aisles on the site of an even older cemetery. The space inside is bounded by the trussed roof, with typical 14th-century polychrome decorations, and extended by the chapels opened in the outer walls, traces of whose capitals survive, between that time (the five large chapels on the left side and the smaller ones on the right side were already in existence by the early 15th century) and the 18th century. The painted wooden ceiling we see now was commissioned by the prior Ugolotto before 1333, the date of his death, and was brought to light

following the destruction of the 18th-century tunnel vault by the "restorers" of the 20th century.

The 20th-century restoration and the church of today. The architect Luigi Zumkeller supervised the work (1929-30) that restored the church to its Romanesque appearance: the demolition of the vault and the lowering of the trussed roof by a meter and a half to its original position, with the recovery of almost all of the hundred decorated joists. Naturally the wooden beams could no longer be relied on and so the painted parts were cut off and attached to new joists with meticulous care, so that the congregation could see the ceiling Ugolotto Altoviti had ordered in the early years of the 14th century, one of the oldest surviving painted roofs in a Florentine church. This intervention, which modified the 18th-century windows, revealing the original splayed embrasures, also altered the interior, among other things by closing the first chapel on the left, which looked like a cube of masonry from the outside. The same thing was done with the floor, lowered by about thirty centimeters to bring it back to the level it had had in the 14th century. Some tombstones that, like the numerous sepulchral monuments, had been moved around the church to meet changing tastes and the requirements of the many structural interventions, were put back in the floor.

Zumkeller's restoration did preserve nine of the ten side chapels that had enriched the simple spatial geometry of the harmonious Romanesque church over the period between the 14th century and the High Renaissance. The main chapel that Giuseppe Richa, in 1756, described as "adorned with stuccoes designed by Giovann'Antonio Dosio" but had previously housed paintings by Spinello Aretino, is no longer visible.

The architects of the 16th century must have been impressed by all this, given that Giorgio Vasari – in his *Vite de' più eccellenti Pittori, Scultori e Architetti* – declares twice, in the preface and in the life of Andrea Tafi, "that Filippo Brunelleschi was not ashamed to use [the church of Santi Apostoli] as a model when he built the churches of Santo Spirito and San Lorenzo [....]."

Severely damaged by the flood of 1966, the church of Santi Apostoli has been subjected to further restoration (the most recent, after that of 1966-68, between 1998 and 2000) which has brought it back to the point where it can be fully appreciated, with the exception of a number of movable works that have not yet returned to their original location. Among the main ones that can be seen in the church are Giorgio Vasari's *Allegory of the Immaculate Conception* – begun in 1540 for Bindo Altoviti – and, in the main chapel, Giovanni Antonio Dosio's *Monument to Archbishop Antonio Altoviti*, who died in 1573. Dosio was also responsible for the late 16th-century renovation of the apsidal section. The two busts of *Antonio Altoviti* and the so-called *Charlemagne* are by Giovanni Battista Caccini.

Documented in Florence in 1578, Caccini was given the job of "restoring" three ancient busts in Giambologna's workshop while the latter was working on Santa Maria Novella, and we know that he was engaged along with Dosio on the decoration of the apse of Santi Apostoli the same year. We also know that the two artists worked on the main chapel from 1578 to 1583, when Altoviti's tomb was completed and the two busts were presumably installed as well: the legendary founder of the church, Charlemagne, and the contemporary Antonio Altoviti, archbishop of Florence from 1548. But on close examination the first bust reveals a peculiarity: it is a skillful restoration of a classical head, probably of Homer. Caccini, who with Dosio had learned in Rome the antiquarian art of salvaging, and completing, antique sculptures (his biographers, Borghini and Baldinucci, recall his ability to assemble pieces from different sculptures), added the nose and presumably eliminated the traditional blind stare.

On the modern high altar stands a polyptych representing the *Madonna Enthroned with Saints* by Jacopo di Cione called Orcagna. Dated 1383, it was brought here around 1950 from the Galleria dell'Accademia,

Giorgio Vasari, *Allegory of the Immaculate Conception*, 1540

facing page
Interior of the church

following pages
Giorgio Vasari, *Allegory of the Immaculate Conception*, 1540, detail

but had originally been in the Minoress convent of Santa Maria at Monticelli until the Napoleonic abolitions. Like Giorgio Vasari's large panel, the work has undergone a demanding restoration that entailed the transfer of the painted surface from the original wooden support to a new one, after the former had been irreparably damaged by the floodwaters of the Arno in 1966.

Giorgio Vasari's described his *Allegory of the Immaculate Conception* as follows "the tree of original sin in the middle of the panel, at its roots, as first transgressors of God's commandment, I painted Adam and Eve naked and bound, and after the other branches I painted, bound hand to hand, Abraham, Isaac, Jacob, Moses, Aaron, Joshua, David, and the other Kings in succession of time [...]. With its tail wrapped around the trunk of the tree I painted the ancient serpent, which having a human form in its upper half, has its hands tied behind it. The glorious Virgin has one foot on its head, treading on the horns, and the other on the Moon, being dressed in the Sun, and crowned with twelve stars. The Virgin, surrounded by radiance, is held up in the air by many small nude angels, lit up by the rays that come from her; which rays, also passing between the leaves of the tree, illuminate the bound figures, and appear to be dissolving the bonds with the virtue and grace that they have from her, whence they come." The picture, which had been inspired by the scholar Giovanni Lappoli called Pollastra (a poet and canon from Arezzo with good connections in Medici circles, where he would be followed by the young

Benedetto da Rovezzano, *Sepulchral Monument to Oddo Altoviti*, 1507

Vasari) – proved a remarkable success, something to which the numerous replicas, copies, engravings and free variations still bear witness today, and was valued by the painters Pontormo, Sogliani and Ridolfo Ghirlandaio at 300 scudi. The client Bindo Altoviti even had a small replica executed by Vasari himself, the following year in Rome.

The image in Santi Apostoli is one of the finest of his representations of literary subjects and complex theological and allegorical themes, for which the artist often turned to scholars and philosophers for assistance. To illustrate the intricate theological theme in detail, and thus take part in the lively debate of the time, the painter looked to the great stylistic precedents of early 16th-century painting, Andrea del Sarto, Rosso Fiorentino and even Michelangelo: the picture contains citations of the *Last Judgment* in the Sistine Chapel and the New Sacristy in San Lorenzo. The presbyterial section is dominated by the plastic volumes of two *Sepulchral Monuments of the Altoviti Family*: the one that Bartolommeo Ammannati erected to Bindo, with a statue of *Charity* at the center, which has also been moved around the church and is now set above the door of the sacristy; and the one to Oddo, carved by Benedetto da Rovezzano in 1507 and representing the ideal of a 16th-century tomb, with sculptural motifs that clearly anticipate the Counter Reformation.

As well as producing numerous works for Santi Apostoli, Benedetto da Rovezzano had worked for the Borgherini family, in whose palace it is still possible to see some of his fireplaces and other decorative elements, and had shared the Altoviti's opposition to the Medici. He carved the sepulcher for Oddo along classical lines, with a large arch enclosing the tomb, pilaster strips with *candeliere*, macabre reliefs and decorative motifs that are also to be found on the Sernigi altar in Santa Trinita, all with a remarkable quality of execution that imparts the softness and preciosity of ancient ivory to the marble.

One last mention should be made of the *Tabernacle of the Sacrament*, commissioned by the Acciaiuoli from the della Robbia workshop, in which the colors tone down the severity of the architectural setting.

Brazier
(13th-15th century)

The first chapel on the left houses a brazier containing stone splinters from the Holy Sepulcher (brought to Florence by Pazzino de' Pazzi after the Crusade of 1088). It is used, from the altar of the cathedral, to light the fire cart (*Brindellone*) that is drawn through Piazza del Duomo by heifers from the Val di Chiana on the morning of Easter Sunday: the successful lighting of the cart (*scoppio del carro*) is regarded as a favorable omen for the harvest to come. An unusual example of gold work, it is assembled from several different parts: the dove was made in the 13th century, while the central part and the overall composition of the object seem to date from the late 15th century. The gilded copper base, decorated with bean and leaf motifs, contains a small brazier to hold the coals used to light the cart. The central element is made of iron, originally enameled in red and green, and encloses the device of the Guelph faction (an eagle gripping a dragon in its talons) within two curved branches. On the top is set the pedestal on which stands the silver dove.

Orsanmichele

*A singular "cube of stone," it was the church of the guilds.
In a celebration of the work that has made Florence great,
art, history and faith are inseparably fused.
A "museum" of Florentine Renaissance sculpture.*

Donatello, *Saint George*,
c. 1417, Guild of Armorers and
Sword Makers. Museo Nazionale
del Bargello, Florence

Via Calzaiuoli

Built in the 14th-15th centuries

*Patrons: Arte della Seta (Silk
Guild), Compagnia dei Laudesi*

"The motives of the Great in ordering very magnificent buildings lie in the desire to demonstrate their power, and wealth, and at the same time an eager concern to increase the beauty of their Cities, and the convenience of Citizens. And in fact it was similar aims that the Florentine Republic had in the majestic, and splendid construction of Or San Michele." The words with which Giuseppe Richa, in his work on the churches of Florence, opens the second chapter on Orsanmichele offer an insight into the nature of this building: located halfway between Piazza del Duomo and Piazza Signoria, it unites the two spirits of the city, its civil and mercantile one with its religious and devotional soul. In medieval Florence the centers of attraction were the cathedral (still fully under construction in the mid-14th century), the Palazzo dei Priori and the Palazzo del Bargello. Along the road linking the three buildings – the new street between the Palazzo del Bargello and Orsanmichele was planned at the end of the 13th century and Via dei Calzaiuoli was widened in the 14th – the Commune embarked on a new planning scheme, aimed at connecting the city's centers of power with the grain market, where the government was anxious to exercise control over prices and ensure the supply of food to the population.

Thus Orsanmichele was born. A church-cum-palace of unusual character, seat of the guilds and ideal conjunction of secular industry and religious veneration, it was a direct expression of the corporative organization of the new civic institutions, which, with the creation of the first magistracy, known as the Priorato, in the 1280s, had begun to play a full part in government. The first association, the Arte dei Mercanti, had been set up by the most active of the tradesmen and artisans to give them greater political representation through their consuls and rectors, and gave rise, at the beginning of the 13th century, to the various specialized guilds: the Arte del Cambio, Arte della Lana and Arte di Por Santa Maria. At Orsanmichele the guilds vied with one another over the decoration of the inside walls and external piers with their patron saints, just as the lower part of Giotto's campanile was adorned with panels representing aspects of human life, from the Creation to the development of civilization through the arts and sciences. As the place chosen for the glorification of the guilds, Orsanmichele stood out as an imposing volume among the city's principal landmarks: Arnolfo's tower, the campaniles of the cathedral, the Badia and Santa Maria Novella and the tower of the Bargello. In the political and aesthetic consciousness of medieval culture, a building had to characterize the panoramic view of the city in which it stood in order for it to take on a representative role, and become a symbol. Testi-

facing page
Luca della Robbia, *Crest
of the Guild of Stone- and
Woodcarvers, c. 1440-45*

MAJOR GUILDS: 1. Judges and
Notaries; 2. Merchants or
Calimala (Cloth Dealers);
3. Moneychangers; 4. Wool;
5. Silk or Por Santa Maria;
6. Physicians and Pharmacists;
7. Vair Traders and Furriers

MINOR GUILDS: 1. Butchers;
2. Cobblers; 3. Blacksmiths;
4. Stone- and Woodworkers;
5. Linen Drapers and Secondhand
Cloth Merchants; 6. Vintners;
7. Innkeepers; 8. Oil Sellers and
Grocers; 9. Leather Dealers and
Tanners; 10. Armorers and Sword
Makers; 11. Belt Makers;
12. Carpenters; 13: Locksmiths;
14. Bakers

14th-century door set in the internal pier of Orsanmichele

facing page
Interior of the church

mony to this is provided by numerous views painted at the time, in which the city is represented solely by its main buildings surrounded by the ring of walls.

The new construction, commenced by the Commune in 1336, lasted throughout the 14th century, and in the 15th century work continued on the completion of its decorations, and above all on the statues that were to occupy the fourteen niches on the outside. Erected on the site of an ancient oratory (9th century) and surrounded by cultivated land, the Orto di San Michele, the 14th- to 15th-century building was a replacement for the loggia, attributed by Vasari to Arnolfo (1284), which, following a series of fires and other mishaps, no longer appeared suited to the requirements of the merchants who used to meet there to trade in grain. The loggia housed an image of the Virgin, probably painted on a pillar and looked after by a lay confraternity (the Compagnia dei Laudesi, a charitable institution founded in 1291 on the feast day of Lawrence, patron saint of bakers), that was greatly venerated by the people, and the decision was taken to give it a more worthy setting. Over forty meters high, the new building was probably the largest grain market in any medieval city, and a magnet for its population as we learn from the lively descriptions of the life that went on around it in the 14th-century Biadaiolo codex. The founding ceremony, held on July 29, 1337, was an important occasion attended by "the Priors and the Podestà and Captain with all the ranks of the Signorie of Florence." In his *Cronica*, Villani preceded this description with the news of the birth of six cubs to the city's three lionesses (the lion, or *marzocco*, was the symbol of Florence), considering this a highly propitious omen for the new construction.

The grain market becomes a church. After Andrea Pisano – appointed master builder of the cathedral as well in 1337 – Simone di Francesco Talenti made substantial modifications to the building of 1336, enclosing the ample loggia on the street (post 1360) with traceries of stone and stained-glass windows and preparing it to house the monumental and solemn marble tabernacle. Carved by Andrea Orcagna, from 1352 onward, to hold Bernardo

Daddi's panel with the *Virgin of the Graces*, this was located in the part where the Virgin had long been honored by offerings and the lighting of candles.

The decorative program, established by a law of 1339, was irremediably altered in 1452 with the removal of Donatello's sculpture of *Saint Louis of Toulouse*. The grain market had been transformed – just as was happening in the cathedral and campanile – into a pantheon of Florentine sculpture with the external tabernacles erected by the guilds and adorned with effigies of their patron saints carved by Andrea Pisano, Donatello, Lorenzo Ghiberti, Nanni di Banco and Verrocchio, among others. On the inside, in the closing decades of the century, the members of the confraternity's board of trustees, including Francesco Sacchetti, laid down the program to be followed by the frescoes, the painted panels to be hung on the piers and the stained-glass windows.

The building, which stands out clearly from its urban surroundings, is structurally so unusual that it has earned itself the definition of a church-palace. This appearance derives in part from the two upper stories, lightened by large two-light windows carved from marble, which were originally used as a grain store and are now a museum. The ground floor is punctuated by the broad and round-headed arches of the original loggia, filled in during the second half of the 14th century with an elegant tracery of arches and decorative motifs, stained-glass windows and panels of masonry. In the walls between the arches are set the fourteen Gothic and Renaissance niches housing the sculptures of the patron saints of the guilds, whose insignia are clearly recognizable in the predellas carved in relief or the colored tondi above. Some of them have now been replaced by copies, or are undergoing restoration prior to their definitive installation in the museum above.

The interior of the church consists of two large halls in a civil style of architecture. Hard to describe as naves, they make it look more like the *salle d'armes* on the ground floor of Palazzo Vecchio: the piers that divide up the large space are similar, as are the arches and ribs that spring from them to form the groin vaults. In the pier near the entrance on Via dell'Arte della Lana

Master of the Biadaiolo Codex, *The Sale of Grain and the Grain Merchant's Shop*, c. 1330, *Codice del Biadaiolo*, fol. 2r. Biblioteca Mediceo-Laurenziana, Florence

facing page
Andrea di Cione called Orcagna, *Dormitio Virginis*, c. 1352. Tabernacle of Orsanmichele, detail

✠ ANDREAS CIONIS PICTOR FLORETIN / ORATORII ARCHIMAGISTER EXTITIT LVI MCCC

The Tabernacle of Andrea di Cione called Orcagna and Bernardo Daddi's Madonna delle Grazie

The complex tabernacle and reliquary – executed by Orcagna and numerous "master carvers" as well as glaziers and mosaicists – is enclosed by a marble balustrade pierced by circles of bronze and bounded, at the corners, by clustered pillars surmounted by light spiral columns with lion's heads at the base, and soaring sculptures of angels. Inside, the square base is decorated with marble panels carved in relief with *Scenes from the Life of the Virgin*, interspersed with small reliefs representing the *Theological Virtues*, *Cardinal Virtues* and *Prophets*. The scenes of the Virgin terminate in large bas-reliefs depicting *Death* and the *Assumption*, which close the rear of the tabernacle. The architecture continues with imposing clustered pillars of the Corinthian order, soaring right up to the trabeation, embellished with high-relief busts of *Prophets*, and the crown with composite spires flanking the pointed tympana decorated with six-pointed stars. Marble drapes serve as a backdrop to bronze grilles that in the past were lowered to close off the arch-shaped openings. A miniature marble staircase leads to the mechanisms used to move them and to the space that contained the strongbox. A skillfully carved tracery of marble, along with gold tesserae and innumerable pieces of green, red and blue glass, ennobles this complex devotional aedicule, of which the painting of the *Madonna of the Graces*, concealed in a secret location and only shown to the people on special occasions, is the corollary. In Daddi's panel the composition of the scene, the *Virgin Enthroned Surrounded by Angels*, harks back to an archaic style, unusual in the Florentine art of the fifth decade of the 14th century: the host of angels arranged in steps is more reminiscent of the *Maestà* of Duccio and Cimabue. In the painting the theme of marriage, symbolized by the Child caressing the Virgin, is associated with that of the Passion, represented by the goldfinch in Jesus's hand, and both allude to the ideals of the confraternity based in the church. Even the choice of Bernardo Daddi, whose work was present in the city's main churches, denotes the desire to find a successful artist capable of painting an altarpiece that would come up to expectations: the devotional icon that the Captains of Orsanmichele wanted to offer to the city. To get an idea of the extent to which the image was venerated, it is sufficient to consider that 1,238,400 candles were sold to be lit on the altar in 1359 alone.

Bernardo Daddi, *Madonna and Child with Angels*, 1347-48, altarpiece of the Tabernacle of Orsanmichele

facing page
Master of the Biadaiolo Codex, *The Sale of Grain and the Grain Merchant's Shop*, detail

is set a door that provided access, by means of a staircase built inside the pier itself, to the upper floors. These were originally used to store grain, which was poured through openings in the walls into the loggia for packaging. The decorations with which they are lined are still fairly legible, including the 14th-century ones on the ceilings depicting *Patriarchs* and *Prophets* and the numerous *Patron Saints* painted on the faces of the piers from the 14th to the 16th century.

On the right stands Orcagna's monumental tabernacle, which frames Bernardo Daddi's gleaming painting on a gold ground, a votive offering for the plague of 1348, in a profusion of spires and pinnacles. Signed and dated 1359, the *Tabernacle* had been commenced several years earlier, perhaps immediately after the epidemic of 1348, as there are references in the documents to a tabernacle in Orsanmichele in the fifties, when the loggia was still partially open and used as a market. On the left an altar houses a marble group representing *Saint Anne with the Virgin and Child*. Carved by the young Giuliano da Sangallo in 1526 to commemorate the expulsion of Gualtieri di Brienne, duke of Athens on the feast day of St. Anne in 1343, it is yet another example of the dual spirit of this singular building, embodying the religious and civil values of the city.

Orsanmichele: the great workshop of statues. In addition to the important commissions for its internal decorations, Orsanmichele became one of the city's great workshops from the 1340s onward, employing the finest sculptors of the 14th and 15th centuries on the execution, for the congregations of the guilds, of niches to house large statues of their patron saints. We should not forget that over the same period in which the guilds were decorating their church, the city embarked on an ambitious public program of sculpture with the project for the ornamentation of the Duomo, and the same artists worked on the majestic cathedral and the building symbolizing the Florentine guilds.

The statues of Orsanmichele, larger than life size and set at a distance that permits a direct relationship with the observer, have been seen as symbols of both Renaissance individualism and corporative ideals. In the same way the tabernacles reflect the architectural styles of the early 15th century: from the Gothic to Donatello's forceful classical manner in the tabernacle of St. Louis. At the center of the artistic debate of the time, the sculptures of Orsanmichele can be inserted into the course of development traced by the new doors of the Baptistery, starting with the competition of 1402.

The creation of the tabernacles proceeded in step with the slow growth of the building: 1339, petition of the Silk Guild and start on the external decoration; 1404, provision of the Signoria obliging the guilds that had right to the "pillar" to execute the sculpture within ten years, on pain of exclusion.

The Signoria's ultimatum produced tangible results: many tabernacles were completed within the ten years, three of them by Nanni di Banco: *Saint Philip* for the Arte dei Calzolai (Guild of Cobblers), the *Four Crowned Ones* for the Maestri di Pietra e Legname (Stone- and Woodcarvers), whose members included sculptors and architects, and *Saint Eligius* for the Blacksmiths, in association with the Goldsmiths; all this while Nanni was working, with Donatello, on the sculptures of the Porta della Mandorla in the cathedral. Contemporary with these were the execution of *John the Baptist* by Ghiberti and *Saint Mark* by Donatello for the Linaioli and Rigattieri (Linen and Secondhand Cloth Merchants), and of *Saint Peter* for the Arte dei Beccai (Butchers), formerly attributed to Bernardo Ciuffagni but recently assigned to Filippo Brunelleschi (Bellosi).

The powerful Arti della Seta, or di Por Maria, and della Lana (Silk and Wool Guilds) had already erected two sculptures, in 1340 and 1377: *Saint John the Evangelist* and *Saint Stephen* (1340). They were both removed to follow new tastes: the former was replaced in 1515 by a new work executed by Baccio da Montelupo and the latter in 1425 by a bronze statue commissioned from Ghiberti, in order to emulate the choice of material made by the guilds of Merchants and Moneychangers. In 1399 the Arte de' Medici and Speziali (Guild of Physicians and Pharmacists) presented the *Madonna of the Rose* to the city, locating it in the large contemporary tabernacle with an unusual covering in the form of a canopy set in front of the seat of the Arte della Lana. Niccolò di Pietro Lamberti carved the tabernacles of

Andrea del Verrocchio, *Incredulity of Saint Thomas*, 1486, Tribunale di Mercanzia (Merchants' Court), entire sculpture and detail on facing page. Museo di Orsanmichele, Florence

the Arte dei Giudici e Notai (Judges and Notaries) and Vaiai e Pellicciai (Vair Traders and Furriers), both with cusps decorated with acanthus leaves and, from the early years of the 15th century, housing works by the same artist, the statues of *Saint Luke* and *Saint James the Greater* (the former was replaced by a work by Giambologna in 1602).

Another great sculptor of saints for Orsanmichele was Lorenzo Ghiberti: he executed the *Saint John the Baptist* for the Arte di Calimala (Merchants), and the *Saint Matthew* (1419-23) for the Cambio (Moneychangers), both in bronze, between the second and third decade of the 15th century. The *Saint John* was the first large statue to be cast in bronze in Florence. In the same years the artist was working on what is now the north door of the baptistery, with the support of the Arte di Calimala, and in his *Commentarii* declares that he made the *Saint Matthew* between 1420 and 1422, a date fully documented in the Arte del Cambio's *Libro del Pilastro*. The last protagonist of the statues on Orsanmichele was Donatello, to whom the Arte dei Linaioli and Rigattieri turned for *Saint Mark* (1413), the Spadai e Corazzai (Armorers and Sword Makers) for *Saint George*, and the Parte Guelfa (Guelph Faction), for *Saint Louis of Toulouse*. The only sculpture in gilded bronze, it was commissioned by the Guelph faction, whose royal patron was Louis, the son of Charles of Anjou, king of Naples, for the huge sum of 3000 gold florins. The proud location chosen for it was the large tabernacle on the façade on Via Calzaiuoli, from where it would be removed in 1452, for obvious political reasons given the advent of Medici rule, and placed in Santa Croce. The Tribunale di Mercanzia (Merchants' Court), the new patron of the tabernacle, would not replace it until 1486, with Verrocchio's *Incredulity of Saint Thomas*. Donatello's other two sculptures – including the *Saint George*, moved to the Bargello in the late 19th century and replaced by a copy in bronze – display a new way of handling the space inside the niches: instead of the static absorption found in the 14th-century sculptures, the saints of the 15th century establish a different relationship with their settings and are, thanks in part to a new awareness of the human body reflected in the calm and relaxed poise of the fig-

ures, innovative, typically Renaissance works. The epitome of the knight, *Saint George* also embodies the ideal of the Renaissance man. The statue, with its proud bearing, is framed in the modest recess of the niche through an original use of perspective. The shield, pivot of the figure's diagonal torsion, determines the movement. The bas-relief at the base, carved in *stiacciato*, represents *Saint George Slaying the Dragon* in the form of a predella, and contrasts the static perspective of a single vanishing point with the potential motion represented by the statue. Like all Renaissance sculpture, the work attained the height of its fame in the 19th century when, following the centenary of Donatello's birth in 1886, the decision was taken to move it (1892) to the hall devoted to the sculptor in the Museo Nazionale del Bargello. The predella was not removed until 1984, following restoration work that had revealed its precarious state of preservation.

The statue itself has recently been restored (2001), giving the figure back the softness of its modeling as well as revealing the remains of an old bronzing that had been inefficiently removed in the 19th century. The presence of reddish stains, alternating with spotless areas, is due to the use of gelatin and oil, to subsequent drastic cleanings and to the substances utilized to take a cast of the statue (Orazio Lulli was the molder who made the cast in 1892, while the sculptor Lorenzo Bartolini had replaced the missing nose in 1852). Other interesting discoveries have been the confirmation of the presence of a sword, with a leather sling, in the saint's hand and of faint traces of gilding used to highlight and embellish the armor, symbol of both the hero and the Guild of Armorers. The intense sculptural activity prompted by the commissions in the cathedral and Orsanmichele (in addition to the competition held in 1401 by the Calimala Guild of Merchants for the decoration of the baptistery door), almost all carried out within the space of a generation, along with the monumental proportions and the civic function of the programs, helps to explain the artistic climate in which the work of building the "*templum in statura et forma Palatii*," as it is described in a document of the Capitani di Or San Michele, was carried out.

Santa Croce

*Franciscan church adorned with masterpieces from the origins of Italian painting:
Cimabue, Giotto and his Florentine followers.
Pantheon of the country as it houses the tombs of many great Italians
(Michelangelo, Machiavelli, Galileo...).*

Cimabue, *Crucifix, ante* 1288.
Museo dell'Opera di Santa Croce,
Florence

facing page
Agnolo Gaddi (?), *Saint Agnes*,
c. 1330, detail of the stained-
glass window of the main chapel

Piazza Santa Croce

Built from 1294 onward

Patrons: Commune of Florence

Great Franciscan basilica, manual of the history of 14th-century painting, illuminated by some of the oldest and most beautiful stained-glass windows in Florence and Italy, filled with works of architecture and sculpture that are among the highest achievements of the Renaissance, a church adapted by Vasari to meet the new requirements of the Counter Reformation and a privileged location for early Florentine moves in the direction of the baroque, pantheon of Florence's great men (from Dante to Michelangelo, from Machiavelli to Galileo, from Alfieri to Foscolo and Gino Capponi): Santa Croce is all this and much more.

Work on the church commenced in 1294, with a subsidy from the Commune of Florence and to a design by the architect and sculptor Arnolfo di Cambio, who in the same years was also in charge of the projects of the cathedral, the Palazzo della Signoria and other Florentine churches (Santa Trinita and San Pier Maggiore). In this case too, the stone and materials used for the construction came from the demolition of the city's second circle of walls, on whose outskirts a new zone had emerged to the east, inhabited by a large number of poor families as well as by the new rich: a densely populated suburb characterized by the presence of commercial, mercantile and banking activities. It was here that the woolen cloth exported all over the world was dyed (and references to this industry can still be found in the names of the streets, such as Via dei Tintori, or "Street of the Dyers"); here that woolen and silk fabrics were woven (Via dei Tes-

sitori, or "Street of the Weavers"); here lived all the people who had moved into the city from the countryside to work in the textile industry, along with the bankers, the Peruzzi and Bardi and other powerful families (Baroncelli, Rinuccini, Alberti...) who had grown rich on the proceeds of that industry. So it is easy to understand why the Franciscans, a mendicant order, chose this site outside the second circle of city walls to erect its Florentine church, located at the center of a newly developed zone with whose inhabitants it was necessary to communicate in a clear language: a language that could be understood by the emerging middle class, the *nouveaux riches* and the poor alike.

The first Franciscan church in Florence, situated in the opposite position to the Dominican Order's first church in the city, Santa Maria Novella, was symbolically dedicated to the Cross, emblem of the sacrifice of Christ, on whose life Francis had modeled his own. So it is obvious that the new church of the Franciscans, built from the foundations up, would have a shape similar to the great *Crosses* painted in those same years by Cimabue and Giotto. It has a nave and two aisles separated by octagonal pillars with water-leaf and composite capitals, roofed by wooden trusses. The nave is higher than the aisles, whose saddleback roofs stretch from one buttress to the other of the seven Gothic arches of which it is made up. The cross-shaped transept has five chapels on each side of the large presbytery. Only subsequently were other architectural elements added to the right and left,

housing the Niccolini Chapel (on the left), the sacristy with the Rinuccini Chapel, the Baroncelli and Castellani Chapels, the corridor of the Novitiate and the Medici Chapel which extend to the right of the building and link up with the Pazzi Chapel, the cloisters, the conventual part and the one in which the tribunal of the inquisition was located.

The construction of the Franciscan basilica must have started from the right-hand end of the short arm of the cross, with the first two chapels, then the next two and subsequently the main chapel and two small ones at its sides. It then continued with the other four chapels and finally the nave and aisles. This system of construction, common to other Florentine churches of the period (e.g. the cathedral), made it possible to start using the church almost at once. Dating of the surviving paintings has shown that the frescoes on the far right of the short arm of the cross are the oldest, and that the work must have proceeded fairly quickly. The interior creates an impression of magnificence. The effect is that of a large hall filled with light filtered through the splendid stained-glass windows, whose vertical thrust is tempered by the gallery which runs along the nave and which was used, in the past, to display the arms, flags and standards of the families buried in the church. Right from the start Santa Croce had been conceived as a giant book in which the stories of the Gospels could be read through simple and clear images comprehensible to all. The technique used to represent the scenes from the life of Christ and St. Francis was the cheapest and most effective: painting the walls in fresco. And so the great decorative undertaking of the 14th century got under way, with the chapels and refectory painted in the space of a few years, in a succession of contributions by the greatest painters of the day, from Giotto – who decorated four chapels, two of which have survived – to his most outstanding pupils (Bernardo Daddi, Taddeo Gaddi, Maso di Banco, Giovanni di Bonino) and the later exponents of the Giottesque current (Giovanni da Milano, Andrea Orcagna, Agnolo Gaddi). In addition to painting the walls, they supplied the cartoons for the stained-glass windows whose iconography supple-

ments the decoration of the chapels with themes dear to the Franciscans. It is for this reason that Santa Croce holds a preeminent place when it comes to "primitive" painting or the "painting of the origins," i.e. a style that reflected the transformation of language which took place at the time of Dante and Petrarch, from the lofty to the vulgar, from Latin to an Italian comprehensible to the new rich and poor: Cimabue with his great *Crucifix*, unfortunately badly damaged by the flooding of the Arno in 1966; Giotto with the Peruzzi and Bardi Chapels; and then all his followers, among the greatest painters in Italy in those years, who gave a new image to pictorial language through the fresco. And Santa Croce, along with Assisi, was the most important center of Franciscan culture and spirituality between the end of the 13th century and the early decades of the 14th.

What remains of the great *Crucifix* painted by Cimabue before 1288, when it is documented as already being in place, hardly conveys any idea of the great innovation with which the painter began to open the way toward a language that was no longer solemn and iconic, but current and understandable, like the Italian language and like the words of St. Francis. A cross on which for the first time hangs a suffering human being, his skin the livid color of death and his body slumped in a plastic pose similar to the sculptures of Nicola and Giovanni Pisano. The sense of grief extends to the Virgin and St. John, represented in the panels at the ends of the arm, absorbed in adoring prayer and mute, incredulous contemplation.

The great 14th-century decoration: Giotto and his followers in Santa Croce. While historians do not yet agree over the chronology of the paintings in Santa Croce, it is likely that the first frescoes executed by Giotto were the ones commissioned by Giovanni di Rinieri Peruzzi for his chapel, with three scenes from the life of *Saint John the Baptist* (*Annunciation to Zacharias, Birth* and *Herod's Banquet*) and three from that of *Saint John the Evangelist* (*Saint John on Patmos, Raising of Drusiana* and *Ascension*). Although badly damaged, the paintings have elements of dress and composition in common with

Aerial view of Santa Croce

facing page
Interior, the main chapel and two side chapels of the presbytery

the *Legend of Francis* first painted by Giotto in the Upper Basilica of Assisi and then in the Scrovegni Chapel at Padua.

The *Scenes from the Life of St. Francis* in the chapel of Ridolfo dei Bardi, comparable in their intensity and subject to the ones in Assisi, date from the years immediately afterward. The walls may have been constructed around 1310 and their pictorial decoration date from a short time later, and in any case prior to Giotto's stay in Naples (1328-32). From the same years dates the execution of the stained-glass windows designed by Giotto and Giovanni di Bonino and representing the *Approval of the Franciscan Rule*, symbolized by the three popes who in alternating positions bless the three great saints of the order: Francis, Anthony and Louis of Toulouse (canonized in 1317). The novelty of these windows lies in the way that the figures are represented in naturalistic architectural settings in the form of aedicules, even if the background remains squared and without depth. The frescoes with *Scenes from the Life of Saint Francis* in the Bardi Chapel have a much closer relationship with the space, into which the figures expand in an almost metaphysic vision, as in the *Appearance of Francis to the Chapter in Arles.* This certainly served as an example for one of Giotto's greatest Florentine followers, Maso di Banco, in the frescoes with *Scenes from the Life of Saint Sylvester* in the Bardi, later Bardi di Vernio Chapel.

The paintings in both of Giotto's chapels have suffered a great deal of damage as a result of their having been plastered over during the Counter Reformation and the insertion of architectural elements, once they were no longer visible, that mutilated them. They were rediscovered in the mid-19th century and restored with the missing parts filled in and repainted by Gaetano Bianchi, according to the taste of the time. Following the flooding of the Arno in 1966, the two chapels have been restored again, following more philological criteria but preserving those of Bianchi's integrations that were located in the room adjoining the sacristy.

After its recent restoration, the Bardi family chapel of San Silvestro, housing the tomb of the client Gualtiero di Jacopo dei Bardi (died in 1331), has revealed the full

Cimabue, *Crucifix, ante* 1288, detail prior to the damage suffered during the flooding of the Arno in 1966. Museo dell'Opera di Santa Croce, Florence

extent of its extraordinary beauty and the way that Maso was able to transform Giotto's style into a new and personal key. Maso's figures, solemn and apparently set in a remote world, act with slow gestures in a metaphysical sphere in which the color imparts an intense luminosity to the rotundity of the masses and the depth of field. The frescoes must date from after 1336, as the theme is linked to the "Beatific Vision," a dogma proclaimed that year by Benedict XII, a fact supported by a recently published document recording the building of the chapel in that same year of 1336. The scene with the *Miracle of Saint Sylvester Bringing the Magi Back to Life* is one of the most gripping examples of 14th-century painting and anticipates not just works from the height of the Renaissance but even the art of the twentieth century. An expressive solemnity and power, an unusual attention to symbolic realism, a perspective that already seems to follow the rules of the central vanishing point and a simple and straightforward language, in which the saint is shown taming the dragon and the acolyte holding his nose at the pungent smell issuing from the ruins. Then the scene is interrupted by a classical column, all that

remains of the temple, and continues with the saint raising the two dead men, shown both lying on the ground and kneeling before him. Noble knights, dressed in vair and armed, look on attentively, each given a personality of his own. The stained-glass window of the chapel of San Silvestro can find a useful stylistic and chronological reference in Maso's frescoes, to which it is also linked in theme. It depicts, from the top, *Saint Sylvester and Constantine*, *Trajan and Saint Gregory*, *Saint Jerome and Theodosius* (who changed places when the window was remounted after the war); and finally *Gratianus and Saint Ambrose*.

Around 1327 (the date inscribed on the funeral monument executed by Giovanni di Balduccio) Taddeo Gaddi began to fresco the Baroncelli Chapel, at the right-hand end of the transept, with *Scenes from the Life of the Virgin*. At the center of the chapel stood the polyptych painted by Giotto and Taddeo at about the same time as the one signed by Giotto, now in the Pinacoteca Nazionale of Bologna. The large stained-glass window at the back represents *A Bishop Saint and a Pope Saint*, *Saint Peter and Saint John the Baptist* and above them *Saint Francis Receiving the Stigmata*, and

was also designed by Taddeo. Beautiful images, later copied by his followers, can be found in this chapel, with the first still lifes in the history of Italian painting in the mock niches, one containing the ampullae and paten for Mass and the other a book and candlesticks, depicted in perspective on the left-hand wall as you enter, and an early nocturne in the *Appearance of the Angels to the Shepherds*. Shortly afterward (around 1330-34) Taddeo painted a large cabinet for relics intended for the sacristy, but now split between Florence's Museo dell'Accademia and museums in Berlin and Munich. The wooden panels, with the paintings enclosed in mixtilinear quatrefoils like those of the baptistery panels, formed the doors of the cabinet executed for the Franciscan Order with *Scenes from the Life of Christ and Saint Francis*. Taddeo also painted the *Crucifixion* in the sacristy, and the large *Tree of the Cross* for the refectory, inspired by St. Bonaventure's text entitled the *Tree of Life*. The saint is seated at the foot of the Cross, writing. Near him are St. Anthony of Padua, St. Dominic, St. Louis, St. Francis embracing the Cross, Saint John the Evangelist, the Virgin and the three Marys. From the tree with the Cross and the Crucified Christ run scrolls and medallions representing saints and prophets. Underneath is the scene of the *Last Supper* and two episodes are painted on each side of the Cross: a *Scene from the Life of Saint Benedict* and *Jesus in the House of the Pharisee* on the left, *The Stigmata* and a *Scene from the Life of Saint Louis* on the right.

Andrea Orcagna painted a *Triumph of Death* on the right-hand wall of the church, now transferred to the Museo dell'Opera di Santa Croce. It dates from the tragic epidemic of plague that broke out in Florence in 1348, reducing the population to its lowest level in history. The fresco was badly damaged during the "modernization" of the basilica to meet the requirements of the Council of Trent, when it was plastered over and mutilated to permit the insertion of altars. Yet it still represents, with all the force of Dante's *Inferno*, the apocalyptic vision of death and the tragedy of poverty, through the extraordinary image of the beggars looking to death to free them from their sufferings.

Three masterpieces by Donatello in Santa Croce. A wooden *Crucifix* by Donatello is first mentioned in 1510. According to Vasari (1550 and 1568) it was executed by the sculptor in competition with the one made by Filippo Brunelleschi for Santa Maria Novella. The "peasant" Christ, as Brunelleschi famously described it according to Vasari, originally located in the chancel of the basilica, is an extraordinary example of physical and psychological force and still retains its original polychromy and the mechanism that allowed it to be deposited in the Sepulcher for the celebrations on Good Friday. Its dating to Donatello's early activity is supported by its affinity with his youthful production, still strongly influenced by Ghiberti.

The *Saint Louis of Toulouse* commissioned in 1423 by the primates of the Parte Guelfa for Orsanmichele and then, after the tabernacle was sold to the Mercatanzia (1460-63), replaced by Verrocchio's *Incredulity of Saint Thomas*, was transferred around that time to Santa Croce, where it is recorded in 1510 set

The Rinuccini Chapel and the Decoration of the Apse

Returning to life after the plague of 1348, Florence saw the arrival of famous painters, one of whom, Giovanni da Milano, was the author of the frescoes in the Rinuccini Chapel, behind its extraordinary railing dated 1365. The *Scenes from the Lives of Mary and the Magdalen with Christ the Judge* (a circular painting so modern in appearance that it has been considered too advanced to really have been executed in the 14th century) are an expression of Giotto's style filtered through the experience of Northern Italy, and in particular of the painting that the artist's influence had diffused from Padua to Milan, Modena and Udine. The elegant women in the *Expulsion of Joachim from the Temple*, fashionably dressed with plunging necklines and high waistlines that emphasize their curves, exhibit a mixture of Giottesque volumes and iconicity derived from Byzantine rows of female saints, in a refined blend of details, gold and colors that must have greatly impressed the Florentines of the time. The pictures prompted the experiments with color conducted by Agnolo Gaddi, author of the frescoes representing the *Legend of the Cross* in the central chapel, painted around 1380 for Carroccio degli Alberti. From Giottesque culture, expressed through Giovanni da Milano, Agnolo moved toward the late Gothic spirit and couched the scenes from the history of the Cross in an attractive narrative style, as are the stained-glass windows of the same chapel with full length *Male and Female Saints* dominated by the *Crowned Virgin* and *Christ* above. In reality, the lower central part of the window of the apse, consisting of four large figures of biblical kings, an almost obligatory theme in the great cathedrals of Northern European, seems closer to Jacopo del Casentino.

Giovanni da Milano, *Expulsion of Joachim from the Temple*, c. 1365, detail. Rinuccini Chapel

on the old and incomplete façade of the church, commenced to a design by Cronaca, and where it remained until 1860, when the façade was completely rebuilt to a design by Matas. It was then moved to the inside of the façade and in 1908 to the Museo dell'Opera, where it can now be seen. The statue is a masterpiece in which the sculptor combines his skill in the casting of bronze with the richness of gilding, an experiment that he was shortly to repeat in the reliquary bust of *Saint Rossore (Luxorius)* and the monument to *Baldassarre Coscia*, in Florence Baptistery.

The *Annunciation* for the Cavalcanti family is subsequent to his journey to Rome, and thus dates from after 1433. It is not certain whether it was originally set against the choir or located on the right wall of the church, as the most recent restoration seems to suggest. It testifies to the undiminished taste for experimentation on the part of the brilliant sculptor, who tries his hand here at an almost full relief and the use of stone and terracotta. Originally it appears to have been painted to resemble precious marble and gold, but this polychromy was removed, in all likelihood, in the restoration of 1884. The scheme proposed by Donatello in the *Tabernacle of the Sacrament* in Rome (St. Peter's) is renewed and rationalized here, with the triangular tympanum replaced by a segmental arch, a solution that would prove very popular in the sculptural decoration of the late 15th century, along with the idea of the putti with festoons on top. It looks like an altarpiece sculpted inside a deep aedicule which houses the angel and Virgin, whose figure is inspired by classical models, carved in stone and then highlighted in gold on many parts of the clothing and hair. Behind the two main figures are two mock doors with decorations also picked out in gold. The gestures and modeling of the putti with festoons and the angels on top seem to be derived from Hellenistic sculpture. The 16th-century sources state that the altar was completed by a predella painted with *Scenes from the Life of Saint Nicholas*, identifiable, according to the most recent studies, with the one in Casa Buonarroti attributed to Giovanni di Francesco del Cervelliera, which Michelangelo Buonarroti the Younger had acquired from the friars of Santa Croce in 1620.

Donatello, *Saint Louis of Toulouse*, 1423. Museo dell'Opera di Santa Croce, Florence

facing page
Donatello, *Annunciation*, c. 1434, Cavalcanti Altar, detail.

The 15th century. Architectural interventions and sculptural decoration. The rebuilding of the monastery, now insufficient for the needs of the monks, commenced after the fire of 1423, which had destroyed the old dormitory. In 1424 the Commune earmarked a large sum for the construction of a new one. This was followed by the largesse of the Medici (probably at the behest of Giovanni di Bicci) which allowed work to start on the Novitiate, the decision of Andrea de' Pazzi to build the family chapel in the first cloister and the Arte di Calimala's commission of a new library. The work was entrusted to Brunelleschi and his team, with Michelozzo responsible for the Novitiate, the cloisters and the library and Brunelleschi himself for the Pazzi Chapel.

The first cloister is partly based on Arnolfo's plans, while the second was built in 1453 to Brunelleschi's design and finished by Michelozzo, on two tiers with columns topped by Ionic capitals that are repeated in the upper loggia.

Grand Florentine pantheon. In 1444, on the death of Leonardo Bruni, chancellor of the republic, Florence decided to pay tribute to him by commissioning from Bernardo Rossellino, a pupil of Brunelleschi who was later to complete several of Alberti's projects, a sepulchral monument worthy of such an illustrious personage. This tomb, so innovative with respect to those of the Gothic period, influenced all the ones that followed. Bruni is represented lying on the sepulcher and covered with a precious drape of brocaded velvet (a type of fabric for which Florence was famous), with ogival meshes enclosing pomegranates, an Oriental symbol of the immortality of the soul. He looks as if he is sleeping on his deathbed, his head wreathed in laurel, just as he was described in the funeral address given by his successor Carlo Marsuppini. The sepulcher is framed by a solemn architectural setting, made up of a round-headed arch underlined by an inlaid band and flanked by fluted responds with Corinthian capitals. Two winged genii hold the inscription on the base of the sarcophagus, while the Virgin and Child, represented at half length and inscribed in a circle, are

Pazzi Chapel, views of the exterior and interior, with detail of the dome

Luca della Robbia (?), *Saint Matthew*, 1445-50. Pazzi Chapel

The Pazzi Chapel

The chapel's scheme of composition echoes the formal solutions of the Old Sacristy of San Lorenzo, but it is likely that the building was finished after Brunelleschi's death and that the pronaos and the roof with dome and lantern are later. Names put forward as continuators include Rossellino and Giuliano da Maiano, who is known to have worked on the building from 1462 onward. The interior was decorated by the della Robbia (Luca executed the glazed terracottas) and Giuliano da Maiano carved the magnificent wooden doors of the portal, realized after the conspiracy of the Pazzi (1478). The chapel is preceded by a portico supported by six Corinthian columns surmounted by a classicizing motif of panels with a central arch. The lower cornice of this attic is decorated with a series of cherub's heads, the work of Desiderio da Settignano. The dome was completed in 1461: it is a drum with oculi crowned by a small lantern. The atrium has a tunnel vault, adorned with coffers and roses. The walls of the rectangular interior are decorated at the top with tondi representing the *Apostles* and Evangelists, attributed to Luca della Robbia. The frieze with a row of cherubs is also attributed to Luca.

flanked by two adoring angels. Above the arch, the crest of the Bruni, surrounded by a rich garland, is supported by two putti. The recent restoration has brought to light the original painting under which the tomb was set, a sort of polychrome baldachin that emphasized the importance of the location and fitted in well with the marble sepulcher, several parts of which were originally gilded. Overall, the work seems to mark the transition from the religious tomb to the civil monument and was certainly influenced by Donatello's monument to *Baldassarre Coscia* in Florence Baptistery.

In 1453 Carlo Marsuppini, supporter of Cosimo de' Medici, friend of Leonardo Bruni and his successor in the post of chancellor of the republic, died too. His sepulchral monument, commissioned from Desiderio da Settignano, was located opposite Bruni's. The extreme refinement of this monument is well suited to this wealthy and cultured man, celebrated in death by Matteo Palmieri. It has the same architectural and decorative elements as the earlier monument, but the whole thing appears steeped in as different cultural climate, from the deceased now deposed on the coffin at an angle to the angel-victories that take the place of eagles, while the sarcophagus resting on lion's paws is adorned with acanthus at the corners, foreshadowing Verrocchio (thought by some to have collaborated on this undertaking). Outside the architectural setting stand two putti with the Marsuppini crest, acting as an invitation to celebration of the poet. There are four panels under the triumphal arch and the red marble alter-

Bernardo Rossellino, *Sepulchral Monument to Leonardo Bruni*, 1444

facing page
Desiderio da Settignano, *Sepulchral Monument to Carlo Marsuppini*, 1453, detail

nates with white pilaster strips similar to the ones that delimit the space externally. The latter are fluted and topped by polychrome Corinthian capitals. The upper lunette is set on a trabeation finely carved with plant motifs and contains a very low relief of the Virgin and the Child inside a clipeus flanked by angels. The arch is decorated with a garland and flanked by two genii supporting a festoon of fruit and leaves that hangs from the center of a vase and reaches three-quarters of the way down the monument.

The Counter Reformation. As in other Florentine churches, Vasari's restoration considerably altered the original appearance of the basilica of Santa Croce. When the Council of Trent came to an end in 1563, Cosimo I, who had close political ties to the pontiff, put its directives into effect by carrying out substantial renovations and alterations of Florence's places of worship. The screens separating the area for the congregation from that used by the clergy were eliminated and altars were built and decorated in the naves and aisles, often accompanied by the construction of a new and majestic high altar.

The work in Santa Croce was begun by Vasari in 1560 and completed, after Cosimo I's death, in 1584. It entailed the elimination of the large choir or screen, the building of side altars with columns and a tympanum, the plastering of the walls and consequent destruction of many 14th-century frescoes and the construction of an enormous new high altar out of wood, demolished in its turn in the 19th century and only partly visible today in the chapel on the left of the transept. On the side altars were set a series of paintings adhering to the ideas of the Counter Reformation and executed by the best artists of the day: Allori, Santi di Tito, Empoli, Cigoli and Ligozzi. Cigoli executed the *Pietà* for the Risaliti (1592). Here the painter reconciled an academic Michelangelesque conception with a new palette of pale and mellow colors resembling pastel. Cigoli also painted the *Christ on the Way to Jerusalem*, for the Serristori Altar (1604), completed by his pupil Bilivert when the artist left for Rome. Jacopo Ligozzi executed the *Martyrdom of Saint Lawrence* for the Salviati Chapel (1611), where the painter from

Giovanni Antonio Dosio and
Pietro Francavilla, Niccolini
Chapel, 1584, detail

Verona introduced an unusual scheme for Florence, derived from Paolo Veronese. The chapel was completely restructured by Gherardo Silvani, who built the altar with decorations of semiprecious stones, much in vogue in those years. Silvani also worked in the Calderini Chapel, between 1620 and 1621. It displays affinities with Roman culture. The ceiling was painted by Giovanni da San Giovanni (1621) with *Scenes from the Life of Saints Peter and Andrew* that reflect the author's interest in Northern European painting derived from his contact with Callot.

The Niccolini Chapel. The client Giovanni Niccolini (died in 1611) had been one of Grand Duke Francesco I's favorites, sharing his taste for pomp and preciosity. To build his family chapel Niccolini had turned first to Palladio, and then to Dosio. Alessandro Allori painted two panels (the *Assumption* and *Coronation of the Virgin*) and Francavilla carved the statues of *Moses* and *Aaron*, alluding to the patron's ancestors and the dedication of the chapel to the Virgin. Begun in 1584, the work was resumed in 1650 by Francesco and finished in 1654 by Filippo and Lorenzo Niccolini, who had the dome decorated with frescoes by Volterrano, Florence's greatest baroque painter. It is one of the masterpieces of the "Roman-style" architecture that was to inspire subsequent baroque chapels erected in Florentine churches.

19th and 20th century. The changes made in Santa Croce in the 19th century related largely to its architecture and sculptures. Between 1845 and 1847 the campanile was erected to a design by Gaetano Baccani and, immediately afterward, the decision was taken to rebuild the church's façade, left incomplete in the 16th century and then demolished. In 1857 the first stone was laid in the presence of Pius IX and Leopold II and the façade, designed by Nicola Matas, was finished in 1863. Inspired by the Romanesque ones of San Miniato al Monte and San Salvatore, it has alternating slabs of white and green marble, interspersed with polychrome marble along

Antonio Canova, *Sepulchral Monument to Vittorio Alfieri*, 1810

facing page
Lorenzo Bartolini, *Sepulchral Monument to Sophie Zamoyski Czartoryski*, 1837, detail

the lines of the campanile of Florence Cathedral. Overall, a harmonious and fitting work that met with a fairly good reception at the time. Inside the church, which already preserved "Italian glories" after the publication of Foscolo's *Dei sepolcri* (1806-07), there was a real competition to erect memorials to the great men of Florence and Italy, notwithstanding the recent laws forbidding burial in the city and requiring the same gravestones for all. The design of the tomb of *Vittorio Alfieri* was entrusted by the Countess of Albany to the greatest neoclassical sculptor, Antonio Canova, who in 1810, after discarding a first project, created a high oval plinth with a pedestal of the same shape but smaller size on top, on which is set the sarcophagus in a classical and almost Etruscan style, decorated with a medallion bearing the poet's profile. *Italy*, a female figure on the right of the monument, looks disconsolately at the tomb while resting her head on her right arm. Among others, Lorenzo Bartolini executed the tombs of *Julie Clary Bonaparte* (1845), widow of Napoleon's elder brother, and *Countess Sophie Zamoyski Czartoryski* (1837), a masterpiece on the level of the beautiful 15th-century sepulchers that inspired it. More classical are the monuments to *Vittorio Fossobroni* (1844), minister of Leopold II, and to *Leon Battista Alberti*, erected in the years in which there were plans to assemble the tombs of Petrarch, Leonardo, Angelico, Colombo, Beccaria and many other great men of the past in Santa Croce. The monument to *Dante*, whose ashes are still in Ravenna, was carved in 1829 by the sculptor Stefano Ricci, while the one to *Gioacchino Rossini* is by Giuseppe Cassioli. Ugo Foscolo's remains were also moved to Santa Croce (1871) and a memorial to him erected by Antonio Berti in 1938.

With the abolitions that followed unification the monastery was turned into offices for administration of the State (Ministry of Finance) and, in 1900, the former refectory, converted into a carpet factory in 1854, was used to house the museum directed by Guido Carocci. It was reorganized in the 1950s and again after the flooding of the Arno in 1966.

Santa Maria Novella

Majestic work of Gothic architecture and principal center of the Dominicans,
it houses masterpieces of painting, sculpture and architecture
by Giotto and Masaccio, Leon Battista Alberti and Pontormo.

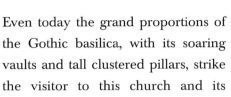

Crest of the Rucellai family, detail
of the façade

Facing page
Masaccio, *Trinity*, 1426-27, detail

Piazza Santa Maria Novella

Built from 1197 onward

Dominican Order

Even today the grand proportions of the Gothic basilica, with its soaring vaults and tall clustered pillars, strike the visitor to this church and its annexes, which house some of the greatest masterpieces of Italian painting (from Giotto to Masaccio to Pontormo), sculpture (Brunelleschi) and architecture (Alberti). Also called Santa Maria della Neve or Santa Maria tra le Vigne, Santa Maria Novella was built on the opposite side of the city to the Franciscan Santa Croce, again outside the second circle of walls, in an area where vines had recently begun to be grown again, as can be deduced from the toponymy (next to it runs Via della Vigna Nuova: "Street of the New Vineyard").

The original church was first mentioned in 983, and was enlarged and modified in 1094, when it was reconsecrated. At the time it was under the patronage of the Florentine canons. In 1219 the first followers of Dominic arrived in Florence and in 1221, through Cardinal Ugolino of Ostia, Dominic himself took possession of the old building of Santa Maria Novella, making it a springboard for his work of conversion and repression of the Patarine and Cathar heresies.

The work was carried on by Fra Pietro da Verona, canonized as St. Peter Martyr, who was based at Santa Maria Novella from 1244 to 1245 and gave a great boost to the struggle against heresy. This fervent activity led to the rebuilding of the monastery in 1221 and its enlargement from 1250 onward.

The Dominican Order began to construct a new church in 1279 at the behest of Aldobrandino Cavalcanti, bishop of Orvieto, who died just as work was starting on the basilica. The plans, according to tradition, were drawn up by the Dominican friars Sisto and Ristoro (although some have suggested Arnolfo di Cambio) and the construction must have proceeded fairly quickly, thanks to contributions from private citizens and the Commune of Florence. In fact many wealthy families resident in the quarter (Minerbetti, Cavalcanti, Strozzi, Ubriachi, Castiglioni, Giudalotti, Tornaquinci, Ricci, Rucellai, Saltarelli, Infangati) vied with one another to finance the new building from the start. Behind all this activity lay the desire of the Order of Preachers, followers of St. Dominic, for large and comfortable spaces in which to carry out the role of teaching that, through the efforts of Remigio de' Girolami, a disciple of St. Thomas Aquinas, had earned the *studium generale* of Santa Maria Novella a Europe-wide reputation as a university in the last decades of the 13th century, only exceeded by that of Paris (where young men were sent to take their doctorate or mastership).

It seems that Dante Alighieri was educated at the Florentine *studium* and so must have attended lectures in the Cappellone degli Spagnoli, formerly the chapterhouse, whose decoration was well suited to Dominican teachings. The highest duty of the Dominicans was to preach the Christian doctrine (in 1217 Pope Honorius III defined them as Friars Preachers) and teachings aimed at the people had to be imparted in the "vulgar" tongue if they were to be understood, just as sacred images illustrating the word of God had to be comprehensible. In effect, right from the earliest decorations the themes selected were of great clarity, striking in

their realism and their visual and emotional impact: an extraordinary example of this is Giotto's *Crucifix*, painted around 1288-89, at the time of Fra Remigio de' Girolami's mastership. Its restoration and location in the basilica at about the height of the roodscreen on which it was originally set have given it back its role and legibility. In 1285, when the Società delle Laudi della Beata Vergine Maria, founded by St. Peter Martyr, commissioned the panel with the *Madonna Enthroned and Child,* known as the *Madonna Rucellai* and now in the Uffizi, from the Sienese Duccio di Buoninsegna, at least part of the building must have been completed. The frescoes in the chapel of San Gregorio (large lunettes) and what is left of the ones on the ceiling of the Gondi Chapel, located on on each side of the presbytery, can also be dated to these years.

Duccio di Buoninsegna, *Madonna Enthroned with Angels (Madonna Rucellai),* 1285. Galleria degli Uffizi, Florence

facing page
Interior of the church

The layout of the church immediately reveals the dominant role of its function, i.e. a place for preaching with a very large space reserved for the congregation. The roodscreen, in fact, was located at the end of the first three arches. There are six of these in all, but the span of the ones in the presbyterial area is much smaller than the ones in the lay part of the church, leaving more room for the public. The same thing happened on the outside, where the square laid out in 1287 and completed during the 14th century was intended to house the faithful during sermons and festivities. The preacher gave his sermons from the pulpit and that of Andrea di Lazzaro Cavalcanti called Buggiano, the adoptive son of Brunelleschi, still survives, set against the fourth pier on the left from the façade, at the level of the old screen. The work was commissioned by the Rucellai and executed between 1443 and 1448 with sculptures representing the *Life of the Virgin,* framed in quadrangular panels of white marble, highlighted in gold. Around 1330 work began on the campanile, built by Fra Giovanni da Campi on the base of a preexisting one and on the orders of Fra Simone Saltarelli, bishop of Pisa and former prior of Santa Maria Novella.

The Strozzi Chapel. Nardo di Cione, a Florentine painter with links to the Giottesque current of the second half of the 14th century, painted *Hell, Purgatory* and *Paradise* on the walls of the Strozzi family chapel in the left transept, dedicated to St. Thomas Aquinas. The hundred or so figures represented in the paintings are given features that define them in an almost naturalistic way, as in the similar theme tackled by the Orcagna brothers in Santa Croce. The theme begins with the *Last Judgment* painted on the rear wall, above and at the sides of the large stained-glass window representing the *Virgin and Child with Saint Thomas. Hell* and *Purgatory* are depicted on the right-hand wall, *Paradise* on the left. Starting out from Maso di Banco and influenced by Giovanni da Milano, Nardo achieved results of great efficacy and refinement that are plainly visible here, despite the precarious state of preservation of the frescoes. On the altar still stands the polyptych by Andrea Orcagna, Nardo's brother, signed and dated 1357, with *Christ* at the center in a mandorla of cherubim and *Saints Michael the Archangel, Catherine, Martha and Thomas Aquinas* on the left, *Saints Peter, John the Baptist, Lawrence and Paul* on the right. The predella contains three scenes: the *Mass of Saint Thomas,* the *Calling of Saint Peter* and *Saint Lawrence Saving the Soul of Emperor Henry.* Echoes of the writings of Jacopo Passavanti, and in particular the *Specchio di vera penitenza,* have been recognized in this panel.

The Cappellone degli Spagnoli. The use of this name – "Great Chapel of the Spanish" – for the huge hall to the north of the Green Cloister, originally the Dominican chapterhouse, dates from 1540, when Eleonora de Toledo, wife of Cosimo I de' Medici, chose it as the place of worship for her Spanish entourage, even before it was dedicated to the patron

Giotto's Cross

Following its recent restoration Giotto's great Cross has been returned to its original location, where for centuries, up until Vasari's intervention, it had hung above the now vanished partition, adding its clear and eloquent voice to that of the preachers when they addressed the people. One of the things that first strikes anyone looking at this immense and beautiful cross is that the man hanging from it is a youth with a vigorous body and a human face, very different from the stereotypes of *Christus Triumphans* or *Christus Patiens* painted only a short time earlier. Ever since Cennino Cennini (an artist active not long afterward and with links to the Giottesque current), it has repeatedly been said that Giotto translated the art of painting from Greek into Latin, or perhaps more accurately into Italian, and the *Crucifix* is a confirmation of this. The restoration has brought to light several details that reflect Giotto's desire to make the image legible and human. For the first time, in fact, the foot of the cross has been widened and the triangle at the end, integral with the cross, added not just as a structural element, but as a representation of Golgotha and Adam's skull, onto which Christ's blood flows. The correspondence with reality becomes complete: Christ's blood redeems the humanity represented by Adam. And therefore makes possible the resurrection of the just at the end of time. This message is closely connected with the Dominican preaching against heresy and the value of the presence of such an image during sermons is clear. The extraordinary decorative elements of the drape, based on silk textiles woven in the Arab world, the halo with its painted glass, the scroll or *Titulus Crucis* with an inscription in Hebrew, Greek and Latin testifying that Christ is the king of all the peoples and the two panels with the charming figures of the Mother and St. John confirm the absolute novelty of Giotto's invention and suggest a date early in his activity (1288-89). Thus this magnificent *Crucifix* must have been painted immediately after the first frescoes in Assisi.

saint of Spain, James of Compostela, in 1592. The hall was built between 1350 and 1355 to a design by Fra Jacopo Talenti and at the expense of the wealthy merchant Buonamico di Lapo dei Guidalotti, who left a considerable sum of money for its decoration in his will: the task was entrusted to Andrea Bonaiuti called Andrea da Firenze, who undertook, in 1365, to complete the work within two years.

On the north wall, opposite the entrance, are painted scenes from the Passion: the *Road to Calvary*, at bottom left, with the city of Jerusalem in the background of the procession accompanying Christ carrying the cross. In the lunette above we see the *Crucifixion*, with Christ between the two thieves and a crowd of onlookers. On the right is the *Descent into Limbo*, where the chosen kneel before the figure of Christ. In the vaulting cells are depicted the *Resurrection, Ascension, Pentecost* and *Saint Peter's Boat*. On the right-hand wall there is a large allegory of the *Way of Salvation* under the protection of the Church and the guidance of the Dominican Order. The Church, symbolized by a model of Florence Cathedral, still under construction at the time, forms the backdrop to ecclesiastic and civil society, represented by the whole gamut of its authorities (popes, bishops, cardinals, emperors, kings, counts, clergy, monks, magistrates, etc.). Here we see St. Dominic urging the Dominicans, symbolized by black-and-white dogs (*Domini canes*), to hurl themselves on the wolves of heresy, in the presence of St. Peter Martyr and St. Thomas Aquinas, who succeeds in converting several heretics. Above is set Christ in a mandorla, with the keys of the church and the holy scriptures. On the left is the *Triumph of Saint Thomas* with an *Allegory of the Sacred and Profane Sciences*.

Brunelleschi's Crucifix. Many people will be familiar with the story about Donatello told by Vasari in the first edition of his *Lives*, when the young sculptor invites Brunelleschi to see a *Crucifix* he has just carved (usually identified with the one in Santa Croce) and the latter complains that the figure looks more like a peasant than a crucified Christ. So Donatello challenges Brunelleschi to get some wood and carve one himself: the result was the *Crucifix* now in Santa Maria Novella. In reality, the perfect proportions of the body, based on the parameters of Vitruvius and represented anatomically, show just how close the understanding was between the two artists, both fully conscious of the new sensibility of the Renaissance. Yet it is also true that, above and beyond this common awareness, the visual results are very dissimilar, and that Brunelleschi's *Crucifix* is far more classical and idealized than Donatello's naturalistic one. It is already apparent that the roads taken by the two geniuses are going to diverge, eventually reaching a point where their collaboration will become impossible.

Masaccio's Trinity. Of all Masaccio's masterpieces, perhaps this is the one that best expresses the concept of Renaissance, a work that coalesces theories of perspective, philosophical ideas and sacred beliefs in a shattering sense of the new and of humanity over which rivers of ink have been spilled. The recent restoration has brought to light the quality of the colors and the interventions made in the 19th-century and has given depth back to the architectural niche framing the scene, a large triumphal arch with a coffered vault that must have greatly pleased Alberti. Under this vault God the Father supports the Cross on which hangs his Son, a man of powerful physique. Standing, and also under the arch, we see the Virgin on the left, looking out at us and inviting us to take part in the scene, and St. John on the right, gazing at Christ. Outside, kneeling, the two donors: on the left an elderly man in 15th-century dress with a red hat and gown (painted in cinnabar, a rare and expensive pigment), recently identified as Berto di Bartolomeo, born around 1377-78 and dying between 1443 and 1447; a prominent member of the guild of stone- and woodworkers, he assisted Brunelleschi in many undertakings and worked as an architect in Santa Maria Novella. On the right is his wife Sandra, about ten years younger than her husband. Figures that for the first time are the same size as

the sacred ones, located outside the sacred representation itself but closely connected with it. The chromatic effect produced by the red and black is enhanced by the modulated and precise contrast of the two colors, located on the left and right alternatively. The same colors are used to underline the architecture, with the sole addition of modulations of white and gray together with the pinkish hues of some details. The balance is perfect and the identical coloring of God the Father, where lapis lazuli is used, emphasizes and clarifies the humanity and realism of the whole. The base on which the donors stand and which constitutes the level of the horizon is painted as if it were an altar table supported by a pair of columns on each side, framing, like an altar frontal, a skeleton lying on a sarcophagus with the inscription: "I ONCE WAS WHAT YOU ARE AND WHAT I AM NOW YOU WILL BE." The fresco's composition is based on a precise scheme of central perspective, which has led to the suggestion that Brunelleschi played a direct part in the design of the architecture: a hypothesis that appears even more credible today, after discoveries made in the archives. The current location of the painting (moved in the 19th century) is the original one. Thus it was immediately visible to the people who, entering from Via degli Avelli, came to hear sermons in the zone reserved for them and separated from the other by the screen. From the pulpit the image, located immediately to the left of the preacher, may have served as a permanent symbol of the theological dogma. During Vasari's renovations of the interior the painting was partly plastered over and covered by a panel (*Madonna of the Rosary*, 1570, painted by Vasari for Camilla Capponi). Over the course of the 19th-century restorations of the basilica, the upper part with the Trinità was discovered, detached along

with the section of wall on which it was painted and moved to the inside of the façade. The missing parts were then completed, as was the practice at the time, by the specialist Gaetano Bianchi. The lower part was not found until the 1950s, confirming the work's original location, and the fresco was moved back again, rejoining the two parts that are so intimately connected. The date assigned by critics has wavered between 1425 and 1428, but sometime around 1426-27 is the most likely, on stylistic grounds. The painting displays such a maturity of composition that it can be compared with the polyptych in Pisa and has even more in common with the *Saints Jerome and John the Baptist* in London, which formed part of the polyptych in Santa Maria Maggiore in Rome (1428).

The Green Cloister. The Green Cloister, whose name derives from the use of green earths to paint the walls, was built in the 1350s. The decoration, for which funds were set aside by Turino di Baldese right from the start of the construction, was probably carried out in the early 15th century by Ambrogio di Baldese, Rossello di Jacopo Franchi and other painters of the school on the south and west sides, while the east side was begun and party executed by Paolo Uccello, perhaps in collaboration with Dello Delli. The first of the five decorated arches represents the *Creation of the Animals* and the *Creation of Adam*, above and below the *Creation of Eve* and *Original Sin*; the second, the *Expulsion from the Garden of Eden*, the *Early Life of Adam and Eve* and, underneath, the *Sacrifice of Cain and Abel* and the *Killing of Abel*; the third, *Lamech Killing His Forebear*, the *Building of the Ark* and, below, the *Entry of the Animals into the Ark*; the fourth, the *Flood* and the *Receding of the Waters* and, underneath, the *Sacrifice* and *Drunkenness of Noah*; the fifth, almost indecipherable, the *Construction of the Tower of Babel*.

It is likely that the scenes were painted before Paolo's departure for Venice (1425) and that the painter, trained with Masolino in Ghiberti's workshop, took from the Door of Paradise many ideas for these paintings, which are constructed like kaleidoscopes in which figures, objects and continually varied points of view produce a sensation of constant transformation, of apprehension,

wonder and fabulous irony. Here the irrational gains the upper hand over Brunelleschian order and composure and the perspective is turned into magic and cabbala that are at once Gothic and Renaissance. A comparison with Masaccio's almost contemporary *Trinity* explains better than any words the fantastic character of Paolo Uccello's use of perspective and optical effects, a relationship that could be likened to the one that unites and separates the experiences of Metaphysical Painting and Futurism in the modern era.

The main chapel and the decoration of the second half of the 15th century. The main chapel was dedicated to Our Lady of the Assumption and was patronized by the Ricci and Tornaquinci. It had been decorated in its entirety by Orcagna when Giovanni Tornabuoni took over the patronage and decided to renovate it with paintings by Ghirlandaio. The work began in 1485 and the decorations executed by Ghirlandaio's workshop proved particularly lively, attractive and modern. The scenes from the lives of the *Virgin* and *Baptist* present a wonderful picture of Florentine life in those years, with beautiful and elegant girls walking haughtily toward the *Visitation*, true portraits in which Giovanna degli Albizi, the wife of Lorenzo Tornabuoni, and Dianora Tornabuoni, married to Soderini, have been recognized. And there are innumerable portraits of men as well: every person in Florence who counted must have been immortalized by Ghirlandaio on these walls, where the workshop displayed great technical skill and mastery, producing pleasing, vivacious and precious results through the use of colors and gold, classical citations derived from Rome and links with great contemporary artists (from Botticelli to Perugino, Verrocchio to Leonardo): a cross section of life and culture that tells us a lot about Florence in those years. The

magnificent windows with *Scenes from the Life of the Virgin and Saints* were also executed to designs by Ghirlandaio around 1491, completing the iconographic themes with the cultivated facility and figurative richness typical of the painter.

Another of the great Renaissance painters who worked in Santa Maria Novella was Botticelli, executing for the Lami family, who had close ties to the Medici, the panel with the *Adoration of the Magi* (in the Uffizi since 1796) and a lunette above it with the *Nativity* (now located over the main door on the inside of the façade). The paintings are generally dated to the mid-1480s, but have also been connected with the conspiracy of the Pazzi (1478).

Filippino Lippi and the decoration of the Strozzi Chapel. Presumably begun around 1497, the decoration of Filippo Strozzi's chapel was completed in 1502, as we are informed by the inscription with the painter's signature above the arch in the scene with the *Raising of Drusiana*. The *Scenes from the Lives of Saints John the Evangelist and Philip* are filled with references to the classical culture that Filippino encountered on his journey to Rome, which must also have prompted him to brighten his palette, now lavish with lapis lazuli and gold, and to paint monochrome "grotesques" in imitation of the ones recently discovered in the Domus Aurea. It has rightly been pointed out that the scenes painted by Filippino contain all the scenographic elements (ambient space, fantastic and realistic works of architecture) of a theatrical stage and are a magnificent prelude to the development of the grand "Manner." In the most important scenes on the two main walls, the *Martyrdom of Saint Philip* and the *Saint Driving Out the Devil* on the left and the *Martyrdom of Saint John* and the *Raising of Drusiana* on the right, there is a repertoire of images and figures described with psychological intensity and richness of detail, a sinuous and harmonious play of lines that clearly reflects the neoplatonic ideas of the day and of Lippi's client. The splendid stained-glass window with themes relating to the *Virgin* and *Saints Philip and John the Evangelist* is also by Filippino Lippi and strongly influenced by Leonardo.

Main chapel

facing page
Domenico Ghirlandaio,
Visitation, c. 1485, detail.
Main chapel

The apartment of the Popes. In 1418 the Commune of Florence had an apartment prepared in the west wing of the large cloister of Santa Maria Novella to receive Martin V on his return from Constance, where he had been elected pope. The accommodation was realized to a design by Lorenzo Ghiberti and Pesello; subsequently, in 1427, the apartment of the Popes was enlarged by Michelozzo with an arcade above the large cloister on the north and east walls and a series of spacious rooms that would be used to house several sessions of the Council of 1439. In this area was situated the so-called chapel of the Pope, dedicated to Leo X de' Medici when he entered Florence on November 30, 1515, to make his appearance in his native city as the new head of the Church. The welcome he received was a magnificent one, as is apparent from Vasari's painting in Palazzo Vecchio and from this chapel, which was decorated by Pontormo, Ridolfo del Ghirlandaio and Cosimo Feltrini over a very short span of time. Pontormo's well-known *Veronica* is one of the most extraordinary examples of 16th-century Florentine painting and the very recent restoration has disclosed the great artist's mastery of painting and drawing, with that highly unusual image of Veronica brandishing the white shroud in which Christ's face can be seen. The scene is set under a canopy, customary at the time, and is depicted in shades of yellow-orange, blue-violet and white. On the ceiling and side walls, also designed by Pontormo, angels and putti hold the arms and heraldic symbols of the Medici family and the pontiff and are interspersed with the "grotesque" motifs so fashionable in those years, executed by Cosimo Feltrini, a true specialist in that type of decoration.

The 16th century and Vasari's modernization. In 1565 Giorgio Vasari, on the orders of Cosimo I de' Medici who had assumed the patronage of Santa Maria Novella, set out to render the church functional and modern, in line with the instructions of the Council of Trent. As in all the main Florentine churches the large screen dividing the zone intended for the public from the one reserved for the clergy was eliminated, the walls were whitewashed, the form of the side altars was regularized and new paintings by the most renowned Florentine artists were installed on them. A coherent cycle of decorations was executed by Vasari himself (*Resurrection of Christ, Madonna of the Rosary*), Naldini (*Birth of Jesus* and *Deposition, Purification of Mary*), Allori (*The Samaritan Woman at the Well*), Santi di Tito (*Annunciation*), Ligozzi (*Saint Raymond Raising a Boy* and *Saint Hyacinth*) and some of the other principal specialists of the period. On that occasion the presbytery was renovated too, only to be altered again in the 19th century. Thus in Santa Maria Novella, as in Santa Croce, Ognissanti and all the major Florentine churches, the spatial and visual unity that had been so severely fragmented by the old choirs and the chapels abutting onto them was restored. The choice of sacred subjects for the decoration of the new altars was left to the clients: however, they were guided by the concept of simplification of form, with the aim of rendering the Christian message clear and intelligible.

The Gaddi Chapel. An extraordinary example of architectural and decorative unity from this period is the Gaddi Chapel, dedicated to St. Jerome and built by Dosio (1575-78). Giovanni Bandini, known as Giovanni dell'Opera, was entrusted with the sculptural decoration, while Alessandro Allori painted the ceiling and Agnolo Bronzino the splendid panel on the altar. A characteristic feature of this chapel is the use of rare marbles from excavations: along with the Niccolini Chapel in Santa Croce, dating from shortly afterward and also by Dosio, it would set the trend for all the rich baroque chapels built in Florence in the years immediately afterward.

The decoration of the large cloister. Construction of the large cloister took place after 1333, but its decoration did not start until about 1570, at the behest of Cosimo I de' Medici who contributed, along with allied noble families and several eminent Spanish prelates (also with links to Medici politics), to the decoration of the fifty lunettes and four corner vaults. They were painted in the 1570s and 1580s, with the exception of a few that were finished in the 17th and 18th centuries. The most famous artists of the day, members of the academy who were already accustomed to realizing collective works, took part in this enterprise. Thus we find paintings not just by Santi di Tito, Poccetti, Allori and Butteri, but also by Fei, Sciorina, Buti, Veli, Simone da Poggibonsi, Gamberucci and Gheri. The lunettes mostly represent themes linked to the life of St. Dominic and the more important Dominican saints engaged in the struggle against heresy (St. Peter Martyr etc.), along with episodes from the *Life of Christ* and many portraits of personages of consequence with ties to Santa Maria Novella, including the depiction of Ferdinando I and Francesco I de' Medici in the guise of *David and Isaiah.*

The library. In 1338-40 a library was built by Jacopo Passavanti on the upper floor, between the cloister of the Dead and the garden, to house the books used in the activities of the monastery and university. It was enlarged by Leonardo Dati in 1421. A new library, set at a right angle to the previous one, was built between 1618 and 1636, to house the donation of over 7000 volumes from the archbishop of Pisa, Monsignor Bonciani. It is a well-lit hall with a vaulted ceiling and gilded shelves protected by a brass grating, above which were set fourteen paintings by Jacopo Vignali, depicting distinguished personages of Santa Maria Novella.

The pharmacy. As early as 1508 the monastery of Santa Maria Novella had an important pharmacy. Temporarily closed at the end of the century (1592), it was reopened in its current location in 1612, when it was entrusted to Simone Marchi, one of the best-known pharmacists of the 17th century who, together

Portormo, *Veronica*, 1515. Chapel of the Popes

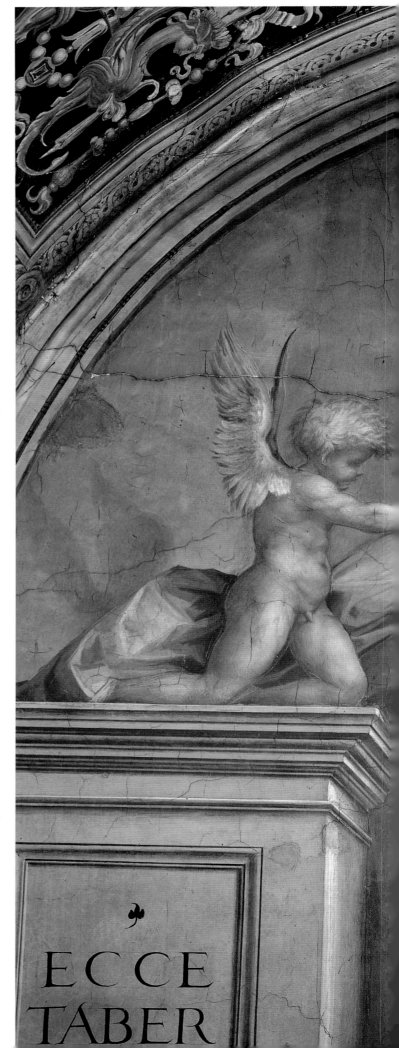

PRETENDI
DÑE·SV

with his successor Angelo Marchissi (died in 1659), made it famous in Florence and beyond. It soon came under the protection of the Medici family, who gave it its own coat of arms, at whose center is set a *Saint Peter Martyr* by Matteo Rosselli. From 1699 onward the pharmacy was subjected to alterations and renovations that comprised the architecture and the external and internal decoration, with Rose of Lima as its new patron saint. In the 18th century it was enlarged again and embellished (salesroom) and earned great fame and prestige thanks to Cosimo Buccelli (died in 1788), inventor of Alchermes and elixir of rhubarb. After the Napoleonic abolition and subsequent return to the ownership of the Dominicans, came, thanks to Fra Damiano Berti (1806-69), the annexation of the chapel of San Niccolò, whose walls had been frescoed by Mariotto di Nardo with *Scenes from the Passion of Christ*, painted for Angiolo and Leone Acciaioli between 1385 and 1405. Since the abolition of monasteries that took place after unification, it has been in private hands and is very well known and appreciated for its ancient pharmaceutical specialties and perfumes, still produced by traditional methods.

Alessandro Allori, *Last Supper*, 1583-97. Museo di Santa Maria Novella

The 19th century. Between 1858 and 1860 a complete restoration of the basilica was carried out in an attempt to return it as far as possible to its Gothic appearance. Vasari's altars were replaced by the present Neo-Gothic ones and lancet windows were opened or reopened and filled with antique-style stained glass, designed by Giovanni Fattori's father Giuseppe. The operation was completed with the laying of the present flooring, eliminating the terracotta tiles and ground-level tombs, which were set in the walls instead, and the construction of the high altar, designed by Romoli as a replacement for the one built by Giuseppe del Rosso in 1804. These were the years in which the monastery was requisitioned and the church taken over by the State. Since that time the history of the complex has been only partly linked to the Dominican Order, which still occupies a number of rooms, while Santa Maria Novella has represented one of the city's first experiments with the transformation of a church into a museum.

The façade

Work began on the façade in 1325 and it was completed at the behest of Guardina, the widow of Cardinal Tornaquinci, and with the money left in Turino di Baldese's will, of which Passavanti was the executor in 1350-51. The large stained-glass rose window with the *Coronation of the Virgin* by Andrea Bonaiuti dates from 1365. Subsequently, the completion of the marble cladding of the façade was commissioned by Fra Paolo Rucellai, at the expense of his family, from Leon Battista Alberti, who executed it in 1470, the year in which he also rebuilt the main portal at the behest of Bernardo Rucellai. The name of Giovanni Rucellai, followed by the date 1470, is inscribed in Roman letters on the pediment of the basilica and marks the conclusion of the splendid façade in white and green marble that harmonizes the lower Gothic part, still linked to the Romanesque coloring of the basilica of San Miniato al Monte, with the upper one of classical proportions realized with an almost musical rhythm by Alberti. At the sides of each of the lateral portals are set three tombs housed underneath pointed arches. The space of each aisle is divided into four by pilaster strips in white marble topped by Corinthian capitals and linked by round-headed arches framing a decorative geometric pattern in two colors. The central, 15th-century arch is bounded by two columns in Prato serpentine with Corinthian capitals. Above this first tier of decoration runs a motif of sails in white and green, symbol of the Rucellai family. On top is a fascia decorated in the same colors with a motif of squares in which circles with geometric decorations are inscribed. The tympanum is tall and flanked by two volutes richly decorated with white and green marble that produce a lacy effect. The large oculus at the center is flanked by pilaster strips made up of horizontal panels of white and green marble and a geometric pattern of rectangles that fills the spaces between them. The upper fascia bears the inscription "IOHANES ORICELLARIUS PAV F AN SAL MCCCCLXX" in capitals, followed by a triangular tympanum with a rayed sun at its center, symbolizing Christ. The marble friezes of Alberti's façade were carved by Giovanni di Bertino, following a precise and complex allegorical and anagogical iconographic program dictated by the famous architect.

San Marco

*Now a state museum, the Dominican monastery was inhabited and made famous by great personages
of the Renaissance: Cosimo de' Medici and Lorenzo the Magnificent, St. Antoninus and Fra Angelico.
The deep mark left by Savonarola is still evident in the church and monastery.*

Crest testifying to Medici
patronage in San Marco

facing page
Fra Angelico, *Annunciation*,
c. 1440, detail. Museo di San
Marco, Florence

Piazza San Marco

*Built at the end of the 13th
century. Renovated in 1436 and
the 16th century*

*Order of the Sylvestrines,
transferred to the Dominicans
(1436)*

Patrons: Medici

Anyone visiting the church of San
Marco in Florence will have the distinct impression of entering a building adhering to the tenets of the
Counter Reformation, such is the extent
to which the pictorial decoration and
architectural alterations dating from that
period predominate. This aspect is in line with the
cultural climate shaped from the moment of the
Dominicans' first arrival by important figures connected with the order, who played a fundamental
role in the history and life of the city: St. Antoninus
Pierozzi, Fra Angelico, Fra Girolamo Savonarola
and Fra Bartolommeo della Porta, great personalities
who left their mark on the layout of this monumental complex through their literary works, preaching
or paintings. In reality the single large hall that
makes up the church of San Marco, with a transept
and apse to which two chapels were added on the
right, has Gothic origins, or rather dates back to the
time of the institution of the order of the
Sylvestrines, sometime in the second half of the 13th
century. Construction of church and monastery
began at the end of the century and by the year 1300
San Marco Nuovo in "Cafaggio" was already a
parish church. To the decoration of the old church of
the Sylvestrines, under the rule of St. Benedict,
belongs the great *Cross*: now on the inside of the
façade, it was originally set on the iconostasis, where
it remained until 1564, the year the screen was
demolished by the Medici at the suggestion of Giorgio Vasari. The scheme of the *Cross* is very like that
of Giotto's *Crucifix* in Ognissanti, but what we have

here is a later painting and an example of the revival of Giottesque prototypes in the second half of the century:
more precisely, it was executed sometime around the 1350s by a painter in the
circle of the Orcagna. Like many Gothic
churches in Florence, San Marco must have had
walls completely covered with paintings that had the
function of conveying ideas linked to Catholic doctrine to the faithful. And in fact on the inside of the
facade, on the right as we enter, we find a fresco
depicting the *Annunciation*, based on the model of
the venerated image located in the nearby church of
the Annunziata. The work was painted sometime in
the 1360s by an artist belonging to the circle of
Jacopo di Cione, close to Lorenzo di Niccolò.

Medici patronage. On January 21, 1436, at the
prompting of Antonino Pierozzi, Cosimo I the Elder
and the young Lorenzo the Magnificent created the
conditions for Pope Eugenius IV to place the complex in the care of the Dominicans. Following a precise plan, the two Medici made San Marco the conclusion of the axis of Via Larga and the representative center of their power and munificence. At the
time Antonino Pierozzi, the future St. Antoninus,
was vicar general of the order and his friendship
with the Medici must have been decisive in obtain-
ing the Florentine church for the Dominicans. Work
began in 1437; the enlargement of the presbyterial
zone to a design by Michelozzo commenced the following year. Signs of those works, which included
the commission of the large altarpiece with the *Vir-*

gin between Saints Cosmas and Damian, Lawrence, John the Evangelist, Francis and Peter Martyr, painted by Fra Giovanni Angelico before 1443 (the year in which the church was solemnly consecrated in the presence of Pope Eugenius IV), remain in the presbytery, where the Medici coats of arms are still visible. The altar, dedicated at the time to those Medicean saints *par excellence*, Cosmas and Damian, had already been dismantled by the end of the 16th century and Angelico's splendid Renaissance panel is now dismembered and divided between the Museo di San Marco and foreign museums. As if in a theatrical scene set in a *hortus conclusus*, the curtain opens onto the Virgin seated with the Son at the center, on a throne in the form of a Renaissance aedicule and flanked by a host of angels, while in the foreground three saints stand on each side, conversing with one another, and Cosmas and Damian kneel, one looking toward us and the other at the Virgin, acting as symbolic intermediaries between the Medici family and the divine. An Oriental carpet articulates the perspective of the space, interrupted in the middle by a "pax" with the *Crucifixion*.

But the works carried out by the Medici affected the monastery even more than the church, turning it into one of the Dominican Order's most important in the city, equaling that of Santa Maria Novella in splendor and surpassing it in modernity and functionality. Between 1437 and 1452, Cosimo I the Elder and Lorenzo the Magnificent entrusted Michelozzo again with the design of the new Dominican monastery. On the outside the building presents a very simple appearance, more or less identical with the original. On the inside there is a spacious porticoed cloister filled with light and dedicated to St. Antoninus. The ground floor houses the common rooms (chapter, refectory, etc.), the second floor the cells of the friars (frescoed by Fra Angelico and his followers) and the large library, with two parallel lines of columns running its entire length and making it look almost like the hall of a basilica. It contained a collection of classical texts acquired from Niccolò Niccoli by Cosimo I the Elder for the Dominican monastery, unfortunately dispersed fol-

lowing its abolition after unification. Today, along with the next room, called the Sala Greca, it houses numerous important illuminated codices, some of them by Angelico and his collaborators. The 18th-century decoration that transformed it by coloring the walls green and characterizing the setting in a luminous and lively fashion has recently been brought to light.

The Annunciation. At the top of the grand staircase we find the *Annunciation*, a theme that Angelico repeated in the third cell as well. Under a Renaissance and Michelozzian portico, very similar to the first cloister or the constituent elements of the library, an angel with multicolored wings addresses the Virgin, the simple figure of a woman seated modestly on a stool who, with her hands folded on her belly, accepts the divine annunciation. A fine flowering sward on the left is bounded by a fence with a dense wood behind it, perhaps resembling the surroundings of San Marco in Cafaggio during the 15th century.

In the first corridor is depicted the so-called *Madonna of the Shadows*, a *sacra conversazione* set in a sort of 15th-century ancona in which the Virgin, seated on a throne with the Son holding a sphere, is flanked by Dominican saints and saints linked with the clients (the Medici): Dominic, Cosmas and Damian, Mark, John the Evangelist, Thomas, Lawrence and Peter Martyr. The picture is generally thought to have been painted by Angelico following his stay in Rome, i.e. after 1450.

On the second corridor are located the three cells of Fra Girolamo Savonarola and seven more, almost all with an image of the *Crucifixion* painted by Benozzo Gozzoli that varies only in the presence of St. Dominic, St. Jerome or St. Peter Martyr.

Fra Girolamo was born at Ferrara in 1452 and took the Dominican habit in 1474. From Bologna, where he spent the first ten years of his monastic life, he arrived in Florence in 1484, launching a fierce struggle against corruption and vanity, which was seen as an open attack on Medici rule and a blatant call for the restoration of the republic and freedom. These ideas were the favorite subject of his fiery sermons,

Interior of the church

Cloister of Sant'Antonio

facing page
Painter of the Orcagna school, *Crucifix*, c. 1360, detail

following pages
Fra Angelico, *Annunciation*, 1440. Museo di San Marco, Florence

Fra Angelico's Frescoes in the Dormitory

Angelico's frescoes in the dormitory, built by Michelozzo in 1437, are a masterpiece of Renaissance painting. True icons of timeless art, their role was to remind the members of the religious community, through the sacred image, of the life and works of Christ. Today we see them as extraordinary examples of an artistic language whose didactic clarity transcends painting, arriving at its pure poetic and moral essence. The effort put into making the sacred images lifelike, with shadows in the places where they would be cast by the light entering through the small windows, brought them alive, turning them into figures and scenes that inhabited the monastery along with the friars. In the twenty cells, following the precepts of St. Antoninus Pierozzi (prior of San Marco from 1439 to 1444), who in all probability was the main promoter of their decoration, Angelico and his assistants (Benozzo Gozzoli, Zanobi Strozzi, Domenico di Michelino) put the *Costitutiones Domenicanae* into effect: "frates non habent nisi unicam cellam pauperem, sine ornamentis aut imaginibus profanis, sed cum imaginibus Crucifixi, Beatae Virginis et Patris nostri Dominici." In effect the Crucifix, Virgin and St. Dominic are the recurrent themes of the decoration, along with others closely connected with them, such as scenes of the Birth, Passion and Resurrection of Christ or related to the life of the Virgin and the Dominican Order. St. Dominic, in fact, is present in almost all the cells, or his place is taken by other fundamental saints of the order such as Thomas and Peter Martyr. Angelico played a direct part in the decoration of the cells between 1438 and 1446, the year in which the painter is documented in Rome. His collaborators must have had considerable room for maneuver from that moment until his return to Florence between 1450 and 1452, and then again when the friar went back to Rome, where he died in 1455. The first cells were all painted by Angelico. There is no continuity of narrative. Rather each picture is an extraordinary personal image, as if the choice of theme had been left to the occupant of the cell itself. The first scene is the *Noli me tangere*, followed by the *Lamentation over the Deposed Christ*, where the episode, set among fantastic rocks, appears to be filtered through the imagination of St. Dominic, portrayed on the left of the composition. In the sixth cell we find the *Transfiguration*, one of the most surreal and metaphysical scenes ever painted by Angelico, in which Christ is depicted standing and dressed in dazzling white, his arms spread to form the Cross, inside a mandorla of white light and on a metaphysical rock. At his feet the disciples (Peter, James and John) look on in astonishment, while alongside we see the Virgin, St. Dominic and the heads of Moses and Elijah, providing a link between the Old and the New Testament.

facing page
Fra Angelico, *The Three Marys at the Tomb*, 1437-40, detail. Museo di San Marco, Florence

View of the dormitory

Cell with a fresco of the *Noli me tangere* by Fra Angelico

leading to his imprisonment and subsequent martyrdom. He was condemned to be burned at the stake – fire was the means he had chosen to destroy heretical books and profane paintings – in Piazza Signoria in 1498. His faith, his preaching and his execution left a deep mark on Florence, influencing its artistic culture from the end of the 15th century through the first twenty years of the 16th. Savonarola was prior of San Marco from 1491 to 1498 and on display in his cells today are several portraits, a painting of his execution in front of Palazzo Vecchio, his robe and the hair shirt that he used to torment his flesh; at the entrance stands a monument in his honor, the work of Giovanni Dupré. Echoes of him are to be found more or less everywhere in this place, as well as in the painting and sculpture of Fra Bartolommeo, Sogliani, Fra Paolino and Baccio da Montelupo, who left many works in San Marco that are strongly characterized by the iconographic rigor of their images.

The common spaces of the monastery were all located on the ground floor close to the first large cloister. It is there, in fact, that we find the chapterhouse with a large lunette frescoed by Fra Angelico, with *Christ Crucified* at the center, flanked by the thieves, and underneath saints linked to the Medici family (Cosmas and Damian, Lawrence) and the city of Florence (John the Evangelist, John the Baptist), along with the Virgin and the three Marys, on the left, and saints linked to the Dominican Order on the right. In the frame, inside diamonds, there is a pelican in the middle and the nine patriarchs and the Erythraean sibyl at the sides. Underneath, in medallions symbolically linked by a vine shoot running from the center where St. Dominic is portrayed, are portrayed the saints and blessed of the order.

The cenacle or small refectory for guests was preceded by a room with a washbasin. The west wall was decorated with the *Last Supper* by Domenico del Ghirlandaio, shortly before 1480. The composition is closely connected with the one dated to the same year and executed by the painter in the Cenacle of Ognissanti. Under an open portico with a groin vault, linking up with the real architectural structure of the

Fra Angelico, *Madonna Enthroned with Saints*, known as the *Madonna delle Ombre* (*Madonna of the Shadows*), c. 1450. Museo di San Marco, Florence

following pages
Domenico Ghirlandaio, *Last Supper*, 1480. Small refectory, Museo di San Marco, Florence

room, Christ and the Apostles are seated at a long table covered with a "Perugian" cloth of heavy white linen, embroidered with a pattern of towered castles flanked by birds and laid with symbolic fruit, bread and tableware made of transparent Murano glass and metal. Below, in the foreground, a cat sits on the checkered floor, symbolizing evil (fought by the *Domini canes*, or "dogs of the lord"), while a peacock is perched in the window to the left. Many symbolic birds (ducks, quails, pheasants, skylarks, goldfinches) fly among the orange and lemon trees, cypresses and palms of the garden behind the seat, outside the portico. Each object, each plant, each fruit, each animal depicted is a precise evocation of the Passion and of the Resurrection of Christ attained through the miracle of the Eucharist, inaugurated at the *Last Supper*.

Next to this refectory was one used by the Dominican friars, painted by Fra Angelico with a *Crucifixion*, according to the custom of the order. When it was enlarged, the wall with Angelico's fresco was demolished and the new structure was decorated by Giovanni Antonio Sogliani in 1536 with the *Miraculous Supper of Saint Dominic*, a theme that combined the traditional subject of Dominican refectories, the *Crucifixion*, with the theme of dining. In addition to St. Dominic, a series of Dominicans presented as true portraits are guests at the supper, while the lay brother on the left, in the foreground, is identified by Vasari as the novice Molletti, client of the painting. In the foreground two angels symbolically carry food to St. Dominic.

Fra Bartolommeo, *Sacra Conversazione* (*Mystic Marriage of Saint Catherine*), 1512. Galleria Palatina, Florence

facing page
Santi di Tito, *Saint Thomas Praying before Christ on the Cross*, 1593

Fra Bartolommeo. Savonarola's teaching had a fundamental influence on the decoration of the church in the first two decades of the 1500s, a century that opened with a series of paintings executed by the *piagnone* (or "wailer," as the friar's followers were called) Fra Bartolommeo della Porta, who, after the "bonfire of the vanities" (1496-97), had taken vows (1500) and started to paint again.

The panel with the *Madonna and Saints*, still on the Cambi family altar of San Pietro Martire (second on the right) is dated 1509 and thus was painted after the friar's journey to Venice: it reflects intellectual developments at San Marco, with a reassessment of Angelico in the "melodious equilibrium of visible things as reflection and image of the infinite truth of the divine" (Paolucci). The intense sense of devotion is underlined by the inscription "orate pro pictore," which from then on became Fra Bartolommeo's signature. Shortly afterward, in 1512, he painted the *Sacra Conversazione* or *Mystic Marriage of Saint Catherine*, sold in 1690 to Grand Prince Ferdinando (and now in the Palatina) and replaced by a copy by Gabbiani, praised by the sources and still in the church. Immediately after his journey to Rome Bartolommeo painted (1515-16) three more pictures for San Marco, all for the presbyterial area: *Saint Sebastian and the Angel* and *Saint Mark*, located on the left and right of the high altar respectively, and *Saint Vincent Ferreri*, which hung above the door of the priests' sacristy. The first painting has been lost, but *Saint Mark* and *Saint Vincent Ferreri* are now both in the Museo di San Marco.

The new guise of the church after the Counter Reformation. Following the construction of the chapel of Sant'Antonino, the friars continued with their plan to create a well-proportioned and regular church: a hall with orderly and uniform altars. So it was in the decade from 1588 to 1599 that much of the history of San Marco was concentrated, characterized by the Dominican theological commitment to clarity, simplicity and verisimilitude that are at the base of Tridentine Catholic aesthetics.

Their greatest interpreter was Santi di Tito, with the panel (signed and dated 1593) representing *Saint*

Thomas Praying before Christ on the Cross, a "tender and lucid painting, cultivated and yet perfectly popular, filled with Venetian influences and yet firmly rooted in the most illustrious Florentine tradition, with effects of almost 15th-century purism [...], it offers itself as an example of total realism" (Paolucci, 1980). The idea of having Christ emerge from the painting in front of which the saint is praying is an extraordinary innovation: Dominican preaching and prayer render the icon human and allow it to communicate, the divine comes down to earth and converses with saints and with ordinary men and women.

The chapel of the Sacrament. It was in these years that the Serragli Chapel, dedicated to the Sacrament (1594-1603) was built next to the Salviati Chapel, first to a design by Santi di Tito, and then (1603) to one by Cigoli, as has recently been proposed by the critics, who have identified him as the man responsible for the marble portal that now forms the entrance and the enlargement of the whole. The center of the vault marks the point of transition: on the left are all the frescoes by Santi di Tito, with the *Gifts of the Eucharist* and *Faith*, while in the middle and to the right are *Christ in Glory, Hope* and the *Delights of Communion*, painted by Bernardino Poccetti, who also executed the decoration of the walls with scenes from the lives of various *Male and Female Saints* whose vocation had particularly close links with the Sacrament, as is illustrated by the monochromes underneath each figure. The panel on the high altar painted by Santi di Tito, but finished by his son Tiberio (1603), depicts the *Communion of the Apostles*, while the canvases on the walls are by Passignano (*The Fall of Manna*), Francesco Curradi (*Supper at Emmaus* and *Multiplication of the Loaves and Fishes*) and Empoli (*Sacrifice of Isaac*) and date from sometime after 1617, the year the architectural work was finished.

The decoration of the cloister of Sant'Antonino. In the cloister of Sant'Antonino, i.e. the first built by Michelozzo from 1437 onward, the *Crucifixion and Saint Dominic* and the panels above the doors with *Christ the Pilgrim, Saint Thomas, Saint Peter Martyr, Saint Dominic* and the *Man of Sorrows*, all

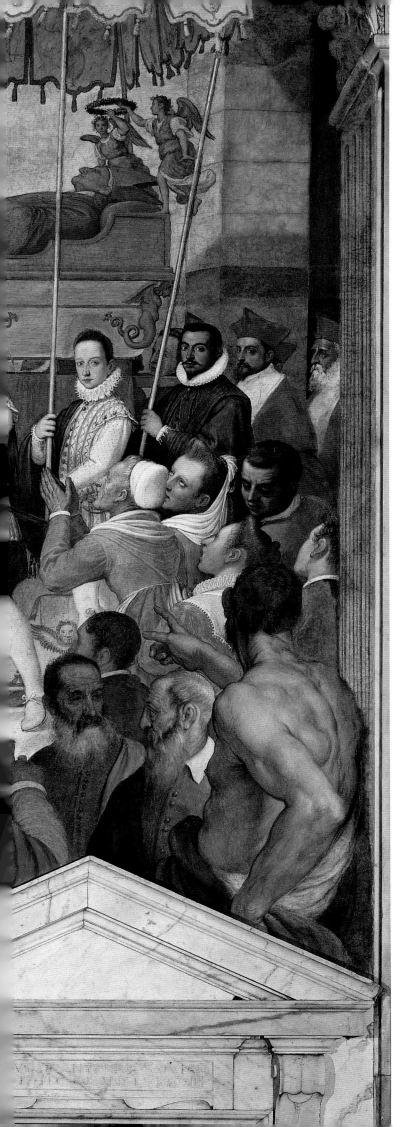

The chapel of Sant'Antonino dei Salviati

The period that left its deepest mark on the church was that of the Counter Reformation, when the plan to create a functional and modern building, worthy of the presence of the incorrupt body of St. Antoninus, was implemented. Antonino Pierozzi, son of the notary Niccolò, was born in Florence in 1389 and was attracted to the order of the preachers by the Blessed Giovanni Dominici. He became prior of San Domenico in Fiesole and was transferred to the new monastery in Florence after serving as governor general of the order in Rome and Cortona. He took part in the Council of Florence (1439) and became archbishop of the city. He fought against abuses and scandals, usury and injustice. He carried out important diplomatic missions at the papal court and died in Florence, bequeathing his writings to San Marco, where

he was buried. In 1579 Averardo and Antonio Salviati undertook to build a chapel of exceptional beauty and opulence in honor of the canonized Florentine bishop. The design was entrusted to Giambologna, who took great care over every detail, as can be seen from the surviving drawings, which show a perfect balance of architecture, sculpture and painting, skillfully blended to form a magnificently harmonious whole. The walls are decorated with episodes from the saint's life, presented in relation to the life of Christ, so that the immediate and intuitive connection brings the message up to date, in line with the proposals of the recent Council of Trent. Alessandro Allori, called Bronzino, was chosen to execute the whole of the fresco decoration, finished in 1588. The panel on the main altar, which was commissioned

from him before 1584, depicts the *Descent into Limbo* and holds a dialogue with the two pictures at the sides, *Jesus Healing a Leper* by Poppi and the *Calling of Saint Matthew* by Naldini. All three were described by Borghini, who emphasizes the rivalry involved in their execution, which was preceded by a large number of drawings. The Salviati Chapel must have been completed after the solemn translation of the body of St. Antoninus, carried out on the occasion of Ferdinando I's marriage to Christine of Lorraine, on May 9, 1589. Immediately after the festivities, Passignano was given the task of painting the two frescoes in the chapel's vestibule, depicting the *Translation* and *Identification* of the saint's incorrupt body, in the presence of Alessandro de' Medici and all the Florentine notables of the day.

Cloister of Sant'Antonino, detail showing Fra Angelico's *Crucifixion*

facing page
Sigismondo Coccapani, *Saint Antoninus Expelling Two False Merchants*, 1613, detail. Cloister of Sant'Antonino

political ties to the Medici. The last scenes were painted around the middle of the 17th century by Cecco Bravo and Giovan Battista Vanni. The decoration was concluded in the 18th century with the final two lunettes, executed by Pier Dandini.

From the baroque to the abolitions of religious institutions. In 1679 the decision was taken to cover the ancient trusses of the church with a modern wooden ceiling with carved coffers. At the center is set a canvas representing the *Assumption of the Virgin*, painted by Giovanni Antonio Pucci in 1725. In the third-fourth decade of the 17th century the tribune of San Marco was enlarged to a design by Pier Francesco Silvani and the high altar, still in existence, was built (1697) on the simplified model of the one Silvani had erected in the Florentine church of Santi Michele e Gaetano. The dome above the new choir was designed by Angelo Ferri. Completed in 1712, it was painted with the *Glory of Saint Mary Magdalen* by Alessandro Gherardini. The work was finished in 1717. The "baroque" image of San Marco was defined in 1780 with Gioacchino Pronti's façade based on 16th-century models, with the tripartite division underlined vertically by pairs of fluted pilaster strips and horizontally by projecting cornices. At the sides of the portal two statues of *Saint Dominic* and *Saint Thomas Aquinas* are set in niches with an aedicule and tympanum; on the second tier there is a window at the center with a segmental tympanum flanked by columns and two flower garlands. The third and highest tier has a bas-relief in the middle, representing a miracle of St. Antoninus. Shortly afterward the abolition of religious institutions led to the division of the Dominican complex. Part of it is still used by the monastic order, while the rest is occupied by the museum devoted to Fra Angelico (1869) and to painting that we could define as Dominican, inspired from the outset by the principles of clarity and simplicity that were to be typical of post-Tridentine language. In 1895 a gallery of finds made during the demolitions in the center at the time Florence became capital of Italy was set up in the former guests' quarters. It has recently been reorganized and can be seen in its entirety.

painted by Angelico, were joined during the period of the Counter Reformation by scenes from the life of the archbishop and saint who had been so committed to the diffusion of Christian doctrine according to the rules of the Dominicans and who had done so much to obtain the monastery of San Marco for the order. Work on them began in 1602, in accordance with a precise iconographic program.

Nobles and benefactors vied to finance the decoration of the cloister's twenty-two lunettes. Many painters were involved, including the most famous of the day: Poccetti (the best versed in the canons of the Catholic Reformation), Ludovico Buti, Alessandro Tiarini, Lorenzo Cerrini, Michelangelo Cinganelli, Fabrizio Boschi, Matteo Rosselli and other painters known for their participation in the decoration of other Florentine cloisters (such as the neighboring one of Santissima Annunziata or the other Dominican one in Santa Maria Novella) or the execution of temporary scenery for the celebration of baptisms, weddings and funerals of important personages with

Santissima Annunziata

Ancient and much venerated Marian sanctuary that grew up around a miraculous image of the Annunciation.
Located in the theatrical setting of Brunelleschi's magnificent square, in dialogue with the dome of the cathedral.
The Chiostrino dei Voti houses the finest permanent exhibition of Florentine "Mannerism."
In the frescoes dedicated to the Virgin the city and its people recount their history.

Symbol of the order of the Servants of Mary

facing page
Our Lady of the Annunciation, detail of the miraculous fresco

One of the most venerated of all sanctuaries, its history is interwoven with that of the order of the Servants of Mary. In 1233 or 1234, and in the name of the Virgin Mary, seven young Florentine merchants decided to form a community amidst the greenery of "Cafaggio," outside the first circle of walls. These laymen had formed a "brotherhood" but, after renouncing their possessions, went to live as hermits on Monte Senario, a choice that marked the beginning of the religious order, the only one in the 13th century that was of purely Florentine origin. In 1250 the seven founders were given papal authorization to build an oratory on the site of their original settlement. Legend has it that it was situated exactly where the revered image of the *Annunciation* is still located. A cult had grown up around the image straightaway. In fact it is said that the seven devotees of the Virgin Mary had commissioned a painting of the *Annunciation* from the artist Bartolomeo but that the latter, when it came to depicting the face of the Madonna, did not feel up to the task. So he asked for divine intervention and fell asleep; when he awoke he found the Virgin's face already painted. Reality and legend soon became entwined, but it is certain that among those who prayed before the sacred image were St. Philip Benizi, who joined the Servites in 1255, and St. Juliana Falconieri, who dedicated her life to the Virgin in 1284. So the place immediately became a venerated shrine and assumed the importance it maintains today. During the 14th century the church was enlarged through bequests and donations, to a design by Giovanni and Neri di Fioravante

(1350). Its decoration must have been entrusted to the major painters of the time: Taddeo Gaddi, Andrea Orcagna (whose polyptych for the Dal Palagio Chapel with the *Madonna and Child between Saints Nicholas, Andrew, John Baptist and James* has survived and is now in the Galleria dell'Accademia) and Nardo di Cione. The revered image must also have assumed its present appearance in those years, at the hands of the same circle of painters (and Orcagna in particular).

The Renaissance. Perhaps it was precisely the Florentine character of the sanctuary that gave it such an important role in city life: this is reflected in the decision of the Republic of Florence to mark the festivity of March 25 from 1416 onward with special ceremonies to be held at the Annunziata. The date, as well as being the feast of the Annunciation, marked the end of the year *ab Incarnatione* for Florence. From that moment on the church and square became the center of religious and civil life, with markets and festivals that are still held on the feast days of the Virgin Mary. Shortly afterward the decision must have been taken to make the church bigger and better suited to the role of devotion it was required to perform: it was enlarged – incorporating the old church – and its form regularized to that of a basilica on the model of the early-Christian ones, with a quadriporticus in front of the entrance, a singe hall with a trussed roof, side chapels and a large dome at the intersection of the nave and transept. A model that Michelozzo, entrusted with the work from 1444 to 1460, must have taken from the

Piazza Santissima Annunziata

Built from 1250 onward.
Modified in the 15th, 17th and 18th centuries

Order of the Servants of Mary

facing page
Andrea del Castagno, *Saint Julian Receiving Absolution from the Savior*, 1454

below
Matteo di Bartolomeo Rustici, *Santissima Annunziata*, 1447-48. Codex in the library of the Seminario Maggiore, Florence

Ridolfo del Ghirlandaio, *View of the Santissima Annunziata*, 1514, detail. Chapel of the Priors, Palazzo Vecchio, Florence

Fra Bartolommeo, *Drawing of the Santissima Annunziata*, 1508. Gabinetto Disegni e Stampe degli Uffizi, Florence

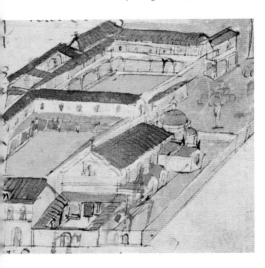

ancient Roman basilicas, which he would have been able to see during his stay in the papal city. Michelozzo also designed the new sacristy (1444), whose construction was financed by Orlando di Guccio de' Medici from 1445 onward. The tribune, begun in the same year, was designed by Michelozzo again, but completed by Leon Battista Alberti to a commission from first Giovan Francesco Gonzaga and then, on his death (1449), his son Ludovico. In 1469 Ludovico Gonzaga entrusted the work on the church to Alberti and in 1477 the first Mass was celebrated.

The "regeneration" of the building also entailed a new disposition of the area of the original oratory, housing the venerated image of the Virgin Mary. The tempietto was built by Michelozzo for Piero di Cosimo de' Medici, between 1447 and 1453. The fresco by Andrea del Castagno depicting the *Vision of Saint Jerome and His Female Disciples* dates from 1454 but was rediscovered in 1899 underneath Allori's altarpiece in the chapel dedicated to the saint. Also by Andrea del Castagno and dating from the same time is the fresco representing *Saint Julian Receiving Absolution from the Savior*, commissioned by the Gagliani family and now under the 17th-century decoration of the Feroni Chapel. In these paintings Andrea exhibits his characteristic manner of "sculpting and carving by painting"; the pale and cold palette in the *Saint Julian* grows brighter and more dramatic in the *Saint Jerome*. Another eccentric and lively presence is that of Piero di Cosimo, author of the panel depicting the *Immaculate Conception with Saints Catherine, Margaret, John the Evangelist, Peter, Philip Benizi and Antoninus* for the Tedaldi Chapel, which entered the collection of Cardinal Leopoldo de' Medici in 1671 and is now in the Uffizi.

Alesso Baldovinetti was also active in the Annunziata, painting the fresco of the *Nativity* in 1460 inside the renovated Chiostrino dei Voti, where Cosimo Rosselli executed the *Investment of Saint Philip Benizi* (1475), shortly afterward the altarpiece for the chapel of the "German nation" and now in the Accademia.

"The church of the Annunziata is most godly and beautiful...." This is how Albertini described it in his "memorial" (1510). Between the end of the 15th

century and the first two decades of the 16th, in fact, the church and its annexes were extensively decorated with panels, sculptures and frescoes by the greatest exponents of early Mannerism. The tribune was renovated and Jacopo Sansovino's altar (1491) installed in it. On the altar was placed the wooden *Crucifix* carved in 1483 by Giuliano and Antonio da Sangallo, now in the church's second chapel on the right: Baccio di Agnolo constructed a complicated setting for it, in the form of an arch of triumph, between 1500 and 1502. This must have contained painted panels of various sizes; the large ones were commissioned first from Filippino Lippi and then from Leonardo da Vinci, who never executed the work. Even Filippino left his panel incomplete (1503-04), dying shortly afterward (*Deposition from the Cross*, finished by Perugino between 1505 and 1507, now in the Accademia). Perugino (*Assumption*, now in the ambulatory) was then entrusted with the completion of the decoration, which he did with the help of assistants (among whom the critics have recognized the very young Raphael).

On the façade was set the coat of arms of Leo X, painted by Cosimo Feltrini on the occasion of the Medici pope's return to Florence in 1515 and flanked by Jacopo Carrucci da Pontormo's *Faith* and *Charity*, which still survive although in a very poor state. The decoration of the Chiostrino dei Voti continued with the completion of the twelve frescoes – executed between 1461 and 1517 – devoted to scenes from the *Life of the Virgin* and the *Seven Founders of the Order of Mary*.

Andrea del Sarto, "flawless painter." In addition to the seven lunettes in the Chiostrino dei Voti and the *Face of the Savior* on the door of the ciborium of the Annunziata's altar, another of Andrea's paintings visible in the sanctuary is the *Rest on the Flight into Egypt*, better known as the *Madonna of the Sack*: one of his masterpieces, it is located above the door that connects the large cloister, called the Chiostro dei Morti, with the church and is signed and dated 1525. It was admired by his contemporaries, as well as by later painters and writers: Michelangelo, Titian, Vasari, Delacroix. A composition of extraordinary harmony and great ten-

The Chiostrino dei Voti

The pictorial decoration of the Chiostrino dei Voti, or cloister of the Vows, is the manifesto of early Florentine Mannerism. After the *Adoration of the Shepherds*, painted by Alesso Baldovinetti around 1460, the decoration continued with the completion of the twelve frescoes devoted to the *Life of the Virgin* and the *Seven Founders of the Order of Mary*. The *Scenes from the Life of Saint Philip Benizi*, general of the Servite Order in 1257, which start with the *Calling and Investiture of the Saint*, painted by Cosimo Rosselli in 1474, continue with five more scenes by Andrea del Sarto representing the *Meeting with the Leper*, *Smiting of the Blasphemers*, *Liberation of the Woman Possessed by a Devil*, *Raising of a Child at the Saint's Funeral* and *Miracle of the Saint's Relics* (dated 1500). On the opposite wall Franciabigio painted the *Marriage of the Virgin* in 1513, Pontormo the *Visitation* in 1516 and Rosso Fiorentino the *Assumption of the Virgin into Heaven* in 1517. The *Arrival of the Magi at Herod's Palace* (1511), with a portrait of Jacopo Sansovino, and *Nativity of Mary* (1514) were painted by Andrea del Sarto. The frame of the lunettes is by the "grotesque" specialist Cosimo Feltrini (1517).

Rosso Fiorentino, *Assumption of the Virgin into Heaven*, 1517, whole picture and detail. Chiostrino dei Voti (cloister of the Vows)

derness in which the Virgin and Child are seated under a depressed arch along with St. Joseph, on the left, his back turned to us and his arm resting on a "sack" that constitutes the fulcrum of the picture.

Executed in the same years and equally appreciated were the panels painted by Fra Bartolommeo for the chapel of the Salvatore, with *Christ the Savior and the Four Evangelists* (1516) and *Isaiah and Job*. Also acquired for the Medici collections (by Giovan Carlo de' Medici), they were replaced by copies by Pugliani (no longer *in situ*) and are now in the Galleria Palatina and Accademia respectively.

The advent of the grand duchy and the Counter Reformation: the church as "vehicle of political propaganda." The large statue of Ferdinando I on horseback, erected by Ferdinando II in 1640 and flanked by colonnades – the ones designed by Brunelleschi for the Innocenti and by Antonio da Sangallo and Baccio di Agnolo for Santa Maria dei Serviti – seemed to be following the road that led directly from the church to Brunelleschi's dome, the highest ecclesiastic symbol in the city, and then to the seat of political power and the Uffizi. A theatrical location, it was decorated for festivities devoted to the Virgin, becoming a spectacle within the spectacle where reality and make-believe were intertwined in a blaze of lights and fireworks. Sacred rites that were opened up to the masses, turning into profane markets and festivals. In the square outside the fruits of nature, inside the church ever more magnificent and precious donations, identifying this place as one favored by the Medici and offering the most complete display of the goldsmith's craft in Florence. In compliance with the political and educational program of the Medici, who saw the ideas of the Counter Reformation as a factor of great importance to political and social stability, the Annunziata was also decorated with major cycles of paintings on the inside and in the adjoining great cloister, commissioned from the principal exponents of this style and doctrine. It was at this time that Giovanni Stradano painted the *Crucifixion* (1569), an expression of the Tridentine religious climate interpreted in a Northern European manner, and

Andrea del Sarto, *Rest on the Flight into Egypt*, called the *Madonna of the Sack*, 1525, detail. Chiostro dei Morti (cloister of the Dead)

Alessandro Allori (who was also entrusted with the task of copying the icon of the Annunziata) painted the copy of Michelangelo's *Last Judgment* (1554-59), formerly in the Montauto Chapel, decorated between 1560 and 1564 with *Scenes from the Life of Christ*. In addition, there was the decoration of the former Pucci Chapel, ceded to Giambologna (1594), who turned it into a burial place for his fellow Flemish artists and decorated it with bas-reliefs representing *Scenes of the Passion*, the *Crucifixion* and *Funerary Angels* (1599).

The chapel of the Annunziata, Medici devotion and the new 17th-century decoration. In the year 1600 Ferdinando I, to thank the Virgin for the recovery of his son Cosimo, donated a precious silver altar frontal with an image of *Cosimo Praying to the Virgin* to the chapel of the Annunziata. It was executed by the grand-ducal silversmith Egidio Leggi, documented as working on it until 1604. In the first decade of the century the entire chapel was modernized at the behest of Ferdinando I and, on his death, Cosimo II commissioned the inlays of semiprecious stones and silver (designed by Matteo Nigetti). In 1618, Don Lorenzo, after being cured of a grave illness, donated to the altar two steps in embossed and chased silver, again to a design by Nigetti. At the center, in a precious frame, was located Andrea del Sarto's *Salvator Mundi* (*circa* 1513), perhaps the property of Don Lorenzo and now on the altar of the tribune.

The patronage of Florentine nobility: the portico, the chapel of San Sebastiano. In 1599 Abbot Alessandro Pucci was given permission to build a new portico of access to the church. The job was given to Giovanni Caccini, who designed it in such a way as to preserve Pontormo's fresco and the Medici coat of arms. Following the client's death in 1601, the work was completed by his brother Roberto in 1604, as the inscription on the architrave attests. It was around this time that the same architect modified the chapel dedicated to St. Sebastian, also belonging to the Pucci family and situated on the right of the façade. Originally a small chapel founded by Antonio di Puccio Pucci in 1452, the oratory had

as its altarpiece until 1857 the *Martyrdom of Saint Sebastian*, painted by Pollaiuolo in 1475. Now in the National Gallery of London, it has been replaced by a copy of the *Nativity of Mary* made by Ludovico Cigoli. In the drum and the pendentives there are frescoes executed by one of the best-known Florentine decorators of the moment, Bernardino Poccetti, who also painted many lunettes in the Chiostro dei Morti (cloister of the Dead), decorated for the most part in the first two decades of the 17th century.

The decoration of the Chiostro dei Morti. This consists of twenty-five lunettes with *Scenes from the History of the Servites*, painted by Bernardino Poccetti, Ventura Salimbeni, Donato Mascagni and Matteo Rosselli between 1604 and 1618 to commissions from the most important families in Florence: a cycle that – in line with the aesthetic principles of the Counter Reformation – was inspired by criteria of didactic efficacy.

The triumph of the baroque. From 1674 onward Cosimo III de' Medici promoted an exhibition of works by artists who, thanks to the Academy, had gone to Rome to study, held in the cloister of the Dead on the feast day of St. Luke (October 18). These works, along with the contemporary ones on display in Florentine collections, soon became a model for the baroque decoration that now characterizes the church. The first renovation took place in the presbytery, when Antonio di Vitale de' Medici commissioned a new design from Alfonso Parigi in 1655. He came up with a large silver ciborium in the form of a tempietto, executed by the grand-ducal goldsmiths Giovan Battista and Marco Antonio Merlini. Next it was the turn of the choir, located at the center of the tribune (1667), clad in marble and decorated by Pier Francesco Silvani. Six marble statues by various Florentine sculptors were set on top of the central enclosure. At the behest of Archduke Ferdinand Charles of Innsbruck, who had visited the Annunziata in 1661, the old roof of the church was replaced with a new carved and gilded wooden ceiling (executed by Pietro Giambelli) on the occasion of the marriage of Cosimo III to Mary Magdalene of Austria in 1664. At its center was placed

Andrea del Sarto, *Salvator Mundi*, 1513. Chapel of the Virgin

facing page
View of the chapel of the Annunziata

Giorgio Vasari, *Saint Luke Painting the Virgin's Portrait*, 1533-35, detail. Chapel of San Luca

Chapel of San Luca

The Chapel of San Luca

Cosimo I de' Medici, at the prompting of Giorgio Vasari, was responsible for the foundation of the Accademia delle Arti del Disegno (Academy of the Arts of Drawing, 1563), and from 1674 until 1767 works of contemporary art were put on display in the cloister every year, for the feast of St. Luke. The chapel of San Luca, erected in the cloister of the Dead and dedicated to the Trinity, alluded symbolically to the essential unity and at the same time practical distinction of the three arts (painting, sculpture and architecture). The chapel, formerly the chapterhouse, which became the seat of the Accademia del Disegno in 1563, was decorated from 1533-35 onward by Montorsoli with statues of *Moses* and *Saint Paul*. It was the sculptor's idea to provide the Compagnia del Disegno with a chapel and common burial place for artists. The room was adorned with stuccoes and paintings by Alessandro Allori (*Trinity*), Giorgio Vasari (*Saint Luke Painting the Virgin*) and Santi di Tito (*Building of the Temple in Jerusalem*). Completed in 1572, the decoration assumed an emblematic role for Florentine art and Mannerism, expressing the dictates of the Council of Trent and the wishes of Cosimo I de' Medici, a supporter of the idea that Church and State should act together to ensure the smooth functioning of politics. In 1823 Pontormo's fresco of the *Sacra Conversazione* (1514) was transferred there from the destroyed church of San Ruffillo.

a large canvas by Volterrano representing *Our Lady of the Assumption* (1670). Around 1680, thanks to the legacy of the prior Donato dell'Antella, Volterrano commenced the decoration of the dome with the theme of the *Assumption of the Virgin* (1683). The high altar was also decorated with a magnificent altar frontal in silver designed by Foggini (1680-82): representing the *Last Supper* and symbols of the Eucharist (with *The Sacrifice of Isaac* and the *Fall of Manna* at the sides, along with lilies, symbol of the Servite Order), it was executed by the goldsmith Arrigo di Bernardo Brunick. The furnishings were commissioned by the fathers and installed on September 8, 1683, feast of the Nativity of the Virgin, when Volterrano's dome was also unveiled for the first time. The work of baroque transformation of the tribune was completed in 1686 with the lining of the walls with marble and gildings. Between 1688 and 1703 the same thing happened in the nave, which was entirely clad in marble. Foggini was also responsible for the restructuring of the chapel of San Giuliano, acquired by the Feroni family in 1691. The iconographic program was dictated by Anton Maria Salvini, linked to Grand Prince Ferdinando and a learned member of the Accademia della Crusca. It was inaugurated in 1693 to genuine popular rejoicing. Foggini was assisted by various pupils in the execution of the stuccoes, sculptures and marble and gilded bronze decorations that adorn the walls and the altar. One of the most important side chapels where the baroque renovation was concerned was the one acquired in 1643 by Marchese Fabrizio Colloredo, Grand Constable of the order of the Knights of Saint Stephen, chamberlain of Ferdinando I and Cosimo II, majordomo and state councilor of Ferdinando II, who had the new chapel designed by Matteo Nigetti in 1647. The architect profited from the experience gained in the chapel of the Princes in San Lorenzo through the use of a sumptuous alternation of precious marbles and semiprecious stones. The dome was decorated by Volterrano in 1650 with *God the Father, Jesus Christ, the Virgin, Saint Andrew and Other Saints Witnessing the Glory of Saint Lucy.* On the altar was placed the picture of the *Martyrdom of Saint Lucy* painted by Jacopo Vignali in 1649, now in the tribune.

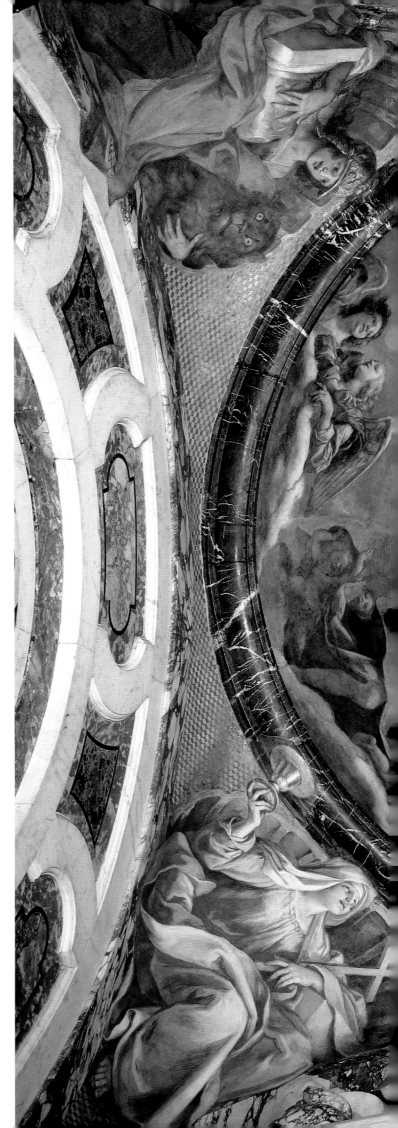

Santa Trinita

*Founded and still occupied by the monastic order of the Vallombrosians, it is an ideal continuation
of the bridge of the same name over the Arno, architectural backdrop to the square. The original location
of Cimabue's Maestà, now in the Uffizi, it houses some of the most suggestive images of 15th-century Florence,
painted by Ghirlandaio in the Sassetti Chapel.*

Symbol of the Trinity, detail.
High altar

facing page
Cimabue, *Madonna
Enthroned with Angels
(Maestà)*, 1301 (?), detail.
Galleria degli Uffizi, Florence

Piazza Santa Trinita

Built in the 11th-14th centuries

*Order: Vallombrosian since the
12th century*

On November 27, 1897, the city authorities were convened for the reopening of the church of Santa Trinita for worship after many years, "radically restored and returned in its essential parts to the form given to it in the 14th century." Everything had begun in the May of 1879 when the painter Antonio Ciseri and the architect Giuseppe Poggi, as members of Florence's Board for the Conservation of Fine Arts, carried out an inspection in Santa Trinita to ascertain the state of preservation of Ghirlandaio's frescoes. Unwittingly, the two men had opened a new chapter in the history of the church. From that moment on, for almost a decade, the question of the restoration of Santa Trinita became one of the liveliest and most significant debates in the city, involving artistic and cultural personalities of international standing. In 1881 the painter and restorer Gaetano Bianchi – author among other things of the interventions in Giotto's frescoes in Santa Croce and Masaccio's *Trinity* in Santa Maria Novella – was asked for his opinion on the restorations: the reopening of the 14th-century two-light windows, the freeing of the arches from decorations, bringing them back to their original pointed profile, the elimination of balustrades from the chapels and reconstruction of their original steps and the removal of Buontalenti's stairway in the presbytery. These were the principal works that the Advisory Committee of Fine Arts approved in their entirety, applying a methodology of restoration that placed no limits on the extent of alterations and eliminations, and indeed justified them with purist intentions.

Throughout the 19th century the interest in "primi-
tive" art found concrete expression in Florence in blanket restorations of medieval buildings, and culminated in the application of marble facings to the façades of Santa Croce and Santa Maria del Fiore. Starting out from the experiences of completion in style practiced by the first generation of architects, the second was to make "restoring" its watchword. Few monuments would be exempted from this pragmatic process of transformation and left to bear witness to the continuity of history through their stratifications.

In Santa Trinita, where the civil engineer in charge of the work had been replaced by the architect Giuseppe Castellazzi (1884), the initial methodological certainty gave way to a more cautious approach. But the more up-to-date views of the members of the consultative committee, in line with the new ideas of conservative restoration, conflicted with Castellazzi's radical interventions, leading to an interruption of the work in February 1885. On one side were the supporters of total restoration and completion "in style," on the other the theorists of conservation and advocates of maintaining the work in the state in which it was found. The English-speaking press made itself the spokesman of this second tendency, railing against this sort of mania for restoration with the backing of the famous Society for the Protection of Ancient Buildings (founded in 1877) which, in the person of William Morris, had already played an active part during the demolitions in the old center of Florence. The views of Giovan Battista Cavalcaselle, scholar and attentive art critic, had no effect: against his

advice, work continued in Santa Trinita on the demolition of the fronts of all the side chapels and the high altar was replaced (today we see a table supported by a marble altar frontal with an interesting medallion at the center representing the *Holy Trinity*, a 15th-century work of Donatellian inspiration clumsily reassembled and completed in the 19th century). The flight of steps of the presbytery, built by Buontalenti around 1574 but regarded as too "frenzied, twisted and bizarre" by Castellazzi, would also be dismantled and reassembled in Santo Stefano al Ponte, where it can still be seen.

A necessary premise to a visit to Santa Trinita – where the ornamental alterations made to the Gothic church from the 15th century to the baroque era have almost all disappeared – is an understanding of the 19th-century restorations described above, which have permitted, amidst doubts and uncertainties, all the Gothic parts of the building to be brought back to light and into harmony, not excluding the reintegration of missing parts that make it an emblematic case: in particular, the elegant motif of the supporting structures of the arches dividing the nave from the aisles, which taper progressively from the square pillars at the base (where all the paintings were destroyed to lay bare the more "primitive" stone), turning into vertical pilaster strips and the ribs of the vaults.

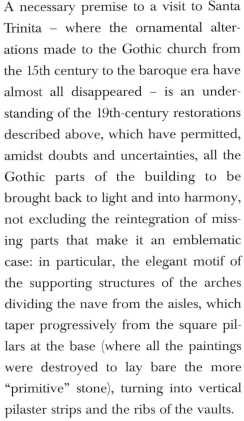

Bernardo Buontalenti, steps of the presbytery, formerly in the church of Santa Trinita, c. 1574. Santo Stefano al Ponte, Florence

facing page
Interior of the church

The origins. The church, built near the river in the Romanesque style, was dedicated to the Holy Trinity, or Santissima Trinità in Italian, but the Florentines have always preferred the Latin form *Trinitas* and called it Santa Trinita. Founded around 1060-70 and erected on the site of the ancient chapel of the Madonna dell Spasimo, it must have presented a very similar appearance to the church of the Santi Apostoli. Of modest size, divided into a nave and two aisles and covered by a saddleback roof, it was constructed out of marble from Tuscan quarries: green marble

from Prato for the columns, white marble from Carrara for the facing of the walls and the floor. Located outside the city walls, beyond the brick gate called the Porta Rossa and close to the Via Cassia from Rome, it became the seat of a Vallombrosian cenoby after 1100 and was included within the ring of walls in 1172-74. The monastery, part of which is used by the university today, extended behind the church as far as what are now Via del Parione and Via del Parioncino. A vast structure laid out around two cloisters, it was founded by Giovanni Gualberto from the noble Florentine family of the Visdomini (later canonized), and occupied by the Vallombrosian monks. An ancient offshoot of the Benedictines, the Vallombrosian Order reached the height of its splendor, in Santa Trinita, in the 14th and 15th centuries.

During the 13th century the small Romanesque church began to play an important role in city life: in 1289 the council of war preceding the battle of Campaldino, at which the Guelph Florentine republic defeated Ghibelline Arezzo, was held there. During the 14th century, perhaps following the disastrous flood of 1333, the Romanesque building was replaced by the Gothic church. Work had already begun, *circa* 1300-30, but only on the first bay to the south (on the left as you enter the church). Following the slow progress of construction, which must have been interrupted during the period of crisis which the city passed through, between the flood of 1333 and the black death of 1348, the Signoria of Florence, at the urging of the monks of Santa Trinita, appointed a six-man Vestry Board in 1383 to oversee the completion of the church. The roofing of the nave and transept dragged on into the first decade of the 15th century: the documents speak of thousands of tiles, produced by the kilns at Impruneta, and the purchase of a chestnut wood in the Valdarno to provide beams for the roof. Architecturally, the church was now finished, but the pictorial decorations and furnishing of the chapels would last for the rest of the century.

The Gothic church. The limpid clarity of the Gothic style of Santa Trinita, probably attributable to Neri di Fioravante, prompts us to make distant comparisons. There is an evident difference from contemporary Flo-

Lorenzo Monaco,
Annunciation, 1424

rentine examples, which all have square bays in the nave and rectangular ones in the aisles. This structure, used in Santa Maria Novella in the 13th century, would be repeated in the 14th century with Santa Maria Maggiore, San Remigio and the more imposing Santa Maria del Fiore. We have to turn to Cistercian churches, like the Sienese abbey of San Galgano, to find a structural analogy with Santa Trinita, although lacking the ring of chapels in the apsidal part. This composite but spacious architecture, at once regular and airy, suggests a unitary design: if not by a single architect, then by a group as well orchestrated as the one headed by Neri di Fioravante may have been in the Florence of the second half of the 14th century. Despite the undoubted quality of the Gothic structure, alterations to its interior were made in the 15th century to meet the wishes of patrons. The construction of the Strozzi, Gianfigliazzi and Sassetti Chapels gave a new atmosphere to the church, only recently completed along 14th-century lines. However much the heavy-handed tampering in the 19th century and the subsequent restorations carried out over the course of the 20th century have altered its appearance and the joins between different periods and styles, these Renaissance insertions seem to seek mediation and conciliation: Lorenzo Monaco in the chapel of the Annunziata – the paintings, altar and railing – provides a clear example of this intention. And Lorenzo Ghiberti was to take the same approach later in the Strozzi family chapel, which would house works by Gentile da Fabriano and Lorenzo Monaco himself. Santa Trinita, Florence's temple *par excellence*, manages to marry the local 14th-century tradition with nascent Humanism: just as it succeeds in counterpoising the Gothic members, synonymous with structural tension, with the pliable, solid geometries of the side chapels. If the 14th-century masonry has reemerged from the vicissitudes to which the church has been subjected over the centuries, very little is left of its Romanesque decorations. The great masterpiece that Vasari tells us used to gleam on the altar of the little church was Cimabue's *Maestà*. The other work from the 13th century is the so-called *Crucifix of Saint John Gualberto*, transferred to Santa Trinita from San Miniato al Monte in 1671.

Cimabue's *Maestà*. The congregation must have been surprised by the wooden altarpiece painted by Cimabue in the last quarter of the 13th century. Grandiose in its measurements, especially in comparison with the works that adorned the city's other churches (with the exception of the *Maestà* executed by Duccio for Santa Maria Novella in 1285), it presents the Virgin on a large throne with a solid wooden structure. The Marian icon – in which the gilded highlights reflect Byzantine influences – is flanked by living wings, four pairs of angels whose sinuous lines, thought to derive from Sienese art, are inserted in an almost architectural setting that the imposing structure of the throne reflects onto the figures. The original location of the work is harder to determine: there is no mention of the large panel – indeed only a wooden crucifix is recorded on the altar in 1360 – until Vasari's reference in the second half of the 16th century. Even bearing in mind the indifference to the works of the "primitives" that was already shown in the 15th century (one thinks of the oblivion to which Giotto's *Maestà* was consigned in the church of Ognissanti), it is difficult to imagine it being placed on anything but the high altar. Moved to the monastery at the time of the 14th-century renovation, it eventually made its way to the Galleria dell'Accademia in 1810 and then to the Sala delle Maestà in the Galleria degli Uffizi in 1919.

Cimabue, *Madonna Enthroned with Angels* (*Maestà*), 1301 (?). Galleria degli Uffizi, Florence

facing page
Fra Angelico, *Deposition from the Cross*, 1422-23. Museo di San Marco, Florence

The pictorial decoration of the 15th century. An ample and exhaustive panorama of 15th-century Florentine painting can still be seen in the church: from Lorenzo Monaco and Gentile da Fabriano to the less well-known Bicci di Lorenzo, Bonaiuto di Giovanni and Stefano di Antonio. Among the major private commissions that were carried out in the church in the early decades, the Bartolini Salimbeni Chapel presents a particularly homogeneous appearance, with the walls frescoed by Lorenzo Monaco with *Scenes from the Life of the Virgin and Saints* and a large panel of the *Annunciation*, set in a gilded frame with pinnacles, with which the same artist concluded the undertaking in 1424. A painting still permeated by graceful late-Gothic forms, in which early Humanistic impulses are enclosed in sinuous outlines, it is charac-

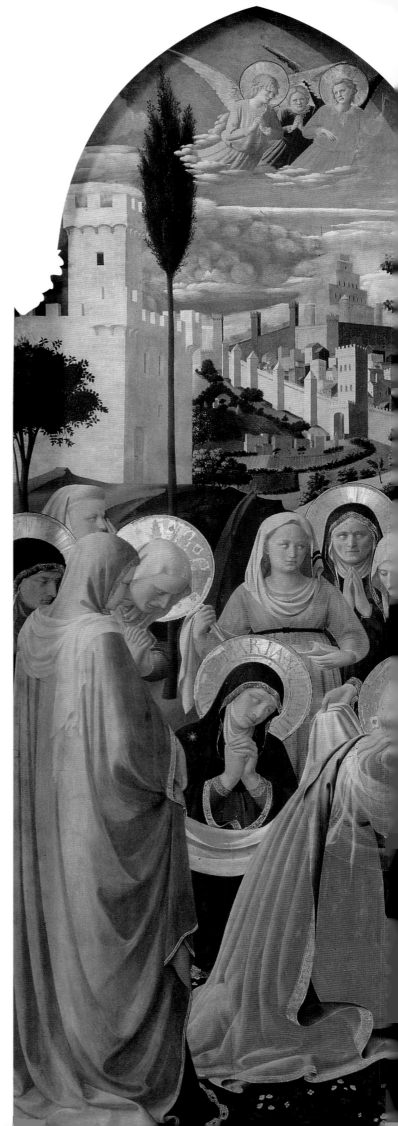

Gentile da Fabriano's *Adoration of the Magi*

A hundred and fifty gold florins was the sum Palla Strozzi, a wealthy merchant active in the faction opposed to the Medici, for which he was exiled, paid to Gentile to execute the panel with a tricuspidate frame to be placed on an altar of the sacristy of Santa Trinita, which had become the family chapel. The rich panel, much admired by his contemporaries and now given a prominent place in the Galleria degli Uffizi, represents an early stage in the work of the painter from Fabriano. Heavily indebted to the Florentine tradition, he chooses a worldly and contemporary setting for the sacred theme. The richness of the clothing, the deliberate inclusion of luxurious and refined details and the attitudes of the figures, absorbed in their important but above all representative roles, make it one of the most eloquent images of wealthy Florence in the early 15th century.

Sassetti Chapel, interior

facing page
Domenico Ghirlandaio, *Miracle of the Child Restored to Life*, 1480-85, detail. Sassetti Chapel

following pages
Domenico Ghirlandaio, detail of *The Confirmation of the Franciscan Rule* with a view of the Palazzo della Signoria, Loggia dei Lanzi and now demolished church of San Pier Scheraggio, 1480-85. Sassetti Chapel

terized by a rich palette and an elegant use of gold in the architectural decorations and clothing.

Making the mental effort required to picture the two large panels by Gentile da Fabriano and Fra Angelico – the *Adoration of the Magi* now in the Uffizi and the *Deposition from the Cross* in the Museo di San Marco – in their original place in the sacristy, transformed into the chapel of the powerful Strozzi family, we can get an idea of the artistic panorama at the highest level the church was capable of presenting: for the first thirty years of the century the church of the Vallombrosians was dominated by the commissions of several families, especially the Strozzi. The sacristy, a sumptuous creation commissioned by Palla Strozzi in execution of the will of her father Onofrio, who died in 1417, seems to be an attempt to rival the contemporary sacristy built by the Medici in San Lorenzo. The construction in Santa Trinita, attributed to Ghiberti, displays a notable harmony and unity of decoration, in which the outstanding elements are the portal and the refined and original *Sarcophagus of Onofrio Strozzi*.

Christian Humanism, represented at its highest levels by Angelico, testifies to the cultural life that centered on Santa Trinita and that was to suffer a curtailment after 1434 when, with the return of Cosimo I the Elder and the subsequent exile of Palla Strozzi, the most popular artists and workshops of the day began to receive commissions for other churches.

In this period Santa Trinita housed works by Bicci di Lorenzo and the prolific workshop of Neri di Bicci, as well as the older Cenni di Ser Cenni: the frescoes in the Doni and Spini Chapels as well as the panels, with their "old-fashioned" frames and structures, representing the *Madonna Enthroned with Saints* and the *Annunciation with the Expulsion of Adam and Eve* (Sercialli and Davanzati Chapels). Conceptually marginal with respect to the more advanced contemporary expressions and usually regarded as backward, this style was very popular in small pictures for private devotion or painted furniture like chests, often attracting commissions from the merchant class. Extraneous to the context of the church, as they come from the nearby San Pancrazio, are the large fresco by Neri di Bicci now in the Compagni Chapel, depicting *Saint*

John Gualberto Enthroned with Saints of the Vallombrosian Order, and the *Tomb of Benozzo Federighi*, with its elegant majolica frame painted by Luca della Robbia.

Domenico Ghirlandaio: the decoration of the Sassetti Chapel. In the second half of the 15th century decoration on a grand scale returned to Santa Trinita. The patrons were the most important families in Florence, who entrusted the city's best-known artists with handing down the memory of their power and their considerable wealth to posterity. While the main chapel, patronized by the Gianfigliazzi, preserves only fragments of the cycle of frescoes that Alesso Baldovinetti painted in it – along with the altarpiece representing the *Trinity and Saints*, in the Galleria dell'Accademia since 1810 (on the high altar today is the polyptych of the *Trinity and Saints* executed for the Davanzati Chapel by Mariotto di Nardo) – the nearby Sassetti Chapel still has its mural decoration with *Scenes from the Life of Saint Francis* (1480-85) and the panel of the *Adoration of the Shepherds*, masterpieces by Domenico Ghirlandaio. When Lorenzo the Magnificent became ruler of Florence, Santa Trinita came back within the Medici sphere and the powerful Vallombrosian Order, along with the leading families of the neighboring quarters, embarked on a patronage of high quality. The protagonists of the *Life of Saint Francis* are the two clients, Francesco and Nera Sassetti, who are portrayed kneeling on each side of the altarpiece, and above all the Florence "that counted," with the Magnificent at the center. Here his role in contemporary Humanistic culture seems to have found the right space and the right location (he is portrayed in the scene of the *Confirmation of the Rule* along with the client Francesco, his son Federico and the gonfalonier Antonio Pucci). Francesco Sassetti (1420-90) spent his life in the service of the Medici: in charge of the Medici bank in Geneva, he became general manager of the bank in 1469, on Piero's death, and the orphaned Lorenzo and Giuliano relied on him for support. Close friend and companion of the Magnificent, Francesco's fortune grew in proportion to Medici prosperity until it reached the levels of

splendor testified by the commission in Santa Trinita (in 1480 he was appointed to the war magistracy called the Balìa, along with Antonio Pucci, and in 1482, after the failure of the Medici bank in Bruges and London, became a partner in the Florentine headquarters).

The allusion to classical subjects and above all the large scenes framed by architectural wings and large urban spaces hark back to the most faithful Florentine tradition, on which Ghirlandaio draws liberally: the plasticism of Masaccio, the movement of Pollaiuolo, the light effects of Verrocchio. Looking at the *Miracle of the Child Restored to Life* (a scene alluding to an event in the history of the Sassetti family and set in Piazza Santa Trinita itself), it is impossible not to recall the large square in the *Raising of Tabitha*

painted by Masolino in the Carmine. And the imposing architecture of Piazza della Signoria in the *Confirmation of the Rule* is clearly reminiscent of Brunelleschi. And the memory of this composition – where we find, in the figures climbing the stairs from the lower floor, portraits of the poet Politian and Lorenzo's sons Giuliano, Piero and Giovanni – will long endure in the *Mass at Bolsena* painted by Raphael in the Vatican Stanze.

Two large and precious tombs carved from touchstone (basalt) in the form of an arcosolium and housing the remains of the clients Nera Corsi and Francesco Sassetti are set in the side walls of the chapel. Executed by Giuliano da Sangallo and the artists of his circle with clearly classical intentions, they are embellished with symbolic reliefs, portraits of

R · P ·
BENOTII DE FEDE
RIGIS ÉPI FESVLANI
QVI VIR INTEGERIMÆ
VITÆ SVMA CVM LAVDE
VIXIT ANNO QVE
M·CCCCL· DEFVN
CTVS EST·

Domenico Ghirlandaio,
Adoration of the Shepherds,
1483-85, whole picture and
detail

Domenico Ghirlandaio's *Adoration of the Shepherds*

The panel was executed by Domenico – perhaps with the aid of Bartolomeo di Giovanni – between 1483 and 1485 (the date MCCCCLXXXV is inscribed on the pillar in the middle). Fundamental to an understanding of this fine picture is the arrival of Hugo van der Goes's *Adoration of the Shepherds* in May 1483, brought by sea from Bruges to Florence to be installed in the church of Sant'Egidio, on the altar of the Portinari family, engaged at the time in trade with Flanders.

There can be no doubt that the large triptych now in the Galleria degli Uffizi, along with numerous other Flemish paintings that made their way to Florence, influenced many of Domenico's figurative choices (see the heads of the shepherds), which he combined here with learned archeological citations.

Ghirlandaio's invention proved very popular in other workshops, where it was used as a model, with minimal changes, for altarpieces like the one in the Florentine church of Santa Lucia sul Prato.

the two deceased in profile and crests alluding to the Sassetti family (two centaurs carrying shields hold a sling surrounded by numerous pebbles, *sassi* in Italian). The choice of the material from a quarry at Prato, which Vasari describes as so glossy that it is more silk satin than polished stone, brings us to Lorenzo the Magnificent. His fabulous treasure included vases made of jasper, amethyst, agate and rock crystal, and there can be no doubt that his links with Francesco Sassetti lay behind the choice of sculptor and the design of these striking funeral effigies.

Santa Trinita between the 16th and 17th century.

The golden age of the 15th century left the walls of the nave, aisles and chapels covered with frescoes. The artistic contributions of the next two centuries would be more limited.

The family altars and chapels were embellished with several panels – including the *Risen Christ between Saints Dionysius and Sebastian* on the Sernigi Altar, and then in the Ardinghelli Chapel, and Agnolo Bronzino's splendid *Pietà* (in the Uffizi since 1925) – but undoubtedly the most interesting intervention of the 16th century was the architectural one made by Buontalenti in the closing decade. In fact Bernardo Buontalenti had been working on the reconstruction of the Vallombrosian monastery and the design of the new presbytery and the façade since 1574.

As had been happening in other churches since 1565 at the hands of Giorgio Vasari, radical alterations were carried out in the monks' choir and this had made it necessary to redesign the whole area of the presbytery. The flight of steps has been preserved in its entirety, but "moved" to the church of Santo Stefano al Ponte. The place of Buontalenti's steps, resembling a piece of temporary scenery, a bat's wing of stone that recalls certain architectural decorations to be found in his windows and portals, was taken in the church by a severe stairway, more in line with the purist and neomedieval ideas of 19th-century architects.

The façade that Buontalenti built after 1592, and which survived the restorations of the 19th century intact, is on quite another scale, but certainly more

rigorous and less original. In keeping with the figurative and stylistic culture of late Mannerism in Florence, the façade has symmetrical lines punctuated, on the first tier, by composite pilaster strips; above the trabeation, a pediment with a central oculus of glass closes the body of the nave,.

In the 17th century interesting interventions in keeping with the taste of the time were made in several chapels. In the first on the left, belonging to Piero di Pandolfo Strozzi and dedicated first to St. Lucy and then to Our Lady of the Annunciation, Giovanni Caccini built (1603) the new structure in a late-Mannerist style and with a complex set of decorations. Sculptures representing *Peace* and *Meekness* were inserted in Poccetti's mural decoration – *Paradise* on the ceiling and *Fortitude, Hope, Wisdom* and *Fear of God* in the pendentives – along with paintings by Jacopo Chimenti called Empoli (*Annunciation*), Pompeo Caccini (*Martyrdom of Saint Lucy*), and Cosimo Gamberucci (*Death of Saint Alexius*).

The small chapel in the left transept created to house the relics of St. John Gualberto is a real gem. The superior of the order, Aurelio Tabagini from Forlì, commissioned Giovanni Caccini (1593-94) to modify the existing chapel. A jewel casket lined with inserts of polychrome marble (covering the whole of the entrance archway and the three sides of the base), it was decorated with paintings by Domenico Cresti called Passignano, an artist with links to the Vallombrosian Order, for which he decorated the important Badia di San Michele in the small town of his birth.

In conclusion, we cannot fail to mention the presence of interesting church furnishings, to be found in many of the city's places of worship, which for reasons of security and the increasing rarity of solemn liturgical ceremonies are confined to the cabinets of sacristies or to inaccessible places, often rendering them invisible to the public and forgotten by scholars. For Santa Trinita the patrimony of textiles is fundamental and includes the chasuble, miter, cope and glove of St. Bernard degli Uberti, the Vallombrosian councilor of Countess Mathilda of Canossa who died in the church of San Salvi in 1085.

top
Chapel of the relics of St. John Gualberto with Passignano's paintings

bottom
Chapel of Santa Lucia belonging to the Strozzi family

Facing page
Agnolo Bronzino, *Pietà*, 1530. Galleria degli Uffizi, Florence

Ognissanti

*Built on the bank of the river where the original religious order of the Humiliati
practiced the craft of weaving, it was adorned with paintings by Giotto, Ghirlandaio and Botticelli.
Its present late 16th-century appearance is due to Cosimo I de' Medici and the arrival of the Franciscans.*

Domenico Ghirlandaio, symbol
of the monastery of Ognissanti,
1480, detail. Cenacle

facing page
Giovanni da Milano, *Coronation
of the Virgin and Saints*, c.
1360, detail. Galleria degli Uffizi,
Florence

*San Salvatore in Ognissanti
Borgo Ognissanti*

*Built from the 10th century
onward. Altered in the 16th*

*Order: 1239 Humiliati; 1561
Franciscan Friars Minor
Observants; 2000 Benedictines*

The church of Ognissanti, on the square of the same name, faces onto the ideal balcony on the river that is at the origin of its history.

In the 12th century, when the city walls had incorporated part of the Oltrarno ("the other side of the Arno"), the river became a passage within the city and, already a primary factor in its foundation, played a leading role in its success. Between the 13th and 15th century the Arno was navigable all the way to the sea, and thus a privileged means of communication for manufacturers, especially the textile industry brought to Florence by the Humiliati, originally a lay community that specialized in the weaving of wool and then a monastic order that came to Florence from Lombardy in 1239, at the invitation of Bishop Ardingo. Installing themselves first in the monastery of San Donato a Torri (then called in Polverosa), the Humiliati moved to Santa Lucia sul Prato (1250). When the small church of Santa Lucia proved inadequate, the Commune, aware of the Humiliati's needs and favorable to their settlement in the city, rented them land on which, shortly afterward (1256), they erected a church and monastery dedicated to the Virgin and all the saints, as well as workshops on the site of the present-day Borgo di Ognissanti. The meadow called the Prato di Ognissanti, which in the Middle Ages extended along the Arno as far what is now "Prato," was a large public area that had not been built on and comprised "insulae" and reclaimed alluvial land, ideal for the wool industry and its related buildings. Wool was worked inside the monastery, and around it, and

the square itself, in the 13th century, was occupied by the friars' scouring troughs. The banks of the Arno were a hive of industrial activity, utilizing the river water for the manufacturing processes and its structures: watermills, fulling mills and drying shops. In 1278 – as Father Tognocchi da Terrinca records (1691) – the Humiliati had become so well established (the church with its Tau-cross plan and campanile had already been built by 1258) that they declared themselves willing to develop the area for the benefit of the Commune, constructing houses for the artisans, a small harbor, a gate on the Arno and a millrace and mills. The wool industry was one of the most important in the city and by the first decade of the 14th century Florence boasted around 300 textile mills, producing 100,000 bolts of cloth.

In 1561, after three centuries in which their presence had characterized the growth of the suburb, its social life and its urban development (on the square in front, which sloped gently down to the riverbed, construction was prohibited in an area of a hundred ells on a side), the Humiliati abandoned the church. After a brief period of cohabitation following their transfer from the monastery of San Salvatore al Monte alle Croci during the siege of Florence, the Friars Minor Observants obtained permission, with the support of the Medici, to take the place of the Humiliati, now very reduced in number (the order was abolished in 1570).

As a mark of the Franciscan presence in Ognissanti, St. Francis's habit was placed inside the base of the

bronze *Crucifix* on the high altar on May 6, 1571, on the orders of Grand Duke Cosimo I. The sacred robe, donated to Count Alberto Barbolani by the saint in 1224, after he had received the stigmata, consists of a very worn cowl of rough cloth with no sleeves. When the Benedictines took over from the community of Friars Minor in 2000, it was consigned to the Franciscan monastery of La Verna.

The 14th-century church. The splendid commissions of the Humiliati: Giotto and Giovanni da Milano. To present an exhaustive picture of the church in the 14th century, when the wool industry – as well as the manufacture of glass – and the economic power of the Humiliati were at their peak, we must speak of the great commissions from Giotto – the *Maestà*, the *Cross*, the panel representing the *Dormitio Virginis* and the decoration of the small chapel next to the main one ("renovated" at the end of the 17th century) where the painter had frescoed *Scenes from the Life of Saint Benedict* – as well as Giovanni da Milano's large altarpiece of the *Coronation of the Virgin and Saints*.

Since the Observants made radical modifications, the present church conserves no trace of the building from the mid-13th century, embellished with paintings and furnishings in the 14th century, except in the sacristy, which houses the large fresco of the *Crucifixion and Saints* (1350) attributed to Taddeo Gaddi, and the Gucci-Dini Chapel. Pulinari's words describe the state of the building on the arrival of the Observants (1561), who found "the church in a bad way, with an ugly choir in front of the high altar." And in fact, a few years later, they "removed the choir, which was in front of the altar, and those screens: which made the church more beautiful."

The fundamental modification was the demolition of the roodscreen (1564) – a high partition between the chancel and nave – and consequently the choir of the Humiliati. Contemporaneously Cosimo I ordered the same thing to be done in the churches of Santa Croce and Santa Maria Novella, in order to meet the requirements of the Counter Reformation that services be visible from the hall of the church

and involve the congregation, previously kept strictly separate.

The screen, fitted with altars and small chapels, which in Ognissanti must have been located in the position where the pulpit now stands, separated the presbytery from the nave, reserving the chancel for the liturgical ceremonies of the monks, and probably housed three of Giotto's panels. This suggests, in spite of the incomplete and patchy documentation, that Giotto – and his flourishing workshop – was the privileged recipient of Humiliate patronage from the second decade of the 14th century onward. The original location of the large *Maestà* and *Cross*, set on top of the roodscreen – a practice that is exemplified by two scenes in the Upper Basilica of Assisi – makes it possible to resolve various questions for which the critics have provided contradictory answers. Thus the *Maestà* was not executed for the high altar of the choir – in fact it is little suited to a central vision, as the composition is designed to be viewed from the left – and it is not very likely that just forty years later Giovanni da Milano would be called on to paint a new polyptych as a replacement for Giotto's imposing altarpiece. It appears equally certain that the cusped dossal representing the *Dormitio Virginis*, ideal in form and dimensions for a small altar table, was located on the altar erected against the screen on the right side of the door leading to the choir.

The substantial number of works and their importance – whatever location they were intended for – bears witness to the exceptional efforts made, in the first half of the 14th century, to decorate the large church that the Humiliati, during their long stay in Florence, had built as a symbol of their economic and industrial power, just as they had already done and were still doing in Lombardy.

The shelving of these works in the middle of the 16th century, due to the profound change in taste that led in Ognissanti, as in many Florentine churches, to radical alterations in the decorations that had determined its original appearance, resulted in damage to many paintings on a gold ground and their subsequent dispersion. In this case it also coincided with the beginning of the decline of the Humiliati and the

Giotto and workshop, *The Crèche at Greccio* and *Verification of the Stigmata*, *ante* 1292, view of the roodscreen with the old panels facing the congregation. Upper Basilica of San Francesco, Assisi

Giotto in Ognissanti

Giotto's presence in Ognissanti at the end of the first decade of the 14th century – mentioned by Ghiberti in his *Commentarii* of 1447 – entailed so many interventions that it suggests a link between the painter and the Humiliati that went beyond matters of art (a document of 1312 records an agreement between Giotto and a certain Bartolo di Rinuccio for lease of a loom). The substantial number of works and their scale make Ognissanti a far from secondary undertaking on Giotto's part, even if the silence of the documents leaves room for many hypotheses. The great *Maestà*, following the definitive abolition of the monastery by the French in 1810, was transferred – after years of neglect in the church – to the Galleria dell'Accademia, where it was put on display, along with many other works from the city's churches (including Cimabue's *Maestà* and Gentile da Fabriano's *Adoration of the Magi* from Santa Trinita, Verrocchio and Leonardo's *Baptism of Christ* from San Salvi and Botticelli's *San Barnaba Altarpiece*, from the church of the same name), before being moved to its present location in the Galleria degli Uffizi (1919). Given pride of place in the first room – following the return of Cimabue's *Crucifix* to Santa Croce – the large altarpiece has

been returned to its full splendor by the restoration of 1989. With the limitation of the damage inflicted by earlier interventions, the work has regained all the plasticity of the bodies and the force of the perspective, however intuitively constructed, revealing its close chronological link with Giotto's work in Padua. Its rich coloring now freed of clouding and darkening, the granitic *Maestà* is set on a light throne, reminiscent of Arnolfo, in which the almost obsessive precision of the decorative elements and precious materials provides a foil to the forceful expression of the Virgin with the Child giving his blessing, ideal center of the representation.

The *Crucifix*, which critics have been inclined to attribute to the workshop, although of very high quality, and the panel with the *Dormitio Virginis*, now in Berlin, can be dated to the second decade of the century and thus are close to the Peruzzi cycle in Santa Croce. In the genealogy of Giotto's crosses, the *Crucifix* exhibits the peculiarity of a profile with curvilinear elements, encountered for the first time in the one in Rimini, although in much simpler form, and its undoubted quality makes it likely that it is the work of one of the master's first collaborators (the so-called "Relative of Giotto").

waning of the entrepreneurial creativity associated with the lay-religious movement. The Gucci-Dini Chapel, at the end of the left transept – one of the few traces of the 14th century still visible in Ognissanti – has over the centuries unwittingly performed the function of a "pantheon" of Giottesque glories, so that Richa, in 1765, records it "used profanely as a store" for the large *Cross*, the *Maestà* and several panels from Giovanni da Milano's dismembered polyptych. At the time of the abolitions (in 1785 and 1810) the old panels, placed in secondary locations owing to the growing lack of interest in the "primitives" and sometimes in a mediocre state of preservation, tended to end up in foreign collections (Giotto's *Dormitio* is now in Berlin) or, in many cases, the city's own museums (like Giovanni da Milano's dismembered *Polyptych* and Giotto's *Maestà*, both in the Uffizi).

The 15th century: Ghirlandaio and Botticelli. In the 15th century, Ognissanti continued its tradition of major commissions and interventions on the part of the Humiliati and, above all, the families with chapels in the church. One of the altars that can still be seen in its 15th-century guise today, only marginally altered by later interventions, is that of the Vespucci, where a plaque still bears the date 1472. It was erected at the behest of the family, which commissioned the fresco of the *Virgin of Mercy* from Domenico Ghirlandaio. It is one of the painter's early works, where he uses his elegant narrative style to portray members of the family, as in his better-known paintings for the Tornabuoni in Santa Maria Novella or the Sassetti in Santa Trinita: the Vespucci's interests in maritime trade meant that they felt in great need of Mary's protection.

The demolition of the roodscreen in 1564 led to the

loss of the wall of the choir: "surrounded by a high wall, in which were two chapels, one on each side of the door," where Ghirlandaio and Botticelli had painted, in fresco, the two icons representing *Saint Jerome* and *Saint Augustine.* Saved from destruction, along with the section of wall they were painted on, they are now set on the walls of the nave. On the architrave of Botticelli's *Saint Augustine* is inscribed the couplet "Sic Augustinus se tradidit ut non / mutatum sibi adhuc senserit locum" ("Agostino was so intent on his sacred studies that he did not notice the change in his location"), in a clear allusion to the move.

The figures of the two saints in their studies represent aspects of the Benedictine rule (to which the Humiliati were subject), emphasizing above all that of study, through the precise description of all the objects present on the desks and shelves: an armillary sphere, codices and scientific instruments; articles of everyday use like scissors and spectacles; and decorative objects, some with symbolic meanings, such as the fruit, glassware and pharmacy jars. Executing them as a pair, around 1480, the two artists, in their attentive analysis of the two figures and their settings, reflected the influence of the examples of Flemish painting visible in Florence in the late 15th century (Jan van Eyck's *Saint Jerome* could be seen in the Medici palace at the time).

The other important monastic commission was for the large *Last Supper* on the rear wall of the refectory, again from Domenico Ghirlandaio, and again in 1480. The majestic room – 32 meters in length – also houses two large washbasins set in a structure of *pietra serena*, dating from the end of the 15th century, thereby uniting in a single space the functions of purification and dining that were usually performed in adjoining rooms. On the rear wall the *Last Supper*, with its two broad arches opening onto a garden, illusorily extends the depth of the space.

1561. The Minors Observants enter Ognissanti. Horrified by the precarious condition in which they found the church, the Minors Observants set out, within the space of a few years, to substantially modify what had been its appearance from its medieval ori-

Domenico Ghirlandaio, *Saint Jerome*, 1480, whole picture and detail on facing page

MCCCCLXXXX

Domenico Ghirlandaio's *Last Supper*

Set under an arcade filled with light, opening onto a luxuriant garden with citrus trees, palms and cypresses and a sky dotted with birds – like the contemporary *Last Supper* in San Marco (1480) – the fresco presents all the details of a luxurious Renaissance interior. The carved ends of the seat delimit the space in which the thirteen are having their meal, their gestures calm and controlled. Here Domenico, as in the *Last Supper* in San Marco, but unlike in the version he had painted at Badia a Passignano several years earlier, shows himself to be an elegant narrator attentive to Christian symbology, but above all that he is able to reproduce a pleasant scene of conviviality.

The care taken by painter over the depiction of the objects on the tablecloth, with its blue pattern in "Assisi needlepoint," the glassware, crockery and food, including cherries, in contrast to the limited interest shown in the expression of emotions, makes it a fine example of a "decorative" piece.

gins up until the middle of the 16th century: the demolition of the roodscreen and consequent reconstruction of the whole of the apsidal and presbyterial part and the erection of aedicules along the walls of the nave gave the church, overall, a strongly Mannerist look.

The main chapel, which was begun in 1574 under the patronage of the Bardi di Vernio, has a lavish lining of polychrome marble – unrolled scrolls of antique marble and recent 16th-century mineralogical discoveries in the panels of the floor, culminating in the marble tracery of the altar frontal – in keeping with the fashion of late 16th-century Florence, where the grand-ducal predilection for colored marble reached its height in the last twenty years, with the construction of the chapel of the Princes in San Lorenzo. The work, which lasted several years, concluded with the sculptural complex made up of a rich and articulated marble partition embellished with two sculptures of A*ngels* by Andrea Ferrucci and four Franciscan saints in the niches. The 17th- to 18th-century guise of the main chapel was completed with the dome decorated by the young Giovanni da San Giovanni, who displayed all the awkwardness of the beginner in the *Glory of Angels* (1616), and with the chancel behind, decorated with *The Expulsion of the Merchants from the Temple* by Giuseppe Pinzani, left unfinished on the artist's death and completed in 1844-45 by Gasparo Martellini.

Among the more important works carried out by the Observants during their renovation of the complex of Ognissanti was the creation of the two cloisters, the first and larger of which replaced the one constructed by the Humiliati in the middle of the 13th century. Built in the late 16th century, utilizing the preexisting structures that had gone through all the modifications we have already enumerated for the church, it consists of an ample loggia with twenty-one columns in *pietra serena*, ribbed vaults and lunettes frescoed with instructional *Scenes from the Life of Saint Francis*. Many of the fresco painters active in the city in the first and second decade of the 17th century took part in the decoration of the cloister, but most of the work was done by Jacopo Ligozzi, a painter favored by the Franciscans and an adroit narrator who, together with Giovanni da San Giovanni and other artists, gave expression to the city's rediscovered optimism through his "skill in dramatization and naturalistic verisimilitude."

The 17th century and the new façade. Following the Mannerist restructuring – which lasted until the closing decades of the 16th century – a new architectural and decorative intervention was carried out in 1627, giving the nave the appearance it has today. The only exception is the large vault representing the *Glory of Saints Francis and Paschal Baylon*, executed between 1769 and 1779 by the *quadraturista* Giuseppe Benucci and by Giuseppe Romei, who painted the central scene.

The 17th-century renovation, ordered by Ferdinando II, was carried out by Sebastiano Pettirossi, who accentuated the spacious effect of a large hall by opening numerous windows and adding a cornice of *pietra serena* that runs the full length of the nave. At the sides of the windows are set paintings on canvas with effigies of *Franciscan Saints*, interspersed with sections of wall decorated in stucco. In 1635, at the same time as the renovation of the interior, work began on a new façade, to a design by Matteo Nigetti that is clearly influenced by Buontalenti. The one we see today, however, is the fruit of a total reconstruction carried out by the Commune of Florence (1871-72) in travertine from Rapolano. The use of this highly resistant material, completely alien to the Florentine context, characterized instead by the golden sandstone called *pietra forte* and the gray *pietra serena*, has resulted in a cold reproduction of the decorative parts executed by Nigetti and the total loss of their expressive qualities, as well as an "authoritarian" insertion into the environment of the city.

Interior of the church

facing page
Domenico Ghirlandaio,
Last Supper, 1480, detail

Chapel of the Santissimo Nome di Gesù, 1722. Right transept

facing page
Matteo Bonechi, *Glory of Saint Peter of Alcántara and Virtues*, 1727. Chapel of San Pietro di Alcantara

The 18th century. Precious interventions "à la mode." In such a diversified setting, reflecting the long and varied history of Ognissanti, in which everyone involved with the church had commissioned works and patronized artists, the 18th century could not fail to leave behind precious examples of contemporary taste. In the right transept the small chapel of San Pietro di Alcantara was decorated, at the behest of the curate Anton Maria da Prato, by Matteo Bonechi, a pupil of Sagrestani, and Vincenzo Meucci. The result is a harmonious architectural and decorative ensemble, in the baroque style, in which the pastel-colored fringes of the painted walls – *Glory of Saint Peter of Alcántara* with *Virtues* on the vault and *Scenes from the Saint's Life* by Meucci on the walls – fit in well with the soft forms of the stucco from which the *Angels* and *Allegorical Figures* that make up the altar are molded. Another chapel – also on the right side – testifies to the high level attained by the 18th-century interventions. Here, prompted by its dedication to the Holy Name of Jesus, Giovan Domenico Ferretti and Lorenzo del Moro painted the *Glory of the Name of Jesus* and Ferretti the two ovals with *Our Lady of Sorrows* and *Saint Joseph*, providing an example of the effervescent rococo painting of which he was one of the finest exponents in Tuscany.

Santa Maria del Carmine

*Situated in the most typical quarter of old Florence, inhabited by workers and artisans,
it conserves the frescoes of Masaccio in the Brancacci Chapel and one of the masterpieces
of the Florentine baroque in the Corsini Chapel.*

Master of the Saint Agatha,
*Madonna and Child with
Two Angels*, 1425-27, detail

facing page
Masaccio, *Saint Peter Healing
the Sick with His Shadow,*
1425-27, detail. Brancacci Chapel

Piazza del Carmine

Built from the 13th century
onward
Reconstructed in 1771-75 by
G. Ruggieri and G. Mannaioni

Order: Carmelites since
the 13th century

The church of the Carmine, a spacious 18th-century interior with luminous vaults painted by Giuseppe Romei, is famous all over the world for the small Brancacci Chapel where Masaccio frescoed some of the *Scenes from the Life of Saint Peter.* The osmosis between the reality of the city and its pictorial representation, which has always struck visitors to Florence, giving them the illusion of living in Renaissance times, reaches its emotional peak in the scenes painted by Masaccio and Masolino in the Brancacci Chapel. The naturalistic representation, combined with an exaltation of form, proposes examples from antiquity coupled with an intense social commentary on sickness, marginalization and poverty. Masaccio's work in the Carmelite church, which Vasari was to call "the world's school," is considered a classic: "an art for everyone, an art for all time, a comprehensible and expressive language, independently of its date," Luciano Berti defined it. Even the urban space that hinges on the church, fascinating and neglected by the imagery of tourism, is different. As early as the 14th century, when the friars obtained permission from the Signoria to turn the space in front of the church into a square, the Florentine urban context, short of large free areas, was provided with an ideal place for preaching. The polygonal apse that still projects into a green space today recalls the site on which the complex was built, expanding with its cloisters and annexes into the gardens and vineyards that filled the area between the last two rings of walls.

The Carmelites arrived in Florence in 1267. In fact the early decades of the 13th century had been characterized by the spread of religious orders that, wanting to establish direct contact with the reality of city life, chose to install themselves in urban settings. This is what the Dominicans, Franciscans, Augustinians and Servites had done, founding the monasteries that gave rise to many of the city's churches: Santa Maria Novella, Santa Croce, Santo Spirito, Santissima Annunziata and Santa Maria del Carmine.

A mendicant order, the Carmelites attained their greatest diffusion with the canonization of Simon Stock in 1265 and were the last to reach Florence, installing themselves outside the walls, where they immediately exercised a great influence on urban development. On June 30, 1268, the bishop of Florence, Giovanni Mangiadori, founded the church dedicated to the revered Virgin of Mount Carmel and the Commune, at its own expense, reopened the nearby Porta San Frediano and reorganized the road system to provide easier access to the new place of worship. The monastery and the church survived until 1771, when a fierce fire destroyed the church. The two arms of the transept were saved, miraculously preserving the chapel of the Brancacci family frescoed by Masolino and Masaccio and, in the left arm, the Corsini Chapel, one of the most interesting examples of baroque art in a Florentine religious building.

The fire of 1771. On the night of January 28 and 29, 1771, flames raged through the inside of the church,

destroying the building that had grown up over the centuries on the site of the sanctuary devoted to the Virgin. However, it was not just the fire that disfigured the vestiges of the past, as is often believed: men anticipated and completed the destruction wrought by the flames. Substantial modifications to the Gothic church had begun in 1568 when Giorgio Vasari had brought the church into line with the tenets of the Counter Reformation by demolishing the roodscreen, just as he had done in Santa Croce, Santa Maria Novella, San Marco and Ognissanti on the instructions of Cosimo I. He also substituted large altars in *pietra serena* for many of the chapels in the nave. In the hall of the church, whose walls were all adorned with old frescoes, the shallow chapels were replaced by large aedicules while the area around them was decorated in fresco; at the same time the wooden railings enclosing the chapels were removed and their altars set against the wall. Here too, just as in Santa Croce and Santo Spirito, a large gilded ciborium adorned with statues, designed by Buontalenti, was erected instead of the original high altar.

The modifications in the first half of the 17th century were few, and of little importance, but the church was clearly in need of restoration and its appearance was no longer in keeping with the taste of the time. From a manuscript uncovered by Ugo Procacci we learn, picking our way through the colorful verbiage of its writer, about the precarious state of the interior: "Our church was reduced by its age to such awful wretchedness that it frightened anyone who entered [...]. What can I say of the ceiling and roof: when it was raining you would have seen more fountains than in the garden of Boboli and in good weather more rays of sunlight than there are stars in the sky. The fine organ built by the Soderini family was so worn out and broken down that it could be used to accompany the discordant concert of cats." So we can understand why the 14th-century trussed ceiling was removed in the 1760s and replaced by a vaulted roof that was to burn down in the fire a few years later. In the 17th and 18th century work started on all the alterations that would, in the space of a few decades and long before the fire, destroy so many works of art. The first to go was the chapel of the Serragli, demolished in 1675 to make room for the fine construction in honor of St. Andrew Corsini. The old Gothic windows decorated with stained glass in the nave were eliminated and then, with the renovation of several chapels in the 1730s, the floor was repaved with bricks and the whole church cleaned and whitewashed. This was the state the interior was in when, in 1736, the decision was taken to conceal the old trussed roof under a rich carved and gilded wooden ceiling with three large painted panels. Giovan Domenico Ferretti, followed by his pupil Alessandro Masini, painted the *Virgin Giving the Habit to Saint Simon Stock*, while Gesualdo Ferri and Filippo Burci depicted several Carmelite saints in the other two panels. When the work was almost finished, and only the gilding remained to be added, the fire broke out. The cause of the disaster of 1771 seems to have been a brazier left burning inside the choir. From here, among the wooden stalls and cabinets, the flames spread into the nave, where the fire reached the wooden framework of the roof and, making it collapse onto the area beneath, turned it into a great pyre. Fortunately, the damage was more limited in the crossing, where the most important works of art were located. To save the Brancacci Chapel "the masters of the guard" opened a gap in the roof, successfully halting the progress of the fire.

The reconstruction. A few days after the fire, the architects Giuseppe Salvetti and Romualdo Morozzi carried out an inspection of the church and, together with the architect Zanobi del Rosso, representing the friars, agreed to demolish the campanile, now unsafe, but leave intact the outer walls of the church which, apart from a few loose stones at the top, were not at risk. At the same time the openings were walled up, leaving only small gaps for access, and both the Corsini and the Brancacci Chapel were closed, to protect them. Without wasting time, the friars decided to build a new church on the site of the old one, and on February 6 of the same year of 1771 the Father Provincial went to Pisa with the prior of the Carmine to deliver a petition to Grand Duke Peter Leopold requesting his support for their plan. Peter Leopold immediately gave his assent and, a few days later, went to see the destroyed church, appointing three supervisors at the

same time. With a promptness unknown to the institutions of the 20th century, on July 1 of 1771 – just five months after the fire! – construction of the new church was begun by Giuseppe Ruggieri, winner of the competition. On July 12 the archbishop of Florence blessed the first stone which, according to tradition, was laid along with two parchments and a number of relics in the foundation of the first pillar on the right.

During the reconstruction, overseen by Giuseppe Ruggieri until his death, numerous finds were made amidst the ancient structure of the church which, partly intact and partly modified, had spanned the five centuries of its history. Walls of chapels, bases of altars and many traces of the frescoes that the documents tell us had decorated the walls between the 14th and 15th century were brought to light.

In the new construction, completed by Ruggieri's pupil Giulio Mannaioni, the principal modification was made in the transept, where the six chapels at the sides of the high altar were replaced by just two. At the time Ruggieri died, in 1772, the new campanile and dome had been finished and all the vaults were already built; the church would be completed a few years later, in 1775. Today, especially on the outside, the building still preserves the sturdy and unadorned structure of the old church. Here too, as in other places of worship in the city, the façade was never finished and the crude front, set at the top of five steps, is stark and severe in its incompleteness (the portal in *pietra forte* was executed by the stonecutter Francesco Sandrini in 1776-77). There are numerous traces of the Gothic church: the front window that is contained within the original central oculus; the profile of the saddleback roof broadened, at the top, by the raising of the building in the 18th century. The interior, one of the largest and brightest in Florence, provides a startling contrast with the essential rigor of the exterior. The new construction, in late baroque forms but markedly classicist accents, was completed with Giuseppe Romei's large and airy painting of the *Ascension* on the ceiling of the nave, framed by architectural perspectives executed by Domenico Stagi. The spacious nave has five chapels on each side, alternating, between pilaster strips and decorative friezes, with the

The Corsini Chapel

same number of confessionals and doors leading into the cloister and a number of side chapels. After finishing the vault of the nave and leaving the field to Domenico Stagi, charged with painting the *quadrature*, Romei went on to decorate the large central dome, the vault of the chancel and the small vaults of the arms of the transept. Thus the church, having assumed a more definitive aspect, was ready for the decorations of its interior. Many families, such as the Arnaldi, Buonaccorsi, Perini, Sassi, Manetti and del Pugliese. reasserted their rights to burial in the church and undertook to meet the expense of decorating the new chapels. A few patrons set paintings on their altars that had been in the old church and, moved to secondary areas during the construction of the ceiling that was there destroyed, had been saved from the fire. To these relics from the 16th and 17th centuries were added works expressly commissioned for the church that was being fitted out in the late 18th century. Under Mannaioni's supervision the ten chapels set in the wall were designed and their altars built in stucco with tympana of alternating form. We do not know the name of the stuccoists who executed the angels in relief, the friezes and the garlands that decorate the upper part of the niches.

The main protagonist of the decoration of the Carmine, perhaps also selected at the suggestion of the grand duke, was without doubt Giuseppe Romei, author of the *Ascension* on the large vault of the nave. Already known for a similar commission, the ceiling of the church of Ognissanti, he displayed a surer and more daring touch in the Carmine with the great *trompe-l'oeil* of almost Roman dimensions. The principal example in Florence of a large ceiling with a scenographic *sotto in su* perspective, Romei's grand composition squeezes Domenico Stagi's mock architecture into the edges of the space. Fresh in its use of pale tones, the structure painted by Stagi exhibits an expert grasp of staging (the artist had also been the author of numerous temporary scenes, including the decorations erected in the Carmelite church for the funeral of Emperor Francis I), painting varied architectural views rich in illusory perspectives in which we see colonnades, arches, balconies, balustrades and stairways, illuminated by a golden light. The decoration of the transept, where the

Luca Giordano, *Glory of Saint Andrew Corsini*, 1682. Dome of the Corsini Chapel

same artists painted the vaults and the choir with the *Glory of Blessed Angiolo Mazzinghi* (right), the *Virgin Giving Her Veil to Saint Mary Magdalene dei Pazzi* (left), and the *Transport of Elijah*, as well as an *Apotheosis of Saints* in the dome, had got under way at the urging of the Corsini family who, intending to rebuild the marble front of the chapel of Sant'Andrea, destroyed in the fire, had entrusted the sculptor Florentine Giovanni Nobili with the design of the work (1774).

The Corsini Chapel: the great Florentine baroque. Dedicated to St. Andrew Corsini, whose remains are contained in the sarcophagus set against the wall of the altar, it represents one of the great examples of baroque art in Florence and the most important 17th-century intervention inside the church. Andrea – born in Florence to Niccolò Corsini and Gemma Stracciabende in 1301 – was a Carmelite friar at the monastery of the Carmine and in 1349 became bishop of Fiesole. Ten years after his death on January 6, 1374, accompanied by stories of miracles and memories of a virtuous life, his incorrupt body was stolen from Fiesole Cathedral, where he had been buried, and taken to Florence. His brother Neri, in

Giovan Battista Foggini, *The Miraculous Appearance of Saint Andrew during the Battle of Anghiari*, c. 1676, detail. Corsini Chapel

accordance with the wishes expressed in his will, had him buried in the Carmine (1385), where he was entombed in the left-hand wall of the nave.

Over two centuries went by before the family, which in the meantime had acquired power and wealth through numerous commercial activities all over Europe, turned its attention to its illustrious forebear again. It was Filippo (1538-1601), followed by his brother Bartolomeo (1545-1613), who, wishing to gain prestige on a par with that of other Florentine families, left a large sum to fund the erection of a chapel and provide a worthy setting for the tomb of the Blessed Andrew. But it was only after his canonization by Urban VIII in 1629 that this desire was realized. In 1636 the Corsini obtained the bare chapel of the Crucifix at the head of the left transept from the Serragli family, and with the subsequent assignment to Pier Francesco Silvani (1675) put the long awaited project into effect. The design was entrusted to one of the architects of the Medici retinue – as the sculptor Giovan Battista Foggini was also to become – who carried out the task scrupulously, especially in view of the family's allocation of 18,000 scudi. The Corsini, who aimed to demonstrate the social standing they had attained with this commission, had delayed assigning the works in the Carmine because of their financial commitment to the purchase of houses on Via del Parione, where their grand palace facing onto the Arno would be built just a few years later. A similar operation would be carried ont, shortly afterward, for the mortuary chapel of Marchese Francesco Feroni in the Santissima Annunziata, commissioned from Foggini again by the *nouveau riche* Francesco, who had won honor and fortune sending his ships to Africa and India.

The internal architecture of the chapel, based on 16th-century elements, reflects the severe taste of the local tradition blended with a baroque exuberance of Roman origin. The small temple, mitigated in its structural rigor by the use of polychrome marble and by the flamboyant dome housing Luca Giordano's pictorial decoration representing the *Glory of Saint Andrew Corsini*, combines the soft light and colors of baroque art with more typically Florentine plasticism, enhanced by Foggini's reliefs. Close in time to the creation of the better-known chapel of the Princes, the

chapel is precious and stunning and must have looked incredibly imposing in the setting of the old Carmelite church. A "fashionable" commission, it employed artists like Foggini, a Florentine sent to Rome to study at the Academy under Ercole Ferrata and Ciro Ferri, as was Carlo Marcellini, who executed *God the Father* at the top of the altar, or the Neapolitan Luca Giordano, whose arrival in Florence was due to the patronage of the city's great families. A prestigious decorator, Luca Giordano was already known in Florence owing to the presence of many of his pictures in private collections, and the Corsini, followed shortly afterward by the Riccardi, who would have him decorate the large gallery of the palace of the same name, turned to him in order to show that their patronage was at an "international" level, placing them in competition even with the Medici family. The completion of the chapel, which was entrusted to Giovan Battista Foggini, entailed the execution of three high reliefs representing the saint's miracles and glory. The artist, studying at Cosimo III's academy in Rome, received the commission from the Corsini before his return to Tuscany in 1676. The three-dimensional representation, which reveals Foggini's appreciation of Roman examples such as the work executed by Ercole Ferrata in the church of Sant'Agnese on Piazza Navona, constituted a novelty for Florence, still unaccustomed to the new baroque style. The *Apotheosis of Saint Andrew Corsini*, located on the rear wall, is flanked by two reliefs depicting the *Appearance of the Madonna to Saint Andrew Corsini during Mass* and the *Miraculous Appearance of Saint Andrew during the Battle of Anghiari*, episodes from Andrea's life that proved decisive in the process of his canonization.

Masolino, Masaccio and Filippino in the chapel of the Brancacci family.

The chapel, originally dedicated to St. Peter and then to the Virgin of Mount Carmel sometime before the middle of the 15th century, had been constructed by testamentary disposition of Piero di Piuvichese Brancacci in 1367, but it achieved its fame thanks to one of his descendants, Felice. A rich merchant of silk cloth, Felice Brancacci was born in Florence in 1382, where he held numerous public posts and was sent to Egypt by the Floren-

tine Signoria as trade envoy (1422). On his return from the mission, which was a great diplomatic and commercial success, Felice entrusted the decoration (1425) to Masolino, whose place was taken, on his departure for Hungary, by his partner Masaccio. The work, destined to remain incomplete as a result of Masaccio's move to Rome, where he died in 1428, was finished several decades later by Filippino Lippi (1431-85). So Filippino's intervention was almost that of a "restorer," or at least was confined to completing the scenes that Masaccio had left unfinished. His painting, realized about fifty years after that of his illustrious predecessors, is inserted with the care and sophisticated adaptation of style required in order not to create obvious irregularities in composition or the handling of the paint. Indeed he was so successful that 18th- and 19th-century critics were convinced, partly as a result of the darkening of the color, that more of the work was Masaccio's than is in fact the case. Further modernizations of the chapel (1746-48) led to the destruction of the four-sided vault and the lunettes underneath, to make room for the dome we see today, representing *The Virgin Giving the Scapular to Saint Simon Stock*, painted by Vincenzo Meucci. Much has been written on the restoration carried out in the chapel since 1980, and completed after about ten years. Following a thorough investigation of the environment and the surface of the paint, using sophisticated technology, the team of restorers have brought a new legibility to the scenes and above all have helped to clarify the terms of the collaboration between Masaccio and Masolino. The dismantling of the 17th-century altar, moreover, has permitted recovery of parts of the decoration that were able to reveal the real coloring of Masolino and Masaccio's paintings prior to the damage inflicted by the fire, and thus be used as samples for comparison during the cleaning of the walls. The new brilliance of color that has emerged from beneath a layer of dirt and heterogeneous substances extraneous to the original pigments has returned the frescoes to the state they were in just after they were painted, providing a new insight into the contributions of the three artists, Masolino, Masaccio and Filippino, now more united and yet distinct and better contrasted than ever.

Masaccio, *Distribution of the Goods of the Community and Death of Ananias*, 1427. Brancacci Chapel

facing page
Masaccio, detail of the *Raising of the Son of Theophilus and Saint Peter Enthroned*, 1425-27, with portraits of Masaccio and Masolino. Brancacci Chapel

following pages
Masolino da Panicale, *The Healing of the Cripple and the Raising of Tabitha*, c. 1425, detail. Brancacci Chapel

The Brancacci Chapel

On the scaffolding together in 1425, Masolino and Masaccio divided between themselves the large expanses of wall to be frescoed according to the client's program: *Scenes from the Life of Saint Peter*. The painters worked on the adjoining scenes in the upper row for several months, allowing them, and observers, to compare two traditionally antithetical, apparently irreconcilable manners. The recent restoration (1980-90) has given the walls a more unitary appearance, in which the color, cleansed of its coating of dirt, has regained its force, smoothing out the differences between the more polished Masolino and the vigorous Masaccio. Here, "where the two cultures that usher in the modern era confront and reflect one another," and after the critical distinctions that have helped separate the two styles, it is helpful to reconcile their vision again by looking at the scenes flanking the chapel's old Gothic window: *Saint Peter Preaching* (Masolino), *The Baptism of the Neophytes*, *Saint Peter Healing the Sick with His Shadow* and *Distribution of the Goods of the Community and Death of Ananias* (Masaccio). The scene of the *Preaching*, which follows Masaccio's one of the *Tribute Money*, corresponds symmetrically with the *Baptism*, complementing it in its landscape and figures.

The *Preaching*, considered by many the work of Masolino, or with minimal contributions from the younger Masaccio, suggests a unitary design of the decoration. The opposite deduction can be made, on the other hand, from a comparison of the famous images of the *Temptation of Adam and Eve* and *Expulsion from the Garden of Eden*. The *Temptation*, frescoed by Masolino in the upper row of the right-hand pier, displays a composed classicism, of cultured Humanistic matrix, characterized by the great figurative potentialities of the naturalistic current; while the *Expulsion* painted by Masaccio on the pier opposite appears tragically modern (both scenes, before their restoration, were covered by sprays of leaves added to conceal the nudity in the late 17th century).

The upper part is completed by two large scenes: on the right Masolino with the *Healing of the Cripple and Raising of Tabitha*, where one of the most frequently reproduced city views acts as a backdrop to two episodes from the Acts of the Apostles; on the left Masaccio with the powerful scene of the *Tribute Money*. The restoration has revealed that both the background and the figures in the elegant scene depicted by Masolino (formerly attributed to Masaccio in its entirety by Cavalcaselle and for the background alone by Longhi

and others) were executed together, in a single day. Scientific analysis has demonstrated, unequivocally, the unity of the backdrop – the Florentine square with buildings, loggias, furnishings and episodes of daily life – and the figures in the foreground, including the two notables dressed in sumptuous capes and headgear. In the row beneath we find the images painted by Masaccio, *Saint Peter Healing the Sick with His Shadow* and the *Distribution of the Goods*, in a setting where we can recognize the typical buildings with rusticated fronts or wooden jutties, common in Florence in the 14th and 15th centuries. In the group of men with St. Peter we can identify contemporary artists like Masolino (with the red hat), Donatello (blue cap and white beard) and Masaccio's brother Giovanni, called Scheggia, Peter's blond companion. It is also possible to interpret the scene of the *Distribution of the Goods* in a contemporary key, as its execution (1427) coincided with fiscal reform and the institution of the Florentine land registry.

On the entrance piers are two scenes attributed to Filippino Lippi: *Saint Paul Visiting Saint Peter in Prison* and *Saint Peter Freed from Prison*. Masaccio interrupted the work in 1427 and silence fell in the chapel,

coinciding with the financial problems of Felice and the fall from grace of the Brancacci. The family, formerly prosperous and honored for its business dealings, was exiled for its opposition to the Medici. Felice, an active member of the Ghibelline faction as well as son-in-law of Cosimo's bitter enemy Palla Strozzi, first imprisoned and then exiled, died in 1447 without ever seeing Florence again. Returning to Florence in 1474, the Brancacci resumed work on the chapel, which would be finished in the eighties by Filippino Lippi. On the left-hand wall, below Masaccio's solemn *Tribute Money*, is set the episode with the *Raising of the Son of Theophilus and Saint Peter Enthroned*. Taken from the *Legenda Aurea*, it tells how St. Peter, imprisoned by Theophilus, the prefect of Antioch, was freed on the promise to resurrect his son, dead for fourteen years. The miracle led to the conversion of all the citizens of Antioch, who erected a new church in honor of the saint. The fresco is the work of Masaccio and Filippino, something Vasari had already made clear, but we do not know whether Masaccio left the fresco incomplete at the time he left for Rome, or if it had been finished but then, following the banishment of the Brancacci in 1435, the parts

portraying the clients and their now politically compromised supporters were destroyed. In this crowded scene, painted with clearly eulogistic intent, the urban or mountainous backgrounds Masaccio had used in the other images are replaced by a conceptually imposing backdrop of architecture in perspective – recalling some of Piero della Francesca's pictures – that is above all a functional setting for the episode. Numerous contemporaries are portrayed: from the resurrected youth (the painter Francesco Granacci) to notable citizens like Tommaso Soderini, Piero Guicciardini, father of the famous Francesco, Filippino's great patron Piero del Pugliese and the poet Luigi Pulci. The prefect Theophilus can be identified as Gian Galeazzo Visconti, ruler of Milan, while the man seated on his right is the Florentine chancellor Coluccio Salutati. In the group on the right we can recognize artists and architects: Filippo Brunelleschi, Leon Battista Alberti, Masaccio and Masolino. The scene concluding the cycle was frescoed by Filippino and depicts the *Disputation with Simon Magus and Crucifixion of Saint Peter*.

Masaccio, *The Tribute Money*, c. 1425, detail. Brancacci Chapel

facing page
View of the Brancacci Chapel

Masolino da Panicale,
*Temptation of Adam and
Eve*, 1425. Brancacci Chapel

Masaccio, *Expulsion from the Garden Of Eden*, 1425. Brancacci Chapel

following pages
Masaccio and Filippino Lippi, *Raising of the Son of Theophilus and Saint Peter Enthroned*, 1425-27 and c. 1481, detail. Brancacci Chapel

Santo Spirito

*Splendid gallery of masterpieces, ideal archive of Christian Humanism,
it is the most majestic 15th-century architectural space in the city.*

Santo Spirito, an ideal showcase of Humanism, houses a genuine gallery of masterpieces in the majestic architectural space created by Brunelleschi. A symbol of the Oltrarno, between the 12th and 17th century the church, its numerous cloisters and monastic buildings grew up alongside the square that the Signoria had already enlarged at the end of the 13th century, just as was done with the spaces in front of the Florentine churches of the mendicant orders, Santa Croce and Santa Maria Novella. In this area, then known as "Caselline," the ancient complex of Santo Spirito, erected by the Augustinians in the second half of the 13th century (1251-96), just after their arrival in the city from the hill of Arcetri, stood amidst fields, vineyards and olive groves. All that remains of this group of buildings today are the refectory with Andrea Orcagna's large fresco of the *Crucifixion* (seat of the Museo della Fondazione Salvatore Romano) and the Corsini Chapel (now the Military Recruiting Offices), but both give us a fairly clear idea of the location of the old church, set further forward but in line with the present one.

The Augustinian Order (1256) was born out of popular religious movements which, inspired by the spiritual heritage of St. Augustine, succeeded with the community of Santo Spirito – already large and prestigious in the 14th century – in placing themselves in the vanguard. The opportunity to make Santo Spirito the symbolic building of the Oltrarno district, which with the construction of the bridge at Santa Trinita was also better connected with the civil and religious center of the city, was provided by Florence's victory over Galeazzo Visconti in 1397, and the consequent undertaking of the Signoria to build, with the backing of the Commune, a new church for the followers of the bishop of Hippo.

But four decades were to pass before, following the commission given to Brunelleschi in 1428-30, work actually started on the new church: a decisive factor was the election of an influential inhabitant of the district, Neri Capponi, as gonfalonier in 1444. Over this long span of time services continued to be held in the old church of the Augustinians – built next to the monastery that had now attained a considerable size – until March 15, 1471, when it was practically destroyed in a major fire. The memory of this ancient structure, where, among others, Cimabue, Lippo Memmi and Taddeo Gaddi had worked, is also that of the great cultural and religious renewal that, thanks to the order's Studium Generale and later on to Florentine Humanistic circles, made Santo Spirito a center of theological and philosophical studies. In the writings of Boccaccio and Petrarch the names of Augustinian friars appear as spiritual masters. The liveliness of the activities carried out at the cenacle also attracted the principal families of the Oltrarno, drawn to culture as a source of social and economic power. And it in this context that we must see the interest shown by the young Lorenzo, later to be dubbed the Magnificent, in the complex, whose fervid intellectual atmosphere provided an ideal setting for his patronage, taking him in a different direction from the family, which had traditionally favored the Dominicans.

facing page
Interior of the crossing with the altar of Giovan Battista Caccini

below
The nave viewed from the main altar

The nave viewed from the façade

following pages
The sacristy with a view of the dome

Filippo Brunelleschi: the project of Santo Spirito between idea and execution. Brunelleschi's design envisaged a building facing onto the Arno and the opposite way round to both the old complex and the present one. His vision was of a new urban basilica on the large square opening onto the river, but this was strongly opposed by the landowners in the area, the Capponi and Frescobaldi families, as well as by the Commune, unwilling to meet the cost of the demolitions this would have entailed, and was not taken up. We know this from Antonio Manetti, Brunelleschi's biographer as well as his successor in the construction of Santo Spirito, who mentions the clients' concerns over the difficulty of finding the funds: "doing well such a thing as we hope may not be affordable."

What Brunelleschi proposed to the members of the building commission was a church with around forty chapel-niches, in the belief that a broader range of patrons would give him greater personal freedom. Mindful of the pressure exerted by the Medici on the design of San Lorenzo, he wanted greater independence in Santo Spirito. This was also what lay behind the idea of starting to build the new construction from the transept, in the secret hope that over time the possibility of a front onto the river would prevail over the interests of the Frescobaldi and Capponi. This, as is clear today, did not happen and the church remained "enclosed" in its quarter, becoming a sort of scenic backdrop to the garden of the ancestral palace of the Frescobaldi in a testimony to their influence as clients. In addition to the plan segmented into numerous chapels, the main innovation of Brunelleschi's building was – according to Franco Borsi's interpretation of the architecture – its modularity: a module of eleven ells on a side constituted the longitudinal and transverse intercolumniation, as well as the distance between the half columns on the outer wall and the vaulted niches set in it. An even number of repetitions of the module led to the emergence of continuity: there was no center, with its consequent bilateral symmetry, just the rhythmic repetition of a single element. In addition to the central column in the apsidal space (on the center line), the most striking results of this constant modularity were the exteriors, with their suggestive succession of curved walls and ingenious intersections. The work of normalization of Brunelleschi's design (he died in 1446 when construction was barely underway) began with the elimination of those external projections and the rectification of the outer walls, and was followed by the roofing with a flat suspended ceiling, instead of the daring tunnel vaulting of both the large nave and the transept. Summing up the complicated but incisive arguments put forward by Franco Borsi, it remains to be identified just what is left of Brunelleschi's design in the rich interior, now a compilation of numerous figurative styles, as well as excellent works of art.

In the 1480s, when the new chapels were practically complete, they began to be assigned on the basis of the old rights in the now demolished 13th-century church: former and new patrons presented themselves, betraying in practice Brunelleschi's egalitarian idea. The Corbinelli acquired a total of four chapels, at the head of the left transept, the Frescobaldi raised the money for three adjoining altars in the apsidal area and the Capponi would do the same in the right transept, re-creating spheres of influence inside the new church. If the structure was essentially in the state we see it today in these years (1481-82), the form of the façade was yet to be decided. The internal structure should have resulted in a front with four doors but, after a long discussion among the citizenry, the views of a group of "consultants" headed by Giuliano da Maiano prevailed and it was built with only three. It should be noted that the façade we admire today is the fruit of the 18th-century plastering (1758) of the bare stone ashlars left by the Renaissance architects.

In the same years the dome was constructed according to Brunelleschi's designs. Executed by the master builder Salvi di Andrea, it was vaulted in 1480 and by 1482 was already finished, leaving the space of the crossing below free for one of the packed sermons of the Fathers of Santo Spirito.

Lorenzo the Magnificent and the new sacristy. The powerful attraction that this center of Humanistic culture exerted on the city and on more distant courts was of great interest to Lorenzo the Magnifi-

cent. While he could do little about the unanimous vote on the external appearance of the façade (the choice between three or four doors), he was able to exercise an incisive influence with his personal financing of the construction of the sacristy. The place was sufficiently important to Lorenzo for him to entrust the work to Giuliano da Sangallo, one of his favorite architects. In December 1489, after Giuliano had built a model for Lorenzo, the foundations of the new construction were blessed. Situated between the chapterhouse and the old sacristy, the structure, linked to the church by a colonnaded vestibule, has an octagonal plan and is roofed with an eight-sided vault. Dying in 1492, Lorenzo was only able to see the outer front completed. The construction of the sacristy, in which the greatest architects and decorators available at the time were involved (in addition to its designer Giuliano da Sangallo, the master builder of Santo Spirito Salvi di Andrea and Giovanni del Betto, while Andrea Sansovino and Simone del Pollaiuolo called Cronaca were among the decorators), continued to benefit from Medici patronage. Piero di Lorenzo, succeeding his father in the government of the city, requested the execution of a wooden model in order to proceed with the work in detail under the direction of Salvi di Andrea. In the sacristy, an example of cultured architecture of classical derivation, Giuliano adopted Brunelleschi's color scheme of white and gray, and with the octagonal form harked back to such lofty models as the Florentine baptistery. In 2000 the *Crucifix* that Michelangelo carved for the high altar was returned to the church, after an absence of about thirty years.

The monastic complex in the 16th and 17th centuries. With the conclusion of the major works in the church, and the shift of attention to execution of decorations by the families with rights of patronage, Cosimo made his awkward presence felt in Santo Spirito. Determined to show himself a powerful and munificent ruler, Cosimo embarked on urbanistic and architectural undertakings (1550) of great significance for the city. Using Giorgio Vasari to put his plans into effect, he opened the great construction site

of the Uffizi – with its annexed corridor providing him a privileged route across half the city – and in the religious sphere, in keeping with post-Tridentine requirements, set about the internal transformation of Santa Maria Novella, Santa Croce, San Marco and Santa Maria del Carmine.

Cosimo had been thinking about Santo Spirito since the sixties when, in view of the urgency of certain works in the monastery, the duke had decided to carry out a complete renovation. Bartolomeo Ammannati was the architect chosen to execute the grand duke's plans which, with the construction of two cloisters, a new refectory, the dormitory and the large kitchen, were intended to put into effect the idea of a "monastery in the form of a city." The reconstruction of the monastic complex of Santo Spirito did not come to an end with Ammannati's work, concluded around 1595. In the 17th century it would be subjected to major architectural interventions, this time by, among others, the Parigi family of architects, who with Alfonso had completed Bartolomeo's project.

With the death of the two architects who had given the complex its 16th-century form, Bartolomeo Ammannati and Alfonso Parigi, in the nineties, the Augustinian Fathers turned to Giovanni Caccini, author among other things of the monumental altar inside the church, Giorgio Vasari the Younger and Lorenzo Sirigatti. The last two were entrusted with a difficult task by the monks: drawing up the whole plan of the monastery and making it "a reliable, well-apportioned and established model [...] which will be observed by all our successors [...] who will not be able to deviate from it in any way." Signed by the Father General, this was a clear message for posterity. This proposition, in which Santo Spirito's vocation to become the place where the whole urban fabric of Florence, or at least significant parts of it, would be molded appears undeniable, remained on the drawing board. In the early decades of the 17th century numerous digressions were made in the new and "irregular" structures of the monastery. This "chaos" was to culminate in 1622 in the building of the Chiostro dei Morti, or cloister of the Dead, by Giulio Parigi.

Michelangelo Buonarroti's *Crucifix*

In the Jubilee year of 2000 Michelangelo's *Crucifix* returned to Santo Spirito, after an absence of over thirty years. In the sixties, following Margrit Lisner's shrewd recognition of Michelangelo's authorship, it had been moved to a museum, that of Casa Buonarroti in Florence. The sculpture, "forgotten" above the portal of a refectory and clumsily repainted, was subjected to a first restoration after the incredible discovery. Its original location had been recorded by Giorgio Vasari: "For the church of Santo Spirito in Florence Michelangelo made a crucifix of wood which was placed above the lunette of the high altar, where it still is." And it is known that Michelangelo had donated it to the prior Niccolò Bichiellini between the spring of

1493 and the autumn of 1494, and therefore when he was aged just eighteen or nineteen. This makes the *Crucifix* Michelangelo's earliest known work. The delicate and slender body, almost that of a boy and surprising when compared with Michelangelo's more mature sculpture, takes us back to a young artist who with great skill – Michelangelo went to the hospital of Santo Spirito to study the anatomy of bodies – reproduces the figure in full relief, sublimating the devotion that guided his work in an image of chastity. Taking equal care over the back of the sculpture, so that it can be viewed from all sides, the artist employed several artifices, such as the slightly overlapping position of the legs which slims down the lower part

and draws attention to the calm expression of the bowed head. Probably painted by the same artist as sculpted it, it is made of lime wood, patiently finished and covered with a thin layer of priming and oil paint in delicate and transparent shades, and displays some interesting peculiarities of execution (the wound in the side and bloodstains are merely traced in red paint, while the hair is made of painted stucco and tow). The softness of the modeling seems to show that the young Michelangelo had taken notice of Leonardo da Vinci's warning: "O painter skilled in anatomy, beware lest the undue prominence of the bones sinews and muscles cause you to become a wooden painter." In 2000, following careful and

painstaking restoration, the work was returned to its original location, in compliance with the legitimate requests from the Augustinian Fathers and in the consciousness of the importance that the original context has for works of art and for their understanding. It was not possible to put it back in the place where Vasari records it, above the high altar, and so, for reasons of conservation and security as well as the change in the architectural context resulting from the insertion of Caccini's new altar, it has been located in the Renaissance Barbadori Chapel in the sacristy, returning it to the function of an object of devotion from which it had been removed, in full harmony with the setting.

Francesco Botticini, *The Three Archangels, ante* 1471-72. Galleria degli Uffizi, Florence

facing page
Cosimo Rosselli, *Madonna and Child between Saints Thomas and Peter*, 1482.

The altars of the church and their "old-fashioned" decoration. The sequence of painted panels with their "old-fashioned" frames of quadrangular shape, predellas, altar frontals painted in imitation of cloth, family crests and glazed windows that we see in the left transept of the church does not appear accidental. Even today a design can be discerned in this unusual uniformity of decorations, despite the variety of artists, clients and craftsmen. Filippo Brunelleschi, who had so quickly been obliged to abandon the implementation of his extraordinary idea for the construction, modified and perhaps betrayed by others, had indicated that the decoration of those chapel-niches, deliberately egalitarian so as not to gain the upper hand over the unitary design he had conceived, should also be consistent. Thus Brunelleschi's chapels, at least in the closing decades of the 15th century, were fitted out in a uniform manner: altarpieces, altar frontals and altar steps, as well as stained-glass windows and coats of arms in the background. All the furnishings display a close cor-

S·TOMAS · M·CCCC° · LXXXII · S·AVGVSTINE

respondence, with one chapel echoing the next in its dimensions, decorative and colored panels and even the composition of the sacred scenes, with an evident attention to the clients. And it was those clients who would get the better of the indications said to have been left by Brunelleschi. If a unitary intent in the decoration and furnishings, presumably taken up by his heir Antonio Manetti, is in fact credible, it is equally evident that the families were going to exert pressure to show off the fruit of their commissions to artists and established local workshops. And if the memory of Brunelleschi's dictate still prevailed up until the end of the 15th century, something that is confirmed by what was going on in the church of San Lorenzo, in the 16th century, and to an even greater extent in the ones that followed, the relationship between architectural structure and decoration was turned on its head, as current taste and the excessive power of the wealthy families gained the upper hand.

Tracing chronologically the entrance into the church of the paintings that were used to decorate the niches around its edges, we find two of identical subject: *The Three Archangels* executed by Neri di Bicci in 1471 for Mariotto della Palla, now in the Detroit Institute of Arts, and *The Three Archangels* by Francesco Botticini, now in the Uffizi, which we know was already present in the new church in 1483. The first panel would be replaced in 1698 by the composition in stucco executed by Giovanni Baratta, who filled Brunelleschi's limpid niche with baroque sculpture.

In 1482, just after the consecration of the church, Cosimo Rosselli's ancona of the *Madonna and Child with Saints Thomas and Peter* was placed on the Corbinelli Altar. Tommaso Corbinelli commissioned the decorations of his chapel from the workshops of Cosimo and his cousin Bernardo. Members of a numerous and versatile family of craftsmen, each of the Rosselli applied his own specialty in the execution of a decorative ensemble typical of late 15th-century artistic enterprise: a panel set in a frame with an architrave on fluted responds and an altar frontal in which the doves of the Holy Spirit surround the tondo with the *Incredulity of Saint Thomas.*

The other workshop that was active in Santo Spirito,

Donnino and Agnolo del Mazziere, *Madonna and Child between Saints Bartholomew and Nicholas of Bari*, with altar frontal representing *Saint Bartholomew*. Corbinelli Chapel

facing page
Donnino and Agnolo del Mazziere, *Holy Trinity between Saints Mary Magdalene and Catherine of Alessandria*, 1490. Corbinelli Chapel

perhaps in collaboration with Rosselli's more famous one, is that of the del Mazziere. Donnino and Agnolo (the latter is described by Vasari as a friend of Cosimo Rosselli) worked for another chapel of the Corbinelli family which, as has already been mentioned, acquired the patronage of four chapels in the new church at moments of particular prosperity. Authors of the altarpiece representing the *Madonna and Child with Saints*, and of the *Holy Trinity between Saints Mary Magdalene and Catherine of Alessandria* for the Corbinelli, the del

Mazziere continued their decorative work in Santo Spirito for the Ubertini Chapel, also in the left transept, painting another *Madonna and Child with Saints Bartholomew and John the Evangelist* (1488). This series of figurative panels, set in "old-fashioned" frames, acts as a foil to the brightly-colored altar frontals in which the same workshops, and the same artists, depicted symbols of saints or family emblems on panels imitating luxurious drapes of silk or velvet, creating a sort of late 15th-century picture gallery. A style of painting whose illustrative, serial and in some ways artisanal character represents the traditional taste of these families of Oltrarno, who saw Santo Spirito, especially up until the 1480s, as a "peripheral" and "closed" artistic milieu, perhaps in a sort of moderation of Brunelleschi's ambitious project. Although close to the Augustinian monastery, a dazzling source of Humanistic culture, of which Brunelleschi's choice was the symbolic but above all structural fruit, a church seems to have developed that reflects in its decorations the taste and pragmatism of the patron families. The Brunelleschian church "looked" onto the square where the great annual wool fair, was staged on November 11, and where the nearby Via delle Caldaie ("Street of the Cauldrons") got its name from the vats used by dyers.

Masterpieces in Santo Spirito: Botticelli, Piero di Cosimo and Filippino Lippi. After the variegated crop of artists who had decorated numerous chapels in the renovated church, we find the first commission to a painter of great prestige, Botticelli. The occasion was provided by the chapel of Giovanni Bardi di Vernio (1483). Belonging to a family closely allied with the Medici, he chose Giuliano da Sangallo for the wooden setting and Botticelli for the panel depicting the *Madonna and Child between Saints John Baptist and John the Evangelist*. The painting, which was removed in 1629 to make room for a canvas by Jacopo Vignali that is still *in situ*, is now in Berlin. A cultured subject typical of Lorenzo's circle, to which the two artists belonged, it refers with its renewed Marian devotion to the contemporary argument over the Immaculate Conception, in which the Augustinians, like the Medici family, took the "immaculist" side.

From the same years, in which the presence of Lorenzo the Magnificent as a member of the church's Vestry Board influenced the choices, dates the execution by Piero di Cosimo of the *Visitation in the Presence of Saints Nicholas and Anthony of Egypt* (National Gallery, Washington) for the chapel of Gino di Neri Capponi; this too was replaced in 1713 by a canvas by Sagrestani and was subsequently sold abroad.

Still in its original place in the right transept we find the superb panel of the *Madonna and Child between Saints Martin of Tours and Catherine of Alessandria* commissioned from Filippino Lippi by Tanai de' Nerli.

The sculpture: Andrea Sansovino for the Corbinelli. In the left transept of Santo Spirito is located one of the finest artistic contributions to the late 15th-century church: in 1491 Bartolomeo Corbinelli entrusted Andrea Sansovino with the erection of the altar destined to house the Holy Sacrament. The Corbinelli, an important Oltrarno family that received the honor of conserving the Sacrament from the Frescobaldi family, who had had the right to it in the old church, were patrons of four altars in the left transept, and with the commission to Sansovino gave the church its most important work of marble sculpture. With the banning of burials in Santo Spirito, in compliance with

IVSTORVM CONVIVIVM

Filippino Lippi's *Madonna and Child between Saints Martin of Tours and Catherine of Alexandria*

Filippino, an artist with a great gift for narration, painted a masterly altarpiece of profound fascination for Tanai de' Nerli (1427-98). Here, as in the *Apparition of the Virgin to Saint Bernard*, now in the Badia Fiorentina, executed for the del Pugliese around 1480, he fully expresses his talents as an illustrator and cultivated interpreter of families with ties to the Florentine Signoria. Surrounded by the rich carving of the gilded frame, made at the same time as Filippino was painting the panel, the large picture presents the sacred figures in the foreground, flanked by portraits of the clients, Tanai de' Nerli and his wife Giovanna (Nanna) Capponi. The figures seem to be pretexts for the imposing architecture of classical reminiscence (see the carved throne on which the Virgin is seated) that frames the scene in the background. The elegant lines of the principal personages are set against a backdrop of four arches that open onto a reconstruction of the city centered on Palazzo Nerli in Borgo San Jacopo, offering a view of Porta San Frediano as well as presenting episodes of daily life. In this setting – which emphasizes the contemporary vision of the client depicted in the dress of a government official – our attention is caught by the image of the father saying goodbye to his little daughter at the door of his house, perhaps a reference to the client's departure on a diplomatic mission to Pisa in an attempt to avert the invasion by Charles VIII in 1494; or simply a more generic allusion to Nerli's status as a citizen who held official posts.

an order of the republic that was respected up until the 17th century, the Corbinelli Altar is unique, with the exception of the *Tomb* of Neri Capponi located behind a bronze grate. Consisting of a marble backdrop that follows the curve of the niche, it encloses, behind a lavish later balustrade (1642), an imposing altarpiece with three classical arches framing the ciborium, figurative reliefs and statues of *Saint Matthew* and *Saint James the Greater*. Under the table an altar frontal in high relief represents the *Pietà*. Little known, the altar underwent a thorough restoration in 2002 that has brought out Andrea's luminous classicizing sculpture and revealed the fine quality of the carving and the use of gold to highlight the decorations.

The 16th century: Raphael's *Madonna of the Canopy* and Rosso Fiorentino's Altarpiece. After the numerous works commissioned from Raffaellino del Garbo by the Antinori, Frescobaldi, Nasi and Segni families in the first five years of the 16th century to decorate their chapels in the church, now embellished with paintings, stained-glass windows and altar frontals along the lines laid down by Brunelleschi, Pietro Dei commissioned a panel for the family altar in memory of his father Riniero in 1507. This was Raphael's painting known as the *Madonna of the Canopy*: never installed in Santo Spirito, it can now be seen in the Galleria Palatina. Raphael left the work incomplete at the time of his departure for Rome in 1508, and the panel made many peregrinations before ending up in the collection of Grand Prince Ferdinando and then the gallery. The same thing happened to the later panel commissioned from Rosso Fiorentino by Piero Dei (1522), which, set in a frame carved by Francesco Ferrucci, is now in Palazzo Pitti.

In the 1530s, with the city's new system of government, Santo Spirito saw a boom in works privately commissioned from artists. Remote from the Mannerist tendencies interpreted by Rosso, they reflected the devotional and religious sentiments that held sway in Florence: Michele Tosini, called Michele di Ridolfo, and Pierfrancesco di Jacopo Foschi. Foschi painted the large panel on the Torrigiani Altar repre-

senting the *Disputation over the Immaculate Conception* (1544-46), the *Resurrection* in the Bettoni Chapel and the *Transfiguration* in the Bini Chapel. The *Disputation*, echoing the heartfelt theological debate in which the Augustinians played a prominent part, was one of the most common Marian subjects commissioned for the church in these years, while the *Resurrection* heralds the iridescent coloring of the early Mannerists. In the following decades great works of Medicean and Vasarian inspiration made their entry into Santo Spirito, including Agnolo Bronzino's altarpiece with the *Noli me tangere*, now in the Louvre, and large paintings by his disciple Alessandro Allori. Allori would paint *The Ten Thousand Martyrs* for the Pitti, *Christ and the Woman Taken in Adultery* for the Frescobaldi and *Saint Fiacre Healing the Sick* for Grand Duchess Christine of Lorraine, on the altar of the sacristy (1596).

In the 17th-18th century this stylistic and temporal variety, common to the decoration of large churches, was broadened by the replacement of several old works by "modern" paintings, in an adaptation to current taste on the part of the orders and patrons. Together with the erection of the large high altar by Giovan Battista Caccini, works by Passignano, Aurelio Lomi, Rutilio Manetti and Vignali, as well as the 18th-century Alessandro Gherardini and Giovan Camillo Sagrestani, would enter the church. Sagrestani painted a brightly colored *Marriage of Mary* that was set on the altar in 1713 as a replacement for Piero di Cosimo's *Visitation*, now in Washington. A brilliant example of the artist's slick but congenial style, it was one of the last additions to the church.

With the return of Michelangelo's early *Crucifix* to Santo Spirito, the panorama of sculpture in the church of the Augustinians has regained the prestige that such a work brings and that is also associated with the artists who made their reputations in the building designed by Brunelleschi, contributing to the fame of the complex, the order and the families that had erected and decorated altars and chapels in it. A center of Humanistic and Neoplatonic culture in the 15th-century city, Santo Spirito still holds a place in the history of its quarter and the whole of Florence as a "city of God, city of man."

Raphael, *Madonna del Baldacchino* (*Madonna of the Canopy*), 1508. Galleria Palatina, Florence

facing page
Rosso Fiorentino, *Madonna and Child with Saints* (*Dei Altarpiece*), 1522, detail. Galleria Palatina, Florence

Giovan Battista Caccini's High Altar

On November 11, 1608, guests at the wedding of Cosimo II and Magdalene of Austria were able to admire the complex structure of the high altar of Santo Spirito. Built by Caccini to a commission from Giovan Battista Michelozzi, senator and member of the Vestry Board of Santo Spirito, its composite and colorful architecture was not unveiled until nine years after the beginning of the work, and four after the death of the client. Conceived in the lead up to the Jubilee celebrations of 1600, the creation of the high altar was a demanding and expensive undertaking for Michelozzi who, as we have seen, never saw it finished. Taking his inspiration for this sumptuous work of interior architecture from Roman taste and from the Florentine precedents of illustrious clients (Bandinelli's contemporary choir for the cathedral, or Orcagna's old tabernacle in Orsanmichele), Giovan Battista Caccini constructed a detailed scale model of the structure that was largely followed, on his death, by his successors: Silvani, Ubaldini and Cennini. Built out of polychrome marble with variegated and lavish inlay work, the altar is composed of a spacious enclosure ringed by an octagonal balustrade on which stand sculptures of angels holding oil lamps, with wooden choir stalls on the inside. At the center, under a baldachin and at the top of a flight of mixtilinear steps, a fabulous ciborium embellished with precious marble and stone - note the columns decorated with strips of lapis lazuli - stands on an altar with a frontal and steps, above the table, decorated with precious marble inlays. This central part was executed by an undisputed specialist, Giovan Battista Cennini, active in the contemporary work that was being carried out for the Medici along similar lines: the chapel of the Princes in San Lorenzo. A controversial insertion into the rigorous symmetry of Brunelleschi's church, the grand altar has attracted criticism, especially in the 1970s, when it was accused of disfiguring the great architect's work. However, it has to be seen in the light of a respect for artistic and cultural stratifications, which help us to gain an understanding of the continuity of history.

Santa Felicita

From ancient basilica to noble nunnery.
Inserted, in the ideal route of the Medici princes, between the places of power and the royal palace,
the church houses Pontormo's great masterpiece, the Deposition, *in the Capponi Chapel.*

Symbol of the convent of
Santa Felicita

facing page
Jacopo Pontormo, *The
Deposition from the Cross,*
1525-28, detail. Capponi Chapel

Piazza Santa Felicita

*Built in the 11th century
1736-39: reconstruction
by Ferdinando Ruggieri*

*Order: Benedictine Nuns
(11th-18th century)*

On October 6, 1736, the abbess and nuns of Santa Felicita, having just started on the work of reconstruction supervised by Ferdinando Ruggieri, made an appeal to Grand Duke Gian Gastone de' Medici, asking him to take the church "under his Royal Protection." The document, conserved in Santa Felicita's extensive archives, provides a fascinating insight into the climate that held sway at the time in the church and the Benedictine convent. There were strong ties between the monastic community, ruling house and Florentine nobility: in fact the nuns were all of noble origin. Often consecrated to religious life not out of choice, but in a pragmatic move to preserve the family fortune, which would have been depleted by too many dowries, they benefited from the financial support and above all influence of their families of origin. Then in 1565 – when Duke Cosimo ordered Giorgio Vasari to build the corridor linking the two Medici residences, Palazzo Vecchio and Palazzo Pitti, through the Palazzo degli Uffizi – the ruling house had officially intervened in this monastic universe. The aerial route traced by the corridor – set against the façade to form its entrance loggia – and the suggestive opening onto the church called the *coretto* represent the best vantage point from which to see the interior that Ferdinando Ruggieri rebuilt between 1736 and 1739, undoubtedly with particular deference to the city's "steadfast rulers." The uniformity we now see is in fact the result of the structure created at that time which, although incorporating two 15th- to 16th-century chapels and the baroque choir, manages to preserve the clarity, sobriety and tradition typical of the Florentine architecture of the early 18th century. Ferdinando Ruggieri, who had already carried out several works for the convent elsewhere in the city, found himself intervening in a decaying complex – most of the building dated from the 11th century – that nevertheless contained some illustrious presences: the Barbadori Chapel conceived by Filippo Brunelleschi and painted by Pontormo, the Canigiani Chapel with the 16th-century frescoes of Bernardino Poccetti and the choir, designed by Ludovico Cigoli at the beginning of the 17th century and decorated with important contemporary pictures by the Guicciardini family.

The church "rebuilt" by Ferdinando Ruggieri. The small Piazza di Santa Felicita, which suffers from the intrusive postwar (1945) reconstructions that have marred the whole of the Ponte Vecchio area, is characterized by the column that stands almost at its center and, above all, the façade of the church with its essential lines that betray, despite the 16th-century corridor, its Romanesque origins. It was from the Romanesque building, in fact, which had survived successive alterations and enlargements into the 18th century, that Ferdinando Ruggieri would start his reconstruction. There can be no doubt that Ruggieri (1691-1741) was the most prominent figure active in Florence at the time and an ideal heir to the architectural tradition of the Renaissance: his designs were in keeping with the prevalent taste, and his position at the body in charge of the grand duke's construction projects, the Fabbriche Granducali, shows him to have had the ruler's

Santa Felicita, Court Church

"I recall how, on the first of August of that year, Duke Cosimo wanted me to start building the corridor running from the Ducal Palace to the Pitti Palace, which begins from the palace and goes over the fabric of the Magistrates, facing the Arno, and over the Ponte Vecchio and from Santa Felicita descends from the palace into the garden of Pitti [...]." These are the words in which Vasari describes the project he carried out for Cosimo I in 1565. This work forged the strong link that would unite the church with the grand-ducal court for over two centuries. It would be Ferdinando I – followed by his successors Ferdinando II, Cosimo III and all the way up to Peter Leopold of Lorraine – who insisted on this public expression of the religious life of the prince, reflecting the desire of the Medici to present themselves as a "Catholic house" in the years following the Council of Trent. Thus first Cosimo, in whose coronation the influence of the pope had played a decisive part, and then his successors set out to demonstrate an attitude

of religious zeal and support for the Counter Reformation, not just in their general political choices but also in their daily lives, something that was to have profound repercussions for their contemporaries. We can recall the sumptuous funerals held in the chapel of the Princes at San Lorenzo, ideal stage for the grand-ducal display of piety. And not even Peter Leopold's construction of the chapel inside Palazzo Pitti, many years later (it was consecrated in 1766), would lead to a noticeable change in the religious habits of the rulers. They would never fail to be present in Santa Felicita, as they did not want to renounce this public exhibition of devotion. The room called the *coretto*, or tribune, from which the court attended religious services, in a sort of theatrical appearance to the people, is located on the inside of the façade. Erected in the first few years of Ferdinando I's reign (1587-1609), it offered a view of the church from the corridor and can be linked with a custom

typical of the 17th-18th century, when, independently of the chapels that existed inside Florentine palaces, the nobility preferred to create a convenient place from which to attend services in the churches closest to their homes. The grand-ducal "presence" in the church is also testified by the monuments and tombstones, many of them still visible, of courtiers or attendants linked to the court: among them it is worth mentioning the tombs of the painter and court musician Arcangiola Paladini, now in the external loggia, Count Silvio Albergati, paymaster

of Cosimo III, the auditor Giacomo Conti and Count Franz von Thurn, state councilor of Emperor Joseph II.

favor. And he was to dedicate his monumental work *Studio di Architettura civile* to Gian Gastone. From this neo-Brunelleschian tradition are derived the geometric clarity and use of two colors, exploited here to define the spacious interior that the nuns wanted and funded, with the tacit support of the grand duke. In this renovation of the decor the architect, although constrained by the preexisting Romanesque-Gothic structure, put late 16th-century schemes into practice. The original wooden trusses of the roof were replaced by a vault, while the nave remained identical; small side chapels took the place of the series of altars and other objects that had accumulated in the building between the 11th century and the early 18th.

Domenico di Michelino, *The Three Archangels and Tobias*, 1493. Galleria de l'Accademia, Florence

facing page
Neri di Bicci, *Saint Felicity with Her Sons*, 1463-64, detail

The interior has a structure rhythmically cadenced by architectural elements of clear 16th-century derivation, in which the older of the main chapels, erected by Ludovico Cigoli in the second decade of the 17th century, is perfectly inserted. In his conscious revival of late 16th-century spatiality, Ruggieri was in reality proposing a "modern" 18th-century architecture: a single large nave with three chapels in the form of tribunes set in the walls on each side, and the setting of the contained main chapel. The classicistic rigor contrasts with a vibrant vertical movement, rising from the pilaster strips into the double arches that subdivide the vault, interspersed with elegant windows in *pietra serena* at the sides. Original the advanced structure of the two small chapels before the transept which, set on pairs of columns, present the central chapel in a focused perspective. With similar balustrades to those on the inside of the façade, the two balconies constitute, together with the upper opening framed by volutes and tablets, the most concrete concession to the baroque. The altars in the chapels of the chancel and nave are of less interest: built in marble and stucco in the 18th-19th century to commissions from the families and the Vestry Board, they are not at the same level as the interior designed by Ruggieri.

The Capponi Chapel (formerly the chapel of the Barbadori)

facing page
Jacopo Pontormo, *Deposition from the Cross*, 1525-28, detail. Capponi Chapel

following pages
Jacopo Pontormo, *Annunciation*, 1525-28, detail. Capponi Chapel

The origins. Following the discovery of remnants of a cemetery and other ancient relics at the time of the 18th-century reconstruction, the work on Santa Felicita attracted the interest of local scholars who, together with the architect, examined the more important finds and set out to save as much of the past as possible from the oblivion to which it seemed destined. During these years, in fact, a total of seventeen inscriptions were uncovered, of which the scholar Domenico Maria Manni has left us an extraordinary account. So the documentation is supplied by a contemporary, who showed a particular interest in such discoveries both as a Florentine man of culture and as an enthusiast for the new historical studies. In the early decades of the 18th century the study of antiquity acquired great prominence and it was at that moment that people began to assemble private collections: in Florence, those of Senator Carlo Strozzi, the Riccardi family (organized by Foggini) and Filippo Buonarroti. A similar example is the "antiquarian" display, still visible in the corridor of the cloister, of the tablets that the 18th-century works brought to light. The rediscovery of the tombstones described by Manni allows us to retrace the origins of the church. An early Christian basilica, erected in the years spanning the 4th and 5th century in a graveyard located in a suburb of the city on the other side of the only bridge over the Arno at the time (at the point where the Ponte Vecchio would later be constructed), it was the first building to go up in the area inhabited by a colony of Greek-speaking people (as is suggested by several gravestones in Greek or with names of Oriental origin found in the 18th century). Subsequently, perhaps as a consequence of the bloody Gothic War of Justinian (536-53), the splendid basilica was replaced by a modest building that would survive, in ruins, until the middle of the 11th century. This is the church that Pope Nicholas II would reconsecrate and rebuild, along with the annexed Benedictine convent, in 1059. And it was in these remote times that it was dedicated to St. Felicity, martyred along with her seven sons during the reign of Emperor Antoninus Pius in the 2nd century AD and often confused in the popular imagination with the mother of the Maccabees, seven young martyrs mentioned in the Catholic version of the Old Testament (170-135 BC). The Romanesque church – of which little survives – had a nave, two aisles and a crypt divided up by small columns. The few Romanesque remains on the surface are only partially visible, as they are concealed between the walls of modern constructions. In the 11th century, a period of full economic and demographic recovery for Florence, the rebuilding and consecration of the convent of Santa Felicita was part of the wave of reconstruction of religious buildings which brought the Romanesque style to its widest diffusion. The topographic location that, as we have seen, had such an influence on the development and subsequent abandonment of the original basilica, was to play an important part in the construction of the new church and nunnery.

From the 14th to the 16th century: the development of the church. The view of the distinctly Romanesque building that is provided by 15th-century images (the Carta della Catena and Jacopo del Massaio's map, *circa* 1470), tallies with the documents and the works discovered inside this ancient but certainly not majestic church. Even though the 18th-century rebuilding resulted in a substantial transformation of the altars and furnishings installed over the centuries, the works still present, or that can be traced to it, reflect considerable activity on the part of the nuns and many families in the parish from the second half of the 14th century on. The desire of private individuals, largely families living on the same square or neighboring streets (the Canigiani, Guicciardini, del Rossi, Barducci and Mannelli), to have an altar or chapel inside their parish church fits into a wider context, which saw wealthy citizens unite faith and prestige in the embellishment of their family chapels. These decorations often involved an expression of gratitude, perhaps through a tomb or a work of art, for having survived the plague of 1348. It is symptomatic, in fact, that the years immediately following the terrible epidemic brought a proliferation of bequests in favor of monasteries, confraternities or religious communities.

It was the convent that assigned the first major commission in 1395: the abbess Lorenza dei Mozzi ordered the polyptych of the high altar and the work of the

woodcarvers would be followed, in 1399, by that of the painters Niccolò Gerini, Spinello Aretino and Lorenzo di Niccolò. A year of great works, 1399: after the polyptych came the frescoes of the main chapel, commenced by Neri d'Antonio, and the large stained-glass window executed by Niccolò Tedesco. Nothing is left of these interventions except the polyptych representing the *Coronation of the Virgin and Saints* now in the Galleria dell'Accademia: an example of Spinello's late activity (here in collaboration with Niccolò di Pietro and

(1427-98), who was Filippino Lippi's great patron in Santo Spirito, commissioned the picture from Neri for the altar dedicated to the titular saint of the church. It represents *Saint Felicity with Her Sons*, with scenes of the *Martyrdom of the Maccabee Brothers* in the predella. Following the change in taste that led to the disappearance of paintings on a gold ground from all of Florence's churches from the late 16th century onward, the work that the delle Colombe family had had painted by Domenico di Michelino was also put aside: represent-

Lorenzo di Niccolò), it is clearly of Neo-Giottesque inspiration, something typical of the works of the last decade of the century, and the solemn figures of the saints at the sides frame a more supple central scene.

Around the same time (1387) the convent had had its chapterhouse decorated by Niccolò di Pietro Gerini: all that remains of the extensive frescoes on the vaults and walls are the multifoil paintings in the crossings depicting the *Redeemer and Virtues* and the *Crucifixion* on the rear wall. The sacristy was built by the Canigiani family sometime after 1473: Brunelleschian in character, it falls within that vast architectural area in which modest executors reproduced the prototypes devised by Filippo Brunelleschi in simplified and often crude forms. Among the important commissions of the 15th century was the sumptuous panel that Neri di Bicci painted, in 1463-64, for the altar of the Nerli family. Tanai de' Nerli

ing *The Three Archangels and Tobias*, the panel had been commissioned in 1493 by Michele di Corso and by the middle of the 18th century had already been replaced by Ignatius Hugford's large canvas depicting *Tobias Restoring His Father's Sight*. Moved to the Accademia in 1810, following the abolition of the convent, Domenico di Michelino's work is an outstanding example of 15th-century painting that offered a scintillating image, inside the church, to the patrons and the congregation.

The Barbadori Capponi Chapel: Brunelleschi and Pontormo in Santa Felicita. An exemplary development inside the old church – which Ruggieri took care not to compromise – was the erection by Filippo Brunelleschi, around 1420, of the chapel of the Barbadori family dedicated to Our Lady of the Annunciation, which in the next century would be

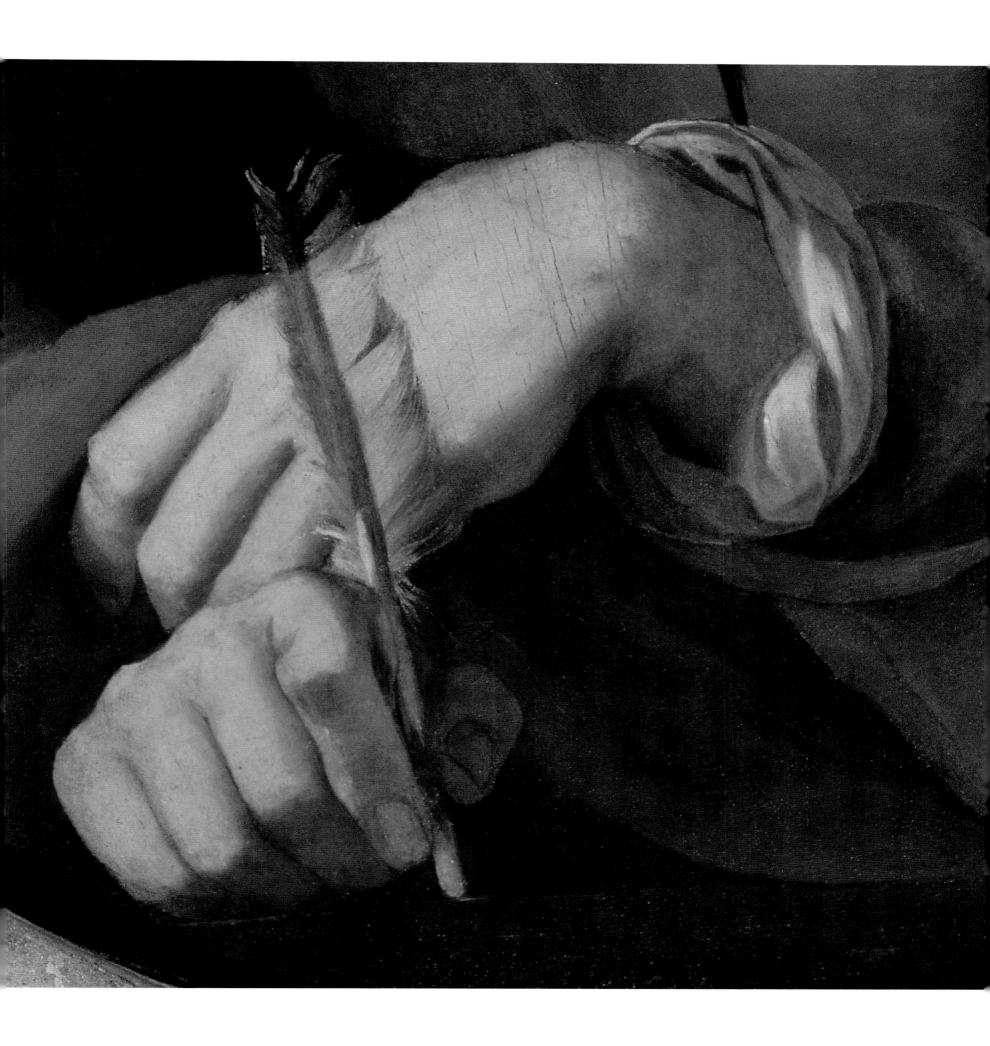

Fab izio Boschi, *Martyrdom of Saint Sebastian*, 1617

Gerit van Honthorst called Gherardo delle Notti, *Adoration of the Shepherds*, 1617, before the damage inflicted on it by the bomb in 1993, detail. Galleria degli Uffizi, Florence

decorated with the most important cycle of paintings to have survived. It was Manetti, Brunelleschi's contemporary and biographer, who attributed to him the execution of "that small chapel that is in the corner of Santa Felicita as you enter by the front door on the right hand, which was a new form at that time and very beautiful," a piece of information that was also handed down by Giorgio Vasari.

The chapel has a square plan with two sides adhering to the corner of the nave, while the other two, with large arched openings, are closed by an 18th-century railing. The roof is a dome, originally hemispherical, resting on four pendentives decorated with the same number of painted tondi; the structural elements are Corinthian pilaster strips with an architrave in which is set an arch supported by Ionic half-columns; shell-shaped paterae are located in the two triangular spaces. Founded between the second and third decade of the 15th century – in close connection with the perspective backdrop of Masaccio's painting of the *Trinity* in Santa Maria Novella – the chapel has been caught up in the trials and tribulations and successive interventions that the church passed through from its medieval origins until its reconstruction in the 18th century. Today, despite some heavy-handed alterations, the 15th-century structure is still clearly visible, thanks to the interventions begun way back in 1936 by the Fine Arts Service of Florence, which have recovered not just Brunelleschi's structural elements but also the decorative and coloristic ones. Motifs of considerable interest have been brought to light, especially if imagined in the original tones of gold and azure, the heraldic colors of the Barbadori, whose richness and vivacity, now lost, created a more harmonious link with the works of Pontormo.

With the decorative intervention in the 1520s – ordered by the chapel's new patron Ludovico Capponi – the structure lost its Renaissance character to become a genuine example of Mannerist dynamism. The explosion of freedom that, especially before the alterations in the 17th-18th century (the superb *Reliquary Monument to Saint Charles Borromeo* executed in marble and semiprecious stone is no exception), must have characterized the interior does justice to the art of Pon-

tormo and his unflagging experimentation, confirmed by Vasari who could not refrain from remarking that "his bizarre and fantastic brain never rested content." The masterpiece of the *Deposition* marks one of the artist's moments of highest spirituality and most intense drama. Pontormo's work, now lacking the hemispherical decoration (*God the Father and the Patriarchs*) in the cupola, destroyed in 1767, covered the entire surface, transforming it: the tondi with the *Four Evangelists* (where *Saint Matthew* and *Saint Mark* were painted in collaboration with Agnolo Bronzino) in the pendentives and the wall on the right with the figures of the *Announcing Angel* and the *Virgin*, filtered by the light from the window with Guillaume de Marcillat's *Transport of Christ to the Sepulcher* (the original is in Palazzo Capponi). Finally, above the altar, the splendid panel of the *Deposition* (or *Pietà* according to the new inscription put up by Ludovico Capponi), an unreal tangle of bodies moving to an imaginary music. The whole thing brings a new dynamism to Brunelleschi's architecture, whose spatiality was too rigorous for the vortex of painting with which the artist filled it. The Mannerist paintings, and above all the *Deposition from the Cross*, dominating the setting, create a surprising decorative ensemble that must have gleamed when the architectural elements were enriched with blue and gold patterns that recalled the emblem of the Barbadori. They must have been very striking, these Renaissance and post-Renaissance chapels, where the place of the severe combination of white and gray that often dominates them today was taken by a riot of color. Superlatives have been lavished on this unique setting, of which the *Annunciation* on the front wall is an integral part, but the words of critics are not able to capture the beauty of the colors with which Pontormo painted these bodies, looking almost as if they are taking part in a dance. Pier Paolo Pasolini has described them in a passage of great poetic force: "colors that blaze in the heart," colors "of poppies, left out in the light of the sun […] of motionless leaves under the surface of the water […] ever more blue, until they turn green." The painter portrayed himself in a secluded corner of the panel, watching the mystical scene.

And so we come to the end of the first part of the 16th

century, in which Santa Felicita had been the hub of developments in the city, and above all, the end of the age of the total autonomy of the church which, in 1565 (the year of construction of Cosimo I's corridor), found itself within the sphere of grand-ducal influence and no longer just that of private patrons. The church, which until then had not attracted much attention from the public, began to play a leading role in both the ceremonies and the daily religious life of the rulers. The first link with the Medici family, established chiefly with the nuns of the annexed convent, was in fact that corridor, which offered a broad view of the interior and which, subsequently, with the construction of a room called the *coretto* or tribune above the chapels at the front, would make possible the presence of the grand duke and duchess and the honor of having them among the "people."

The 17th century. If the 16th century had brought radical changes to the ancient church, the 17th century would limit itself to modest modifications dictated by the new taste in architecture and decoration. Ludovico Cigoli, author of the design for the new main chapel, patronized by the Guicciardini since 1606, was given the most important task. The other interventions – the Badii Cioli Altar in the transept and the reliquary monument to St. Charles Borromeo, inserted in Brunelleschi's chapel – are only interesting examples of the Florentine taste for polychrome marble. While the canvases present on the three altars on the left, Fabrizio Boschi's *Martyrdom of Saint Sebastian* (1617), Ignatius Hugford's *Tobias Restoring His Father's Sight* and Simone Pignoni's *Saint Louis, King of France* (1682), offer a high-quality sample of 17th-century Florentine painting, on the altar in the transept is set one of the most important altarpieces that the families commissioned for the church: the *Assumption of Mary with Saints Catherine of Siena and Margaret of Cortona*, painted by Volterrano for Caterina Cioli Poltri and Eleonora Badii Poli in 1677. In its current form, the main chapel has a large central archway, designed by Lodovico Cigoli in the first decade of the 17th century to a commission from the sons of Angelo Guicciardini, Piero, Francesco and Girolamo, but surmounted by the bro-

ken pediment and coat of arms that Ferdinando Ruggieri added during the 18th-century reconstruction. Piero Guicciardini – who had left for Rome in 1611 to take up the post of ambassador – devoted particular attention to the works in the family chapel, in his position as a privileged interlocutor of the architect, who was also in Rome, where he had been summoned by Pope Clement VIII. Guicciardini had the canvases that were to decorate the walls of the apse executed in Rome as well, by followers of Caravaggio (the vault had been frescoed by Michelangelo Cinganelli with the *Coronation of the Virgin and Saints* between 1617 and 1619). They included the *Adoration of the Shepherds* by the Flemish artist Gerrit van Honthorst, acquired for the Galleria degli Uffizi in 1835 and almost destroyed in the explosion of 1993.

The 19th century and decay. The new construction, which barely a century before had won the admiration of contemporaries, coincided with the beginning of the church's decline. The only exception was the commission, by the Vestry Board, of the large canvas depicting *Saint Felicity and the Martyrdom of the Maccabees*, placed on the third altar on the left in 1863. With this work Antonio Ciseri took his academic style of painting to its greatest height: the beauty of the forms and the smoothness of the flesh tones, steeped in a warm light and set against a dreamy classical backdrop, recall the works of Ingres. The Benedictine nunnery, the driving force behind the activities and interventions, had gradually lost its influence owing to the decline in the number of sisters and then was swept away by the political and religious events that, with the advent of the House of Lorraine, overtook Florence and the whole of Tuscany. The church, after this forced scission, lost its most active and vital function, which had taken it through the centuries from a fundamental center of aggregation in Oltrarno, in the ancient Borgo di Piazza, to the position of parish and grand-ducal church, always supported by the convent from which it had sprung. Thus, when the *maire* of the city of Florence decreed the definitive closure of the monasteries of Santa Felicita and Santo Spirito on October 6, 1810, Santa Felicita had reached the epilogue of a glorious past.

Antonio Ciseri, *Saint Felicity and the Martyrdom of the Maccabees*, 1863, whole picture and detail on facing page

San Miniato al Monte

The majestic Romanesque building, today an ideal "balcony" overlooking Florence,
has preserved its ancient charm intact;
as closely bound to the heart of the city as it is physically distant.

Crest of the Arte di Calimala,
patron of the basilica of San
Miniato from the 12th century
until 1770

facing page
The façade, 12th century, detail

Viale dei Colli

Built in the 11th-13th century
(1013-1207)

Order: Cluniac Benedictines from
the 11th century; 1373-1553
Olivetan Benedictines; 1697
Jesuits with the "House for
Spiritual Exercises"; 1783
Olivetan Benedictines

Patronage: Arte di Calimala
until 1770

The façade of the basilica of San Miniato, splendidly framed between the Palazzo dei Vescovi and the fortified walls of the city, illuminates the hill of Monte alle Croci at the top of the flight of steps designed by Giuseppe Poggi which leads up from the Viale dei Colli. Set in a semi-fortified context – a star-shaped perimeter surrounded by cypresses and occupied on the inside by the monumental cemetery of the Porte Sante (1865) – San Miniato and its monastic complex immediately call to mind their function in the 16th century, when Michelangelo built ramparts there to defend the city against the troops of Charles V (1529).

A mute spectator, San Miniato overlooks the bowl of the city along a line of sight that was given to it in the 19th century, when Poggi, redesigning the ancient system of roads climbing the hill, commenced what would later come to be seen as a distortion of history, canceling the view of the church surrounded by its green hill that John Ruskin had painted in his Romantic watercolors.

Bishop Hildebrand and the construction of the church dedicated to the martyr Minias. Built on a site where a place of worship dedicated to the martyr Minias had existed since the 8th century, the church was founded by Bishop Hildebrand of Florence, who installed a community of Cluniac Benedictines there around 1013.

With the support of Emperor Henry II of Saxony and his wife Cunegond, Hildebrand had the church and monastic buildings – a donation from Charlemagne himself – restored after discovering, according to tra-

dition, the martyr's remains on the hill near Florence. For hagiographic reasons, given the scarcity of historical information about Minias – a Christian martyr during the reign of Emperor Decius (250 AD) and described in the apsidal mosaic as king of Armenia – Hildebrand got the abbot, the monk Drago, to write the *Passion* of Minias. With its emphasis on the legendary elements, this was to form the basis for all the subsequent writings. Even the investigations by scholars in the 18th and 19th centuries (G. Lami, P. Lugano, *Acta Sanctorum*, R. Davidsohn) brought nothing new and fully documented to light, leading to the conclusion that in the hagiography of martyrs what matters is not their lives, but their deaths. Drago recounts how Minias, decapitated at the gates of the city, picked up his own head (and thus was a cephalophore martyr, i.e. carrier of his severed head) and walked to the hill where he was then buried. It is in this guise that he is depicted – on the altar in the right-hand aisle – in the altarpiece by Jacopo del Casentino.

The importance of the church of San Miniato, one of the earliest major religious buildings constructed in Tuscany, lies in the fact that it stems, at least where the structural parts are concerned, from a unitary design. The date 1207, inscribed on the floor, can therefore be taken as the year of conclusion of the work. Thus the important building project was undertaken during a period of great expansion of the city, testified by the larger ring of walls constructed between 1172 and 1175. Acknowledging the contemporaneity of the phases of construction and decoration with marble, we can divide up the process into four stages: 1011-68 crypt;

1070-93 first tier of the façade, walls of the aisles, chancel; 1128-50 wall and arches of the nave, second tier of the façade; 1175-1207 pediment of the façade and floor. Having also established that nothing was preserved of the early-Christian building and that Hildebrand had the church built from scratch, the documents of 1180 telling us that the works were still being carried out by the Vestry Board of San Miniato, under the supervision of the Arte di Calimala, are decisive. The early-Christian church probably remained in use during the fist two phases, occupying the area between the façade and the presbyterial part. The new aisles enclosed the old church, which was not demolished until the new chancel was finished and the religious functions could be transferred there (much as would be done later with Santa Reparata and the cathedral).

So the basilica of San Miniato, built over the span of around 200 years, does not appear to have been an isolated and precocious example of the importation of Lombard construction techniques, as had been proposed by critics in the early 20th century, but a conscious product of the classical Florentine tradition fused with the Romanesque style of Lombardy. What predominates in this architecture is the taste for ornamental decoration in two colors that was very widespread in Tuscany. A scheme of Middle-Eastern origin (the use of polychrome in the area of Muslim influence was derived from Islamic art), it was very popular in architecture from the Middle Ages to the Renaissance, and even beyond (during the revivals of the 19th and 20th century for instance), and the façade of San Miniato is one of its most significant examples.

The façade. Built in three successive stages, it is divided into tiers. The lower one is defined by five round arches – three of them with doors – supported by columns of green marble with Corinthian capitals

View of the hill of San Miniato showing the façade of the casi... and the nearby Palazzo dei Vescovi

facing page
Interior of the church

and bases of white marble. The lunettes and two blind arches are filled with a geometric motif. The result, simple and clearly of classical derivation, is similar to the marble facing of Florence Baptistery. The second tier, in a more picturesque and fragmented style, consists of a central section, corresponding to the nave, flanked by two gables. The central part, divided up by four fluted pilaster strips, has a window in the form of an aedicule, surmounted by a mosaic representing *Christ Giving His Blessing between the Virgin and Saint Minias.* The upper tier, the pediment, presents figured decorative motifs of inlaid green and white marble: a series of nine small arches framed by strips of marble in two colors serves as the base for five square and two triangular panels, decorated with the same symbolic figures that we find in the floor of the basilica: animals facing one another between interlaced flowers, lions and griffins, with two putti in the middle, perhaps the Gemini of the Zodiac. At the sides two dragons, which also appear on the iconostasis in the presbytery, and at the top a white cross on a green ground framed by six candlesticks. The decorative elements and methods of execution in this part of the façade are very like the ones we find inside and suggest that they were realized around the date of 1207 that is engraved on the floor of the nave.

On the summit of the façade still stands the eagle clutching the *torsello* (bale of twelve bolts of cloth) in its talons, symbol of the Arte di Calimala which had supervised the work on San Miniato since the 12th century and continued to administrate it until 1770.

The existence of a monastery next to the church is recorded since ancient times. Belonging to the Cluniac monks until 1373, it would be assigned by Pope Gregory XI to the Benedictines of Monte Oliveto who, after a series of absences and presences, still occupy it today.

In 1295, at the instance of the bishop of Florence, Andrea de' Mozzi, the Palazzo dei Vescovi was constructed "on the site of the houses of said monastery." For almost a century the out-of-town residence of the Florentine bishops, it would also be transferred to the Olivetan monks in 1373, when work started on a major restructuring of the monastic area, continuing into the first few decades of the 15th century.

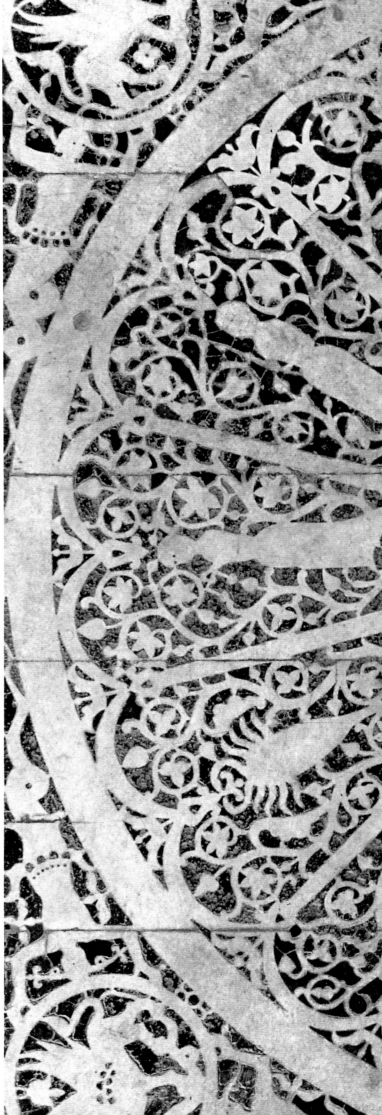

Detail of the iconostasis, early 13th century

facing page
The floor with the wheel of the Zodiac, c. 1207

The interior. The church, on a basilican plan with a nave and two aisles and no transept, echoes the traditional classical model in its trussed roof and rigid dimensional proportions (the nave is twice the size of the aisles). The interior, where the nave and aisles are separated by nine round-headed arches, is spaced out by clustered pillars that support the transverse arches. The latter, in the absence of a vaulted roof, are reduced to simple articulations, subdividing the church into three bays of which the last, raised one constitutes the presbytery. The aisles have flat endings, while a semicircular apse with a conical roof closes the nave. The apse, with a hemicycle divided into round arches by six columns, is illuminated by five large windows filled with slabs of translucent marble and, like the whole area of the presbytery, is raised about three meters above the level of the church. It is accessible by two flights of steps at the ends of the aisles. Originally built of stone, the steps were clad in marble in the 15th century and lead to the ambulatory in front of the presbytery, from which it is separated by the marble iconostasis (a screen between the presbytery and the nave and aisles that reaches a height of almost three meters), where the large pulpit is located on the right. On the other side of the screen the presbytery is split into a nave and two aisles by two pairs of columns and two half-pillars in green marble from Prato; the columns are the only ones in the basilica to have been salvaged from Roman buildings, as were some of the capitals in the nave.

The walls of the right-hand aisle, in the chancel, are covered with frescoes, while on the other side the walls of *pietra forte* have been left bare, with the exception of a fresco on the rear wall. Also from the 14th century is the decoration on the trusses of the roof, which we

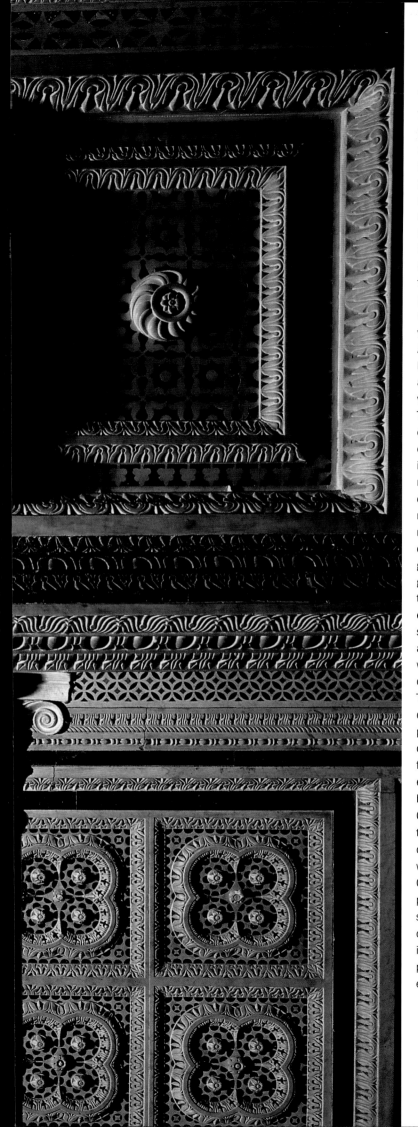

The Presbytery and the Apse

The area of greatest artistic interest inside the church is unquestionably that of the raised presbytery. A prominent part of the basilica – it takes up almost half of the space – and substantially intact in its profusion of carved marble, inlays and mosaics, it is partly concealed from anyone entering the church by the structure providing access to the crypt underneath, consisting of a white and green trabeation. Above, in the ambulatory, this houses a seat in white marble, a sign that the congregation was allowed access in the past. The plutei – the marble enclosure of the altar and chancel – are richly subdivided into square panels in white marble with green inlays, decorated with mixtilinear rosettes inside frames of plant motifs. At the top is set a cornice with a frieze of inlaid green and red marble in geometric patterns that terminate, at the sides of the entrance to the choir, in symbolic figures: a little devil in a bizarre pose confronting two winged monsters with long curling tails.

The Christian symbol of the fish closes the decoration of the plutei: Christ prevents the diabolical representation of evil from entering the chancel. It is easy to see the connection between this decoration and Oriental textiles, which helps us to interpret the rich ornamentation extending the whole length of the iconostasis. On the right pluteus is set the pulpit: with the projecting part supported by two slender columns in brecciated marble, it has two carved and inlaid panels with central rosettes on each side; at the top runs a projecting cornice composed of motifs and moldings in green and white marble. The lectern in the form of a telamon standing on a lion-shaped console is extraordinary and echoes the reliefs of male figures on the façade at the sides of the central tympanum, accentuated here by the liveliness of the eyes in glass paste. The pulpit, a jewel of Tuscan Romanesque art, can be dated to 1209 and is comparable to the older one of Sant'Agata Mugello, now dismantled, and, in its structure, to the contemporary one, but with more richly carved panels, of San Pier Scheraggio, now in San Leonardo at Arcetri. Of particular importance, notwithstanding the numerous interventions of restoration, is the mosaic in the apse, a notable example of the figurative use of the medium, partly in virtue of a meticulous technique that produces effects similar to painting (unlike the mosaics in Ravenna, extremely small tesserae were used to represent the flesh tones of the faces). Dated 1297 – but probably older, from the sixties: the inscription has been tampered with and is now partially lost – it depicts *Christ Enthroned and Giving His Blessing between the Virgin and Saint Minias with the Symbols of the Evangelists*, and appears closely linked to the work of the mosaicists active in the baptistery in the same years. Filled with symbolic references, it portrays Christ Pantocrator in a traditional pose, of Byzantine derivation, like the one that can be seen in many apsidal conches decorated with images in mosaic: in San Lorenzo fuori le Mura and Santa Maria in Trastevere in Rome and in Cefalù Cathedral. There is no documentation relating to the client (although a kneeling male figure, on a smaller scale, can be seen on the left side), to the artists who prepared the cartoons or to the mosaicists who inserted the glass tesserae with such skill. It is worth recording the fact that it was the powerful Arte di Calimala which supervised the execution of the cycle of mosaics in the baptistery, and that in the administrative books of the guild relating to the building in Piazza San Giovanni appears the name, among others, of the master mosaicist Apollonius of Florence, put forward by the critics for San Miniato as well. Even the great arch that frames the mosaic is rich in symbols that recall the ones used on the archway leading to the rectangular apse of Florence Baptistery. A visual and interpretative analysis of the apsidal conch reveals the use of a complex symbology: in addition to the well-known symbols of the Evangelists, it is in the heavenly garden that we find a real profusion of concepts: animals and plants traditionally alluding to salvation (peacock–immortality; phoenix–resurrection; pelican–Messiah; tree of life–mystery of the Eucharist; dove–innocence; banana tree–from which the souls in the guise of birds feed) occupy the mystical place taken from the Oriental repertory, whose symbols have passed into Christian art.

View of the apse showing the mosaic representing *Christ Giving His Blessing between the Virgin and Saint Minias*, second half of the 13th century know to have been replaced and redecorated at that time (their present appearance was conferred on them by a heavy-handed 19th-century retouching). The church is illuminated by narrow and splayed single-light windows that run along the upper walls of the nave and have a painted decoration imitating inlays. All that remains of the old floor, which was probably made of concrete mixed with pozzolana, crushed brick and pieces of marble and is dated by an inscription to 1207, is the strip of inlaid green and white marble that runs from the central door to the chapel of the Crucifix. Contemporary with that of the baptistery, it presents the same motifs of Oriental origin, brought to the West by the extensive trade in textiles. The two floors seem to be the work of the same craftsmen, who made use of similar, if not identical designs. In the eight surviving panels that indicate the main route from the entrance we find geometric shapes rich in Oriental decorative elements and Christian symbols, alternating as if in a precious piece of lacework. In good condition – compared with that of the Baptistery where the wear has been greater – the fine inlays of the floor reach their peak in the fourth panel representing the wheel of the Zodiac. A Judeo-Christian symbol, the circle of the Zodiac is an allusion to the twelve apostles and the centrality of Christ. Present in the East since antiquity, it was used in Florentine churches not only for its clear theological significance, but also for reasons of a practical character. It is thought, in fact, that in San Miniato it had the function of a sundial, as it certainly did in the baptistery, with the shadow cast by the gnomon – a slender metal pole – indicating the hours of the day.

Agnolo Gaddi, *Saint Minias and Saint John Gualberto, Scenes from the Life of Christ*, 1394

facing page
Michelozzo, Luca della Robbia, Maso di Bartolomeo, chapel of the Crucifix, 1448-51

The chapel of the Crucifix and its pictorial decorations. The artistic addition of greatest interest to the basilica of San Miniato is, without doubt, the elegant tabernacle that Michelozzo and Luca della Robbia executed with the assistance of Maso di Bartolomeo in 1448, to a commission from the Arte di Calimala, in order to house the miraculous *Crucifix of St. John Gualberto*. Piero de' Medici met the expense of the work and traces of his emblem can be found in many parts of the small chapel: the trabeation is decorated with the motif – in green and white marble – of three plumes with the Medicean ring and the motto "semper"; on the rear face is carved a falcon gripping the diamond ring with three feathers, and even the metal grate that encloses the ciborium has an open-worked pattern representing the ring. The omnipresent eagle of Calimala towers above the vault. The chapel, located in the middle of the nave and "closing" the descent to the crypt, is covered by a broad tunnel vault with a ceiling of della Robbian white and blue coffers and an external decoration of scales in the Medicean colors of white, green and red. Supported by a rich marble architrave, the vault stands on two pairs of columns and fluted pillars with composite capitals. It houses a panel painted by Agnolo Gaddi in 1394 as a setting for the venerated *Crucifix*; in 1448 it was rearranged in order to fit into Michelozzo's tabernacle and after 1671, when the image was transferred to the church of Santa Trinita, organized in its present form. The so-called *Crucifix of Saint John Gualberto* – which popular tradition holds to be the miraculous image that bowed its head to persuade the saint to forgive the murderer of his brother – is now in the church of Santa Trinita and cannot be stylistically analyzed as it has been heavily repainted at unknown dates. Agnolo Gaddi's reassembled panel forms the splendid gold backdrop of the tabernacle: *Saint Minias and Saint John Gualberto* occupy the central space, with numerous *Scenes from the Life of Christ* in the surrounding panels.

The events that led to the transfer (1671) of the miraculous image should be linked with the military function that San Miniato performed from the 1550s onward. In the presence of the garrisons occupying the fortress, the Olivetan monks abandoned the church and monastery (1553), allowing it to fall into a state of neglect and decay. The precarious condition of the complex – turned into a lazaretto during

the plague of 1630 and then a sort of rest home for private citizens for several decades – persuaded Cosimo III to have the miraculous *Crucifix* moved with a solemn procession.

Following the interventions on the inside walls in the early part of the 20th century (1917, 1930), the decision was taken to remove the plaster and paint that covered the walls of the aisles, exposing numerous frescoes that had embellished the walls of the church over the centuries. The decoration, which must have once occupied the whole wall of the aisle as far as the presbyterial part, although only fragments of it can be seen today, leads us to the wooden panel depicting *Saint Minias and Scenes from His Legend* located on the altar at the head of the aisle. An early masterpiece by Jacopo del Casentino, it can be dated to around 1315; at the sides of the solid image of Minias – a full red mantle cloaks his sturdy limbs, firmly occupying the space – are set scenes from his legendary life, with colorful architectural settings in the manner of Giotto.

The crypt. Inside this venerated place are kept the bones of St. Minias, under a Romanesque altar table. The crypt is divided into a nave and six small aisles by thirty-six slender marble columns, on which rest the groin vaults decorated with multifoil images of *Saints and Prophets*.

There are numerous documents relating to the works carried out in this part of the basilica: in 1337, with a legacy of a hundred florins from Monna Zecca, the Sienese Petruccio di Betto – a craftsman very active in those years, when he also made the railings of several chapels in Santa Trinita and Fiesole Cathedral – executed the wrought-iron

Jacopo del Casentino, *Saint Minias and Scenes from His Legend*, 1315

facing page
The crypt with its vaults frescoed by Taddeo Gaddi and the railing of Petruccio di Betto

enclosure of the mortuary chapel, and in 1341 Taddeo Gaddi carried out the pictorial decoration of the vaults. The work, acknowledged as one of the artist's masterpieces, was only brought to light, underneath the plaster with which it had been covered, at the beginning of the 20th century, and seems close to the frescoes in the Baroncelli Chapel in Santa Croce, as well as the surviving fragments of Taddeo's paintings in the Camposanto of Pisa.

The sacristy. A fine set of cabinets, made in 1470 by the woodworker Jacopo Monciatto, lines two walls of the sacristy, along with a series of benches (the stalls are a Neo-Gothic addition from 1860), inlaid with subtle geometric motifs. The room is roofed by a groin vault with ribs decorated with geometric patterns that extend all the way to the ground, underlining the corners and delimiting – as in the Upper Basilica of Assisi – sixteen panels on the walls frescoed by Spinello Aretino. The scenes with *The Life of Saint Benedict* and the vault with the *Four Evangelists* in the cells were painted by the artist from Arezzo – mentioned nowhere in the documents – to fulfill the last wishes of the merchant Benedetto degli Alberti (died in exile in 1388), who had bequeathed his property to fund the decoration and endowment of the sacristy of San Miniato. Leaving instructions for the execution of the stained-glass window that portrayed him life size (but destroyed during the plague of 1630) and everything else to do with the furnishing and officiation of the sacristy (paintings, cabinets, altar, plate), the client had exercised such a profound influence that he even brought about an original modification of the episodes represented, in order to have the life of the saint intertwine with his own. Spinello, who in San Miniato painted the first major cycle in Tuscany devoted to the life of St. Benedict, derived the iconography from the Rule of Gregory and Jacobus de Voragine's *Legenda Aurea* (1255-66), but introduced significant innovations. We should not forget the great power wielded in the city by the degli Alberti family, which made it easy and rewarding for the painter to come up with a personal interpretation

The sacristy with the frescoes of Spinello Aretino

Facing page
Spinello Aretino, *Scene from the Life of Saint Benedict*, c. 1387, detail. Sacristy

of the historical events of which Benedict had been the protagonist: in those years it appeared natural to "read" the episode of *Benedict Leaving His Father's House* as an allusion to degli Alberti's recent exile following the riot of the Ciompi in 1378.

The chapel of the Cardinal of Portugal. Built at the behest of Jacopo of Lusitania (1433-59) – son of Isabella of Aragon and Pedro duke of Coimbra –, the chapel was dedicated to Sts. James, Vincent and Eustace and constructed following the death of the prince while on a journey from Rome to Mantua to take part in the council convened by Pope Pius II to promote the crusade against the Turks. During his brief stay in Florence, the young cardinal and cousin of King Alfonso V of Portugal, who had already distinguished himself by the deep religious feelings he had displayed at an early age, expressed the desire to be buried in the church of San Miniato. Gravely ill, he chose the site in the hills, refuge of the Olivetan monks to whom felt spiritually close, as his last resting place.

The architectural scheme of the Old Sacristy, built in San Lorenzo by Filippo Brunelleschi and imitated in many different parts of Italy, has in the chapel of the

deceased and is reflected in the arch framing the marble altar, housing a copy of the large panel by Antonio and Piero Pollaiuolo representing *Saint James the Greater between Saints Eustace and Vincent* (the original is in the Galleria degli Uffizi). Framed by drapes held by angels (painted by Alesso Baldovinetti, who was entrusted with the decoration of all the spaces of the chapel, including the beautiful panel of the *Annunciation* on the left-hand wall), it echoes in the steep floor of the Renaissance terrace on which the three saints stand the fine decoration and taste for colored marble that are characteristic of this interior. It was in this context that Luca della Robbia executed the lining of the vault: the intense coloring of the *trompe-l'oeil* ceiling of polychrome tiles – in which are set five bas-relief medallions depicting the *Four Cardinal Virtues and the Holy Spirit* with round frames made of blue scales of decreasing intensity – emphasizes the brilliance and richness of the setting. The floor with Cosmati motifs made from tesserae of different kinds of marble that, brought from Rome and Tuscany, were composed by Roman craftsmen, the disks of porphyry that extend symbolically right under the cardinal's tomb and the panels that act as a backdrop to the bishop's throne (allusively echoed in the *Annunciation* above) all help to create a cunningly balanced blend of the various elements, and produce an extraordinary effect.

The artistic and symbolic fulcrum of the chapel is the cardinal's tomb, executed by Antonio Rossellino in 1461, on the right-hand wall. The man's virtues are in fact the subject of the frieze, of classical reminiscence, carved at the base: moral force opposed to lust (the youth killing a bull), and the victory of rationality over the irrational (the allegory of the soul is represented by a winged youth driving a chariot).

It is clear that the executors of the will wanted the large sum of money invested to be matched by a dazzling display. Through the use of costly materials and refined techniques of execution – highlights of gold made the marble drapes look like precious fabrics – the young prelate, who had given up the privileges of his birth for purity and sanctity in his earthly existence, received a worthy celebration.

Cardinal of Portugal – erected in San Miniato to a design by Antonio Manetti, but under the direction of Antonio Rossellino (1461-66) – one of its most important examples. Square, roofed by a domical vault and with pilaster strips at the corners framing the arches of three shallow rectangular chapels with tunnel vaults and the entrance, it has a centric cruciform layout whose most lofty precedent is the mausoleum of Galla Placidia in Ravenna. Again we find a profusion of polychrome marble, a feature extraneous to Florentine 15th-century architecture.

The entrance to the chapel – through a large arch with coffers decorated with gilded rosettes – is surmounted by a lunette with the coat of arms of the

Antonio Rossellino's Tomb of the Cardinal of Portugal

When the cardinal's body was laid in the tomb on September 12, 1466, leaving to posterity, as we are told by Vespasiano da Bisticci, a reputation of sanctity for the short life he had led with uncommon moral force, the mausoleum in San Miniato was concluded. It had taken seven years and the skillful direction of Antonio Rossellino to carry out such a demanding joint undertaking. And the work in the chapel must have been done as a team, since the program of the decoration is so coherent and concerted that it suggests a choice of the most stylistically consistent artists active in the city. This resulted in a variety of ideas, but also in successful stylistic and decorative correlations between the various elements, creating an overall effect of resplendent polychromy, in keeping with the tastes of the client and the Portuguese bishop Alvaro, executor of his will.

The tomb is a superlative example of Rossellino's art. Above the sarcophagus a pair of angels, holding the "crown of virginity" and the "palm of victory over the world" (now missing), kneel at the sides of a sacred stone – probably the stone from the cardinal's portable altar – set between the oval depicting the Virgin, in a sumptuous frame with cherubim and a festoon, and the body of the deceased. The marble plinth is rich in classical citations: a frieze with winged genii and unicorns facing one another, as well as symbolic scenes on the sides, it proposes themes taken from Roman sarcophagi, reinterpreted in a Renaissance key. The effigy of the dead man – and the whole structure, which is reminiscent of other important Florentine sepulchral monuments, framed by an arch and by carved drapes – is characterized by a waxy softness that Antonio Rossellino derived from the sculpture of Desiderio da Settignano, while the sumptuous decoration of the cardinal's pall and dalmatic almost echoes that of the Pollaiuolo brothers' painting of *Saints*.

GENERAL BIBLIOGRAPHY

In addition to the bibliography specific to each church, a number of texts fundamental to an understanding of the history of Florence and its places of worship are indicated below.

1568
Giorgio Vasari, *Le Vite de' più eccellenti Architetti, Pittori et Scultori Italiani scritte da M. Giorgio Vasari pittore e architetto aretino, di nuovo ampliate con i ritratti loro e con l'aggiunta delle vite de' vivi et de' morti dall'anno 1550 insino al 1567*, Giunti, Florence 1568, annotated edition by Gaetano Milanesi, Sansoni, Florence 1878-1886, 9 vols. English trans. by Gaston C. de Vere, *Lives of the Painters, Sculptors and Architects*, Everyman's Library, London 1996 (1912), 2 vols.

1677
Federico Bocchi and Giovanni Cinelli, *Le bellezze della città di Firenze scritte da M. Francesco Bocchi e ora ampliate da M. Giovanni Cinelli*, Florence

1678
Federico Leopoldo del Migliore, *Firenze città nobilissima illustrata*, Florence

1754-62
Giuseppe Richa, *Notizie istoriche delle chiese fiorentine divise ne' suoi quartieri*, Florence, 10 vols.

1758
Giovanni Lami, *Sanctae Ecclesiae Florentinae Monumenta*, Florence

1765
[Gaetano Cambiagi], *L'Antiquario fiorentino ossia guida per osservar con metodo le rarità e bellezze della città di Firenze*, Florence

1776-78
[Marco Lastri], *L'Osservatore fiorentino sugli edifici della sua patria*, Florence, 1st edition

1789-1802
Vincenzo Follini and Modesto Rastrelli, *Firenze antica e moderna illustrata*, Florence, 8 vols.

1798
Guida per osservar con metodo le rarità e le bellezze di Firenze, Gaetano Cambiagi, Florence

1819
L.F.M.G. Gargiolli, *Déscription de la ville de Florence et de ses environs*, Florence

1824
Luigi Biadi, *Notizie sulle antiche fabbriche di Firenze non terminate e sulle variazioni alle quali i più ragguardevoli edifizi sono andati soggetti*, Florence

1841-45
Alfonso Ademollo, *Marietta de' Ricci ovvero Firenze al tempo dell'assedio*, historical account with corrections and additions by L. Passerini, Florence, 6 vols.

1842
Federico Fantozzi, *Nuova guida ovvero descrizione storico artistica critica della città e contorni di Firenze*, Florence

1847
Luigi Santoni, *Raccolta di notizie storiche riguardanti le chiese dell'Arcidiocesi di Firenze*, Florence

1894
Arnaldo Cocchi, *Notizie Storiche intorno antiche immagini di Nostra Donna che hanno culto in Firenze*, Florence

1897-1927
Robert Davidsohn, *Geschichte von Florenz*, Berlin, 7 vols. Italian trans. by Giovanni Battista Klein, *Storia di Firenze*, Florence 1956-68, 8 vols.

1903
Arnaldo Cocchi, *Le chiese di Firenze dal sec. IV al sec. XX*, Florence

[1905]
Vittorio Alinari, *Eglises et couvents de Florence*, Florence n.d.

1910
Walter Limburger, *Die Gebaude von Florenz*, Leipzig, 2 vols.

1929
Francesco Lumachi, *Firenze. Nuova guida illustrata della città e dei dintorni di Firenze*, Florence

1940-54
Walther and Elisabeth Paatz, *Die Kirchen von Florenz*, Frankfurt am Main, 10 vols.

1970
La Chiesa fiorentina, ed. by Carlo Celso Calzolai, Florence

1972
Mario Lopez Pegna, *Le più antiche chiese di Firenze*, Florence

1973
Giovanni Fanelli, *Firenze Architettura e città*, Florence, 2 vols.

1974-93
Alberto Busignani and Raffaello Bencini, *Le chiese di Firenze. Quartiere di Santo Spirito*, Florence 1974; *Quartiere di Santa Croce*, Florence 1974; *Quartiere di Santa Maria Novella*, Florence 1974; *Quartiere di San Giovanni*, Florence 1993

1974
Marilena Mosco, *Itinerario di Firenze barocca*, Florence

1976
Luigi Zeppegno, *Le chiese di Firenze*, Perugia

1980
Osanna Fantozzi Micali and Piero Roselli, *Le Soppressioni dei conventi a Firenze*, Florence

1990
Cappelle barocche a Firenze, ed. by Mina Gregori, Cinisello Balsamo

1993
Firenze e Provincia, Touring Club Italiano, Milan

1997
Klaus Zimmermanns, *Florenz: Kirchen, Palaste und Museen in der Stadt der Medici*, Cologne

2001
Storia Arte Fede nelle chiese di Firenze, Florence

BAPTISTERY OF SAN GIOVANNI

1994
Cristina Acidini Luchinat, *Il Battistero e il Duomo di Firenze*, Milan

Il Battistero di San Giovanni a Firenze, ed. by Antonio Paolucci, Modena, 2 vols.

1996
Il Bel San Giovanni e Santa Maria del Fiore. Il centro religioso di Firenze dal Tardo Antico al Rinascimento, ed. by Domenico Cardini, Florence

Antonio Paolucci, *Le porte del Battistero di Firenze alle origini del Rinascimento*, Mirabilia Italiae, Modena

1997
Michael Viktor Schwarz, *Die Mosaiken des Baptisteriums in Florenz: drei Studien zur Florentiner Kunstgeschichte*, Cologne

2000
Anna Maria Giusti, *Il Battistero di San Giovanni a Firenze*, Florence. English ed. *The Baptistery of San Giovanni in Florence*, Florence 2000

SANTA MARIA DEL FIORE

1971
Marvin Trachtenberg, *The Campanile of Florence: "Giotto's Tower,"* New York

1983
Margaret Haines, *La sacrestia delle messe del Duomo di Firenze*, Florence

1994
Cristina Acidini Luchinat, *Il Battistero e il Duomo di Firenze*, Milan

Il restauro della cupola di Santa Maria del Fiore, Florence, January 30

La cattedrale di Santa Maria del Fiore a Firenze, vol. I, ed. by Francesco Gurrieri, Florence

1995
La cattedrale di Santa Maria del Fiore a Firenze, vol. II, ed. by Cristina Acidini Luchinat, Florence

2001
La cattedrale e la città. Saggi sul Duomo di Firenze, vols. I*, I**, ed. by Timothy Verdon and Annalisa Innocenti, Acts of the International Symposium for the VII Centenary of the Cathedral of Florence (Florence, June 16-21, 1997), Florence

La cattedrale come spazio sacro. Saggi sul Duomo di Firenze, vols. I*, I**, ed. by Timothy Verdon and Annalisa Innocenti, Acts of the International Symposium for the VII Centenary of the Cathedral of Florence (Florence, June 16-21, 1997), Florence

Santa Maria del Fiore. The Cathedral and its Sculptures, ed. by Margaret Haines, Acts of the International Symposium for the VII Centenary of the Cathedral of Florence (Villa i Tatti, June 5-6, 1997, Fiesole), Florence

SAN LORENZO

1827
Domenico Moreni, *Pompe funebri celebrate nell'Imp. e Real Basilica di San Lorenzo dal secolo XIII a tutto il regno medicceo*, Florence

1979
La cappella dei Principi e le pietre dure a Firenze, ed. by Umberto Baldini, Anna Maria Giusti and Anna Paola Pampaloni Martelli, Milan

1984
San Lorenzo. La basilica, le sagrestie, le cappelle e la biblioteca, ed. by Umberto Baldini and Bruno Nardini, Florence

1989
La Sagrestia Vecchia di San Lorenzo e il "Martirio di San Lorenzo" di A. Bronzino dopo il restauro, Florence

1993
San Lorenzo. I documenti e i tesori nascosti, exhibition catalogue (Florence), Venice

1998
La Sagrestia Vecchia di San Lorenzo. Il restauro delle tarsie lignee del Quattrocento, Florence

1998
Licia Bertani, *San Lorenzo, Cappelle Medicee, Biblioteca Laurenziana*, Florence

BADIA FIORENTINA

1981
Un parato della Badia fiorentina, ed. by Dora Liscia Bemporad and Alessandro Guidotti, exhibition catalogue, Florence

1982
Ernesto Sestan, Maurilio Adriani and Alessandro Guidotti, *La Badia fiorentina*, Florence

1992
Francesca Carrara, "La Badia fiorentina e la congregazione cassinense," in *La Chiesa e la Città a Firenze nel XV secolo*, exhibition catalogue, Florence, pp. 105-18

SANTI APOSTOLI

1931
Luigi Zumkeller, *I Restauri della Basilica dei SS. Apostoli in Firenze*, lecture given on April 26, 1931. in Santi Apostoli in Florence

1992
Giampaolo Trotta, *Gli antichi chiassi tra Ponte Vecchio e Santa Trinita*, Florence, see the articles by Giampaolo Trotta, Alessandro Guidotti and Lisa Venturini

2001
La Chiesa dei Santi Apostoli e Biagio: restauri recenti, Florence

ORSANMICHELE

1978
Lorenzo Ghiberti. Materia e ragionamenti, catalogue of the exhibition, Florence 1978-79, Florence, pp. 161-205 (with specific bibliography)

1996
Orsanmichele a Firenze, ed. by Diane Finiello Zervas, Modena (with previous bibliography)

Diane Finiello Zervas, *Orsanmichele. Documents 1336-1452*, Modena

2000
Licia Bertani and Muriel Vervat, *La Madonna di Bernardo Daddi negli horti di San Michele*, Florence

SANTA CROCE

1967
Giotto e Giotteschi in Santa Croce, Florence

1968
Primo Rinascimento in Santa Croce, Florence

1983
Il complesso monumentale di Santa Croce. La Basilica, le Cappelle, i chiostri, il Museo, ed. by Umberto Baldini and Bruno Nardini, Florence

I Musei di Santa Croce e di Santo Spirito a Firenze, ed. by Luisa Becherucci, Milan

1993
Il Pantheon di Santa Croce a Firenze, ed. by Luciano Berti, Florence

1996
Santa Croce nel solco della storia, Florence

1998
Maso di Banco. La cappella di San Silvestro, ed. by Cristina Acidini Luchinat and Enrica Neri Lusanna, Milan

SANTA MARIA NOVELLA

1966
Stefano Orlandi, *Santa Maria Novella e i suoi Chiostri monumentali*, Florence

1981
Santa Maria Novella, La Basilica, il Convento, i Chiostri monumentali, ed. by Umberto Baldini, Florence

1983
Arte e Storia in Santa Maria Novella, ed. by Roberto Lunardi, Florence

1997
Margarete Dieck, *Die Spanische Kapelle in Florenz: da trecenteske Bildprogramm des Kapitelsaals der Dominikaner von S. Maria Novella*, Frankfurt am Main

2000
Marco Dezzi Bardeschi, "Leon Battista Alberti e Giovanni di Paolo Rucellai: da Santa Maria Novella a San Pancrazio," in *Anagke*, N.S., 1999 (2000), 27-8, pp. 10-19

2001
Giotto. La Croce di Santa Maria Novella, ed. by Marco Ciatti and Max Seidel, Florence

Martin Germ and Leon Battista Alberti, "Santa Maria Novella in Florence and Nicolaus Cusanus," in *Umeni*, 49, 2001, pp. 11-18

2002
Andrea Baldinotti, Alessandro Cecchi and Vincenzo Farinella, *Masaccio e Masolino. Il gioco delle parti*, Florence

La Trinità di Masaccio. Il restauro dell'anno 2000, ed. by Cristina Danti, Florence

SAN MARCO

1980
Antonio Paolucci, in *La Comunità cristiana fiorentina e toscana nella dialettica religiosa del Cinquecento*, exhibition catalogue, Florence

1989
La chiesa di San Marco a Firenze, vol. I, Florence

1990
La chiesa e il convento di San Marco a Firenze, vol. II, ed. by Giorgio Bonsanti, Florence

1998
Savonarola e le sue reliquie a San Marco: itinerario di un percorso savonaroliano nel Museo, Florence

2000
La Biblioteca di Michelozzo a San Marco tra recupero e scoperta, ed. by Magnolia Scudieri and Giovanna Rasario, Florence

SANTISSIMA ANNUNZIATA

1971
Eugenio Casalini, *La Santissima Annunziata di Firenze. Studi e documenti sulla chiesa e il convento*, Florence

1987
Tesori d'Arte dell'Annunziata, exhibition catalogue ed. by Eugenio Casalini, Maria Grazia Ciardi Duprè Dal Poggetto, Lamberto Crociani and Dora Liscia Bemporad, Florence

1992
Francesca Petrucci, "Santissima Annunziata," in *Le chiese di Firenze*, Rome

SANTA TRINITA

1887
Giuseppe Castellazzi, *La basilica di Santa Trinita, i suoi tempi ed il progetto del suo restauro*, Florence

1897
F. Tarani, *Cenni storici e artistici della chiesa di Santa Trinita*, Florence

1987
La Chiesa di Santa Trinita a Firenze, Florence

OGNISSANTI

1972
Mina Gregori, "Giovanni da Milano: storia di un polittico," in *Paragone*, 265

1992
Ferdinando Batazzi and Anna Maria Giusti, *Ognissanti*, Rome

"La 'Madonna d'Ognissanti' di Giotto restaurata," in *Gli Uffizi. Studi e Ricerche*, vol. 8, Florence

2000
Vincenzo Vaccaro, *Il restauro della facciata di Ognissanti*, Florence

SANTA MARIA DEL CARMINE

1932
Ugo Procacci, "L'incendio della chiesa del Carmine del 1771," in *Rivista d'Arte*, S. II, pp. 141-232

1987
Leonida Pandimiglio, "Felice di Michele vir clarissimus e una consorteria: I Brancacci di Firenze," in *Quaderni di restauro*, 3, pp. 12 *et sqq.*

1990
Umberto Baldini and Ornella Casazza, *La cappella Brancacci*, Milan. English trans. by Lysa Hochroth, *The Brancacci Chapel*, New York 1992

1990
Lucia Monaci Moran and Silvia Meloni Trkulja, "Cappella Corsini in Santa Maria del Carmine," in *Cappelle Barocche a Firenze*, ed. by Mina Gregori, Cinisello Balsamo

1992
La chiesa di Santa Maria del Carmine, ed. by Luciano Berti, Florence (with bibliography)

1998
Mario Carniani, "La cappella Brancacci a Santa Maria del Carmine," in *Cappelle del Rinascimento a Firenze*, Florence

2002
Andrea Baldinotti, Alessandro Cecchi and Vincenzo Farinella, *Masaccio e Masolino. Il gioco delle parti*, Florence

SANTO SPIRITO

1991
Elena Capretti, *Il complesso di Santo Spirito*, Florence

1996
La chiesa e il convento di Santo Spirito a Firenze, ed. by Cristina Acidini Luchinat, Florence

2000
Il Crocifisso di Santo Spirito, Comune di Firenze, Assessorato alla Cultura, "I Restauri", vol. 5, Florence

2002
Il restauro dell'altare del Sacramento. Presentazione del restauro sull'altare Corbinelli, April 17, 2002, ed. by the Opificio delle Pietre Dure, Florence

SANTA FELICITA

1986
Francesca Fiorelli Malesci, *La chiesa di Santa Felicita a Firenze*, Florence (with previous bibliography)

SAN MINIATO

1988
Francesco Gurrieri, Luciano Berti and Claudio Leonardi, *La Basilica di San Miniato al Monte a Firenze*, Florence (with previous bibliography)

1995
Franco Pratesi, *La splendida Basilica di San Miniato a Firenze*, Florence

1998
Giovanni Matteo Guidetti, "La Cappella del Cardinale del Portogallo a San Miniato al Monte," in *Cappelle del Rinascimento a Firenze*, Florence (see for its specific bibliography)

INDEX OF ARTISTS